TOM KINDRE

The Boys
From New Jersey

*Tales of love, fear, bravery
and survival, from one of
the world's most acclaimed
archives of World War II*

Printed in Victoria, Canada

Note for Librarians: a cataloguing record for this book that includes Dewey Classification and US Library of Congress numbers is available from the National Library of Canada. The complete cataloguing record can be obtained from the National Library's online database at:
www.nlc-bnc.ca/amicus/index-e.html
ISBN 1-4120-2592-3

TRAFFORD

This book was published *on-demand* in cooperation with Trafford Publishing. On-demand publishing is a unique process and service of making a book available for retail sale to the public taking advantage of on-demand manufacturing and Internet marketing. **On-demand publishing** includes promotions, retail sales, manufacturing, order fulfilment, accounting and collecting royalties on behalf of the author.

Suite 6E, 2333 Government St., Victoria, B.C. V8T 4P4, CANADA

Phone	250-383-6864	Toll-free	1-888-232-4444 (Canada & US)
Fax	250-383-6804	E-mail	sales@trafford.com
Web site	www.trafford.com		

TRAFFORD PUBLISHING IS A DIVISION OF TRAFFORD HOLDINGS LTD.
Trafford Catalogue #04-0420   www.trafford.com/robots/04-0420.html

10   9   8   7   6   5   4   3   2   1

The Boys
From New Jersey

Tom Kindre

TRAFFORD PUBLISHING CO.
Victoria, BC, Canada

Dedicated
to the memory
of the
236 Rutgers men
who gave their lives
in World War II.
Their stories,
unlike ours,
will never be told

To Anne with love
from one of the boys who
became her Uncle!
Semper Fie

Vince - Page 95 and 222

ACKNOWLEDGMENTS

This book would not have been possible without the commitment of the almost 300 men and women who, late in life, took the time and mustered the courage to tell their wartime stories. Many of those stories had been locked away and were only fully revealed to the tellers with the telling. For some the exercise proved cathartic, and for most it has added a new dimension to their lives, giving families and the historical record a treasure that would otherwise have been lost. I am also deeply indebted to Sandra Stewart Holyoak, Director of the Rutgers Oral History Archives of World War II, and her assistant, Shaun Illingworth, for their devoted help with photos, suggestions and fact checking; Professor John Whiteclay Chambers II of the Rutgers History Department, who championed the Oral Archives Project from its beginning; Kurt Piehler, the Project's founding director, who got things up and running; Thomas Frusciano, Rutgers University Archivist, for his advice and counsel; Rutgers University, which granted permission to use the material in book form; the dozens of Rutgers student interns who participated in the interviewing and editing process as part of their course work; and my wife Marie, whose tireless proofreading and helpful insights made the task lighter.

AUTHOR/EDITOR'S NOTE

This work is based on the interview transcripts on the web site (http://fas-history.rutgers.edu/oralhistory/orlhom.htm) of the Rutgers Oral History Archives at the time of publication. (List of interviewees ff. p. 322).

I alone am responsible for the choices that resulted in this compilation. With some 15,000 pages and more than 4,000,000 words to choose from, it was a daunting task, and a morally difficult one because every interview not represented is as much a part of legitimate history as those selected.

In working with the transcript excerpts, I have edited out repetitive phrases, the stammerings and backtrackings that often accompany our spoken speech, and have in some cases shifted material from one point to another to make a more cohesive narrative, but I have added nothing, so there are no words here that were not spoken by the storytellers themselves.

COVER AND BACK COVER designs by Shaun Illingworth
PHOTO CREDITS Cover: John Berglund; Charles Mickett,Jr.; Morton Burke; Peter Sarriaocco; William Godfrey; Russell Cloer; John Archibald; Crandon Clark; Jerome Selinger; Vincent Kramer; Irving Pape; Edwin Kolodziej; Charles Getty; Nathan Shoehalter; Ogden Bacon; George Claflen; Franklin Kneller; Livy Goodman; James Essig; Frank Gimpel. Back Cover: Robert Owen, James Essig, Ephraim Robinson, Livy Goodman.

FOREWORD

"The real war does not get into the history books," said the poet Walt Whitman, fresh from the bloody job of nursing wounded soldiers on Civil War battlefields. His lament, fortunately, is no longer valid. Over recent decades, historians have discovered that while the grunts and swabs who do a war's dirty work tend not to write, they and other ordinary citizens can often be persuaded to talk, and out of that discovery has come the modern practice of oral history.

The result is a democratization of the historical record. While the history of wars was once mostly that of statesmen and generals, garnered from official records, military documents and the memoirs of high-ranking personages, we now have genuine voices from the foxholes as well.

This new wealth of material has been a treasure trove for scholars and authors. The Rutgers Oral History Archives of World War II has posted nearly 300 comprehensive interviews on its web site, and more arrive as quickly as they are processed.

The Archives are being used not only by those interested in World War II and its military component, but also for genealogical research, and for sociological studies that include immigration history, the GI Bill and Rosie the Riveter.

But members of the public, while they may have computer access to the web, are likely to find it a daunting task to wade through the equivalent of 15,000 pages and some four million words of interview transcripts currently on the web site.

Tom Kindre's book, *The Boys From New Jersey*, overcomes that difficulty for the average reader. What the author has done is mine the Archives for their most poignant, dramatic and personally revealing stories of wartime experiences and behavior. He has arranged the material chronologically, following scores of New Jersey boys from the neighborhoods of their youth through growing up, college days, training camps, battlefields and the distant places where duty sent them. And the stories are all in their own words.

Many of the insights are arresting. A GI on Okinawa, overcome by the chaos of battle, muses that "Somebody must have been in charge. Maybe it was the Good Lord pulling the strings." A captured B-24 pilot who was marched along a road while German civilians threw rocks and spat at him, says, "I understood how they felt. I might have killed their brother or their father." A Seabee in the Pacific who was hit by shrapnel as he waded across a river observes, "You know something's happening, but you don't want to know."

The author, himself a World War II veteran and a participant in the Archives, brings an informed commentary to the presentation. His viewpoint with respect to the times and the material is "we" rather than "they," and in his introduction to each section, his personal experiences are often brought to bear. In "The Far Side of the World," he notes that "The places we went, the people we met, the assignments we were given, were beyond anything our imaginations could have conjured."

The immediacy of oral history is one of its most appealing attributes. Some experiences have been repressed for years and are revealed for the first time in the interviewing process. Many interviewers have expressed the awe they feel from being present at moments of personal catharsis, when the person speaking is obviously reliving the experience and feeling once again the emotions that accompanied it.

But in the interview transcripts, it is sometimes difficult to recapture that immediacy in its fullness. The typical interview is discursive, full of lost beginnings and unfinished thoughts. The interviewer asks questions to provoke memory and attempts to follow interesting trains of thought by asking, in effect, "What happened next?" Often the complete recounting of an experience comes out piecemeal as the doors of memory are gradually opened, and the story unfolds in fits and starts, between the interviewer's questions and comments on other points.

To the researcher dispassionately seeking nuggets of information, finding his way through this barrier is simply part of the job, but the average person looking for entertainment or historical insights may not have that kind of patience.

The author of *The Boys From New Jersey* has attempted to work around that roadblock by means of careful editing, deleting the interviewer's questions and the hems and haws of normal speech to give us a more or less seamless story from each speaker. He has sometimes shifted material from one place to another, he tells us, to make a more cohesive narrative, but he states, "I have added nothing, so there are no words here that were not spoken by the storytellers themselves."

Scholars, in reviewing wartime sources, are frequently looking for insights into motivation, morale, discipline and obedience to orders, and how those factors might have influenced the outcome of the battle or the war.

For the interested reader, those qualities are there to be analyzed, if one wishes to do so, but perhaps more rewarding is the pure storytelling, of a very personal sort, that goes right to our own emotional depths, makes us aware that these boys were no supermen but ordinary individuals like the rest of us, and makes us wonder what we would have done under the same circumstances. This, too, is the reaction most often expressed by undergraduates involved in the interviewing process.

The generation whose stories have been recorded for the Rutgers Oral History Archives of World War II were born after the "Great War," or the "War to end all wars," as the First World War was known. Their stories begin with memories of life in their home communities, the towns and farms where they grew up. Their voices speak of family legends and myths, customs preserved or lost, of best friends, favorite pastimes, hard work, hard times and hope. They lived in a small, insular world which for some had expanded only to the college campus before the December 7, 1941, attack on Pearl Harbor.

Their generation will be remembered for their humility when asked to recall their experiences of war, and for their deep sense of commitment to comrades, their families and their country. Today's generation is asked to think "outside the box," but the generation of the war years never knew there was a box, as evidenced by their adaptability and ingenuity both during the war and in the years following.

Their stories fascinate scholars. Scores of researchers across the world tell us through email, telephone calls and research visits that they are utilizing the Archives materials. Many ask to be put in touch with interviewees to further develop their research. The material is being used in scholarly journals, monographs, exhibitions, documentaries and books such as the 2003 Pulitzer Prize-winner, *An Army at Dawn: The War in North Africa*, by Rick Atkinson.

Most intriguing, perhaps, is the impact on today's generation. At Rutgers, an undergraduate history seminar, The American Experience in World War II, is based on the Archives. Students participate in the interviewing process, edit interviews and prepare research papers on subjects derived from the interview materials. Occasionally they meet in small, informal seminars with the interviewees themselves. Tom Kindre finds that opportunity remarkable: "It's the equivalent of our having been able to talk with Civil War veterans when we were in school."

The Boys From New Jersey is a wonderful entree to the oral histories being recorded in the History Department and housed in the Alexander Library's Special Collections and University Archives at Rutgers, the State University of New Jersey. After reading this book, you will want to read more. You can find us online at http://fas-history.rutgers.edu/oralhistory/orlhom.htm.

Sandra Stewart Holyoak
Director, The Rutgers Oral
History Archives

CONTENTS

PROLOGUE

We were born around the dawn of the Roaring Twenties but too late to enjoy their new freedoms. Before we reached our teens, the whole gaudy era-- flappers, speakeasies and all-- vanished into history. It was supplanted by the mournful tones of "Brother, Can You Spare a Dime?" and the Great Depression was upon us. Our society, before we had even taken our places in it, had gone from jazzy exuberance to something approaching desperation.

For some, the Depression meant a little less of everything; for others, it brought a corrosive undermining of self-worth and a strain of family ties. But the strongest families were made stronger, and as children we learned an invaluable lesson: work is necessary to support life.

When it was time for college, not all could afford it, but by scraping where we could, many found a way. From the farms of western New Jersey, the coastal towns of Bayonne, Elizabeth and Perth Amboy, from sparsely populated South Jersey and from the northern commuting suburbs, we converged on New Brunswick, at the state's geographic center. There, at the old college of Rutgers, we pursued our studies while the world overseas slowly collapsed into madness.

Meanwhile, Time's conveyor belt was moving us along re-

lentlessly, and it dropped us off, fresh and innocent, on the threshold of the US entry into World War II at the perfect age for combat-- old enough to master the M1 rifle and the .30-caliber machine gun, but young enough to be confident in our own immortality.

Preparing for a career while the world fell apart was disconcerting at best. Imagine trying to keep your mind on your books when you're 20 years old, Pearl Harbor has been attacked, 78,000 American soldiers have surrendered on Bataan and Col. Jimmy Doolittle is bombing Tokyo. All that took place in my Class of '42's senior year.

Academic life soon gave way to sobering new realities as the nation struggled to prepare itself for all-out war, and, one after another, we traded the campus for the training camp.

Over the next four years, the needs of the military and the luck of the draw sent us across the Atlantic and the Pacific, and wherever American forces fought, some of us were there.

Of the 7,618 Rutgers men who served in World War II, 236 did not return. Those who did went about their lives and work with hardly a thought to commemorating what they had done, and few were inclined to talk about it. For some, the GI Bill now made college a possibility for the first time.

Then, beginning in 1994, Rutgers alumni and others associated with the University began to tell their long-shelved stories to a team of interviewers. The historical compendium that resulted is the Rutgers Oral History Archives of World War II. All the stories in this book are drawn from that source.

Now we are in the twilight, but as we look back through more than three-quarters of a century of turmoil, we are awed by what we experienced in the twentieth century's seminal event-- World War II. I think I can speak for most when I say that we have at least one belief in common-- we are grateful that we survived, and sometimes astonished that we did so.

ANCESTRAL TRAILS

We grew up in small towns or on farms, mostly sheltered from evolving world history. But the ancestral trails that led to the communities of our youth were amazingly diverse-- failed homesteaders; fifth or sixth-generation dirt farmers looking for something better; new immigrants from Italy, Germany and Poland; young Russians fleeing the Czar's military service; merchant seamen yearning to come ashore.

New Jersey, conveniently close to a major port of entry, had a patchwork of ethnic enclaves grafted to its basic native stock. Most had one thing in common: they wanted their offspring to do better in life than they had done.

But not all felt the same about themselves. Frank Kneller's German parents hid the German newspaper out of shame for World War I, while Joe DeMasi ran home to his Italian mother on the first day of school to report a surprising discovery: "Mom, they don't speak our language."

What they seemed to share, though, was the desire to be assimilated. While emigres might cling to the old country tongue across the kitchen table, they wanted their offspring to be Americanized as quickly as possible. There were no "second language" issues.

Latent inventiveness, stifled under centuries of European tra-

dition, often sprang to the fore in the new world. Emigres in many ways had to reinvent themselves, and their willingness to do so may have helped to spark the independent American streak in the next generation. Lew Bloom got a new name when his father, Abraham Berezowsky, enlisted in the Army. The Irish sergeant who swore him in couldn't cope with the spelling, so he simplified it. Norm Brandt's father, fresh from Poland, knew only the 13-month lunar calendar of his youth. Faced with a question about his birth date, he plucked one out of the air-- November 11, Armistice Day.

What our parents and grandparents endured to reach this land of opportunity was the stuff of our childhood stories, and it fueled a pride in country that made it easy for us to leap to the nation's defense when we were called on to do so.

Whether the streets were believed to be paved with gold or not, the desire for a better life in America was so powerful that families tore themselves apart to achieve it. D. Robert Mojo's Spanish grandfather was nine years old when his country was wracked by a plague. His parents took him to a ship captain headed for America and said, "Get him out of here and put him wherever you can when you get to America." My grandmother in rural Ireland was taken to the port of Cobh by her family and put on a ship for New York in 1863. She was 16-- alone, penniless and illiterate.

Those who made it to New Jersey settled in almost every part of the state, so each town, each county, was a miniature UN, with a collection of little ethnic neighborhoods-- Italian, Polish, Irish, Jewish, German. In childhood, we stuck pretty much to our roots, but high school and college became the melting pot that spawned typical American marriages--German/Italian, Jewish/Irish, Irish/German, Polish/English and virtually every other possible combination.

"My father was on the docks in San Francisco and he saw a sign that said 'Firemen Needed.' That's how he started going to sea."   --John F. Ambos

Sometime around 1910 my grandfather homesteaded out in a little town called McCoy, Colorado. It was up on a high mesa, about 9,000 feet. And the only way you could live up there was to farm. So he and a group of other people from Golden went up there, and they spent all winter cutting trees, cutting up wood, making a sluice to bring water out of what was called the Grand River then, but it's now called the Colorado, to their farmlands. They worked a whole damn year on this, and when they opened it up they found that someone had made a mistake and the water wouldn't flow.

They had a hard life. My father used to tell about the salesman who comes through in the spring with his wagon, and you would order a couple bolts of cloth, a sack of salt, some coffee, sugar and what not, and they would deliver it in the fall. That's all they had all year.

My grandfather must have been a tough guy, because my father left home when he was 16. I'm sure he left because he couldn't live with the old man. His older brother had already left home. My father went to work with some local ranchers. He moved around, worked here and there. He told me he was in

5

San Francisco, walking along the docks, and he saw a sign that said, "Firemen Needed." He went aboard the ship and became a fireman, shoveling coal in the boilers, and the ship went over to the China area. That was how he started going to sea.

He was in the merchant marine when World War I came, he was working on a transport in the Atlantic, and he just went from New York to points in Europe. After the war was over, he took a job with Tidewater Oil Company on a tugboat in New York Harbor. That's why we lived in Bayonne.

In 1933 Tidewater decided to sell off their tugboats and hire out the service, and my father got a job on a deep-sea tanker. It was a miserable life for a man like that. He liked to be digging in the dirt, he wanted to be a great farmer, wanted a farm, and the tanker trip took 16 days, eight days down, eight days back. Then he'd be home for 24 hours. By that time we had a home and some land in New Market, New Jersey, and my father, being the avid farmer, would lay out the garden, buy the seeds, and I did the work. (laughter)

When World War II came along, he was still on tankers. And while he was on duty, his ship was sunk by a German raider, and he was picked up by the rescue boats. And they took all the survivors over to Japan. By the time they got to Japan, they had sunk quite a few ships, and they had 400 or 500 prisoners. And my father spent the rest of the war as a prisoner in Japan. He was there three-and-a-half years, something like that.

But we didn't know about that until much later. All we knew at the time was that he was missing in action. We were finally told what happened by the captain of his ship. The captain and six or eight men got off in a boat by themselves and got back to Capetown, which was about 500 miles away. And from there he came back home, and he came out to visit us.

He said the torpedo that struck them had hit just underneath my father's cabin. And he said my father had bought a monkey in South Africa and normally at that time of day he'd be training the monkey, so he thought my father was in the cabin, and we

6

thought for sure he was killed.

It was only much later-- maybe a year-- that we got word that he was alive. He normally weighed around 215 pounds, and was a little taller than I am. He came back weighing about 140, terribly malnourished. But he always said to me that the Japanese didn't treat their own soldiers any better than they treated their prisoners.

"My mother was engaged to marry my father's brother. When he was killed, my father said, 'Well, then, I will marry her.'" --Peter M. Saraiocco

My father and mother came from Italy, from a little hill town called Casoli. It's near Aquila, a very mountainous region. My father came to America as a boy of 14, by himself, in 1900. And he went to the Port Richmond area of Philadelphia, where there's a little enclave of Italians. It's kind of squeezed between a large Slavic, Polish group of people and a large number of Irish. It was a very interesting little enclave, because it was composed of two major groups, those from Abruzzi and those from Apulia. Then later, after I was born, we moved to Paulsboro, New Jersey.

My father lived with a family from Casoli. The obvious question: well, what's a 14-year-old boy going to do? Well, he rented there; I suppose he was a boarder. I can't even remember all the things he did. He went to Canada, and he became a boxer, among other things. He did all kinds of things, because there was no one there to tell him he couldn't do it. And later, when he was about 30, he went into the US Army, and he was in Del Rio, Texas, under General Pershing. And he used to tell me about their expeditions into Mexico, chasing Pancho Villa.

Now I have to tell you the other side of the story, about my mother. My mother was engaged to marry my father's brother, whose name was Peter. And Peter was in the Italian Army, and near the last day of the war-- World War I-- he fought and was

7

killed at the Battle of Caporetto. And my father said, "Well, then, I will marry her." And so, they married by proxy. He was here and she was there. And then she came over.

I don't know whether he'd ever met her, but I doubt it. He was then about 33. My mother used to say, "Well, see, he was as old as our Lord was when he was crucified." (laughter) She was about 22. He probably knew the family. They both came from the same town.

So when I was born, I was named Peter, because that was the name of the man that she normally would have married. I suppose that was the kind of thing they did in those days.

I went to Italy and tried to find where they lived, and I did. My mother always used to say they lived under the church, and I couldn't understand that. But sure enough, the large church was at the very top of the town, and their little house was down below it.

"Paul Robeson was a giant of a man. He would grab my father and say 'Archie,' and practically lift him off the ground." --John L. Archibald

I was born July 30, 1921, in Bridgeton. My father was teaching vocational agriculture at the Bridgeton High School. My dad was a graduate of Rutgers, Class of '17. He majored in agriculture. He had been born on a farm. I always thought that his parents were quite extraordinary, inasmuch as probably both my Grandfather Archibald and Grandmother Archibald had, I would say, maybe, an eighth or tenth grade education, but they sent both of their boys to Rutgers.

My father was the older one, and he went to Rutgeers, and after graduation he served in World War I. The Class of '17 went right into the service, as our classes did. My father was discharged as a first lieutenant in the field artillery. He went to Bridgeton, where my brothers and I were born, and then, in 1926, he was asked to come to Rutgers as an associate professor at the School of Agriculture, so we were college brats.

We lived in the little village of Middlebush, just five miles west of New Brunswick, but Rutgers was very much the center of our world, you might say. They had swimming courses for the college brats on Saturday mornings and we went to the Rutgers gym and the Rutgers concerts, the football games, sports, and so forth.

My mother was a local girl. I know my father had met her while he was a student at Rutgers. He lived with his uncle, John Thompson, who was a minister at the Middlebush Reformed Church, and at that time, with funds as they were, he lived in the parsonage and commuted by train into New Brunswick.

My father and Paul Robeson were very good friends. Robeson was a giant of a man. My father was a little smaller than I am, and I can remember going to concerts where Paul Robeson would sing at the gym, and my father would take us backstage with him. Paul Robeson would come down, he'd grab my father by the shoulders and say, "Archie," and practically lift him off the ground, (laughter) and they had great mutual respect. My father had great compassion for Paul, for the fact that when the college football team traveled, he could not room with the other boys because of his color. He always understood how Paul was disillusioned with the life that was dealt him.

Selman Waksman was behind my father, I'm not sure exactly what class he was. They were both at the College of Agriculture, and Dad and Selman Waksman were good friends. Selman Waksman was a very poor boy when he arrived at Rutgers. Nobody realized that he was living in an attic in downtown New Brunswick. They really hazed the freshmen in those days, and, when Waksman came-- I guess all the men wore a tie and jacket-- they cut their neckties off.

Well, anyway, they cut Waksman's tie off, and when he went to chapel the next day, he had his collar up, covering his cut necktie, and I think the next day, they took his shirt. So, the next day, he arrives with just the jacket, and then they realized

9

that the poor man only had the one necktie and one shirt, and they also realized he was practically eating bread and water in these attic lofts. I think it's amazing how that man turned the tables and made a great discovery *(Waksman became co-discoverer of streptomycin).*

"My father's name was Max Abraham Berezowsky. The Irish sergeant who enlisted him couldn't spell that so he wrote down 'Bloom.' " --Lewis M. Bloom

My father came from a village in what is now Belarus. In his time, 1910, it was the province of Lithuania in Czarist Russia. My father was intelligent. He wanted to be an engineer. He was in his late teens. He was Jewish. And the local authorities resisted his going beyond Gymnasium. My grandfather had done everything, including bribing some local officials to get him accepted by some engineering institute, but it fell through. And he wasn't getting anywhere.

The only thing he could do, as a Jew, was apprentice out as a tailor. Then he was told that he had to serve in the Czar's army, and Jews were heavily persecuted in the army. So he upped and left.

A great aunt in Brooklyn sponsored him. Her husband was a wholesale butcher. They lived in a large brownstone, three or four stories high, and the first floor was devoted entirely to a refrigerated area for meats. My father was put into the refrigerator the first thing next morning to work with these carcasses. He lived in the attic, and at the end of the week he asked if he could get paid. His aunt's husband told him a greenhorn like him does not deserve any pay, he's teaching him a trade, he bought him a pair of pants and a shirt, and therefore he should dispel any ideas of getting paid for quite a while.

Well, my father was a very independent person who could fend for himself. At four o'clock the next morning he packed up, walked across the bridge and made his way to Whitehall Street.

My father spoke Russian, Polish, Lithuanian, Yiddish, German and Hebrew. As he walked down the street, he saw signs that said "Join the Army and See the World" in all those languages, including Yiddish. Well, that was his first indication that anybody treated Jews on an equal basis, so he enlisted.

His name was Max Abraham Berezowsky. They put him in a reception station on Governors Island. After a week, he complained to the first sergeant that his name wasn't being called at reveille. They found out that the Irish sergeant who had enlisted him couldn't spell his name. The first thing he could think of was "Bloom," so he put down Bloom, and that has remained with the family ever since.

His outfit was the 29th Infantry Regiment. They'd just come back from the Philippines a year or so before, and they were being trained as horse infantry. I don't think the US army was over 120,000 men at that time. It was a repository for all sorts of nationals; very few of them could speak English. My father learned English and the equivalent of a high school education in the Army.

He left the Army about six months before his enlistment was up because he wanted to get married. You could buy your way out of the Army for about $100 in those days, anybody could, and that's what he did.

Through a series of events, he ended up as a manufacturer of women's apparel in New York. After that broke up, he went into a number of other ventures, one of which brought him to New Brunswick. That's how we ended up living in Highland Park.

"My parents were first-generation German-American, but they wouldn't let me speak German or read a German newspaper."   *--Franklin J. Kneller*

My parents were first-generation German-Americans, and they were embarrassed about World War I. They wouldn't teach me German. They wouldn't allow me to learn German. They

11

spoke German once in a while between them, when they didn't want me to know, but they wanted to be Americans. They wouldn't even have the German newspaper in the house, and they told me that they would have days when they would be embarrassed on the bus because people would look down on them if they were reading a German-language paper. They didn't want to do anything German. They wanted to be American.

"My mother flew bombers to Gander, but she couldn't fly into the combat zones, and she groused and grumbled about that."   *--Franklyn Johnson*

My father was born in a place called Honeoye Falls, near Rochester, New York, and my mother was born nearby, in Mendon-- small villages in the western part of the state. Our family were farmers from way back, from the 1600s in New York and before that in New England.

My father was a Pfc in the Fourth Marines in World War I, and after that much of his career was spent in Florida as an immigration border patrol inspector. Then, because the folks on the family farm were getting older and needed help, we went up to New York State. He had been a reserve officer in the Florida National Guard and when the CCC, the Civilian Conservation Corps, came along, they pulled in Army officers to supervise. He was, at that point maybe a first lieutenant and he had three different camps. So he could do his work and then go home on weekends to help the old folks.

In the meantime, my mother, Olyve Eckler Johnson, had been taking flying lessons, mainly for her own amusement. She got a Piper Cub first, and then a Cessna, and this hobby was turned into military service in the Civil Air Patrol. She had been frustrated by being just too old to join the WACS.

I remember my father by this time was in the Pentagon, on the planning staff, and was now a lieutenant colonel, and she begged him to intervene for her, but of course they had to have a rule. So she missed out on the WACs but instead went into the Civil Air Patrol. She was adjutant of the New Jersey wing, and she flew planes, including bombers, out from a place called Manhattan, Kansas, from the factory, and she'd fly them, on occasion, to Gander, Newfoundland.

Another irritant on top of the age problem was the fact that they wouldn't let her fly planes into the combat zone, so she groused and grumbled, and tried to extort from my father some promises that the rule would be changed, but it wasn't changed.

So, they had, both of them, rather colorful careers, and then, that led up, I guess, to my being in the service from ROTC, as a double ROTC graduate. I went to a military academy called Riverside, down in Georgia. I didn't have a commission, but I had three years of ROTC, and I came up to New Jersey and was an academic sophomore, but a military senior in the Rutgers ROTC regiment, which had some interesting results. My superiors in the fraternity were under me as second lieutenants in A Company, which I commanded.

"My father was just ripe for the Czar's military arrangements, and being Jewish, he'd have been sent to Siberia."   *-- Mark Addison*

Both of my parents came from Lithuania, although it was Russia at that time. My mother arrived in 1893; my father, I think, in '94. They met here, and were married around the turn of the century.

My mother arrived here alone from Lithuania. It was quite a journey at the age of 13. She was technically an orphan. Her father had passed away after he had remarried, and she had a very lovely stepmother. But she also had a married sister here, in the United States, in Tuckerton, in Ocean County. And they sent her a ticket. And she came alone, which was quite a journey at that time. My understanding is that she traveled to Hamburg, took a boat to a port in England, and then came to Philadelphia. She

13

didn't land at Ellis Island.

My father, on the other hand, came at the age of 19. He was just ripe for the Czar's military arrangements. And he was not an only son, so therefore he was eligible. And what very often happened to Jewish young men, they were sent to Siberia and nobody ever heard of them again. There were a number of Jewish people in southern Ocean County, and they wanted someone who would be able to teach their children Hebrew and something about Jewish tradition and prayer. He had been attending a rabbinical school, commonly called a yeshiva, and so they sent him a ticket and got him out.

That brought him into the same area where my mother had previously landed. Eventually, when she grew up, they married. Tuckerton is not large today; it was even smaller then. So it wasn't hard to meet. After all, the Jewish community was rather small. And anyone who arrived from the other side was apparently immediately grabbed, brought into a house with food and whatever and plied with questions about relatives in the old country. So obviously, they met rather soon after he arrived.

"My grandmother and a girl friend came from Germany in the 1880s and set out for California. Their courage was astonishing." --Frank Dauster

My father was born and lived, until he was an early teenager, in a godforsaken little town in Pennsylvania coal country. He quit school when he was 12 to go pick slate under the coal-breakers. And I've been back there. I'll never go back there again. The coal dust is ingrained into everything. There's no grass, it's just horrible, still. Just awful.

I just recently found out something I hadn't known about my father's mother, and it's astonishing. I knew she'd been married previously and my father had some half-brothers and half-sisters, but I didn't know the rest. It seems that she came to this country from Germany with another girl, a friend, and they set

14

out for California. This had to be sometime in the 1880s. The courage of two young women doing this is just astonishing.

They got as far as Iowa, they met a couple of farmers out there, and my grandmother married one of them. They wound up in Pennsylvania. He worked in the coal mines and was killed.

Then she married my grandfather, who was also a miner and after he was given up for dead the third time in a coal mine collapse, she said, "That's it, I'm leaving. I'm taking the children. You can do what you want."

So somehow they both wound up in Bloomfield. I remember that my grandfather had blue marks all over his hands and all over his head, and his neck. And I thought he had been tattooed, but they were scars from where coal had fallen down and cut the skin and the coal dust had just gotten ingrained. There was no medical treatment, so he had these blue marks all over. It was horrifying.

If they hadn't left, I could have grown up in a coal town, Mahanoy City or Ashland, or the town my father was from, which was called Locustdale, a little, tiny place. I wouldn't have lasted there very long. That's not my thing.

I don't know how they got to Bloomfield. I have a vague recollection that some friends from Pennsylvania had moved down here. They had some kind of connection. At one point, my father, who was 16, was working in a factory. He was the only employed member of the family. He was supporting the whole family, which was both his parents and a variety of siblings.

Eventually my grandparents had a little mom and pop grocery store for a while. And then my grandfather got a job as caretaker of the football field for Bloomfield High School, and they moved over to East Orange, and that's where I grew up.

We lived on the second floor of my grandfather's house. He lived on the first floor with one of my uncles, who was unmarried. And my mother took care of the whole house, and did all the cooking, all the laundry, and all that sort of thing for everybody. And while my father was out of work, I guess my grand-

15

father, through his pension and my uncle, who was working, provided the groceries.

Now that house is directly underneath the Garden State Parkway. So as I drive down the Parkway and go past it, I keep remembering that old John Barrymore film, I don't remember the name of it, where he is running away and at the end he looks at the house he's been trying to get and he says: "Good-bye, my house," and I feel very much like that.

"My father jumped ship in Halifax and bummed his way across Canada, working as a waiter, busboy, night clerk and boxer."   *--Frederick Wesche II*

My father was one of 10 children-- the oldest, in fact. My grandfather had gone from Germany to England around 1900 and went to work in one of the famous hotels in Brighton, called the Metropole. My father and most of the other children were born in England, in either Brighton or London. Come World War I, my grandfather still had something of a German accent and with the feeling against Germans at that time he decided to pull up stakes and come to America.

In the meantime, however, my father, the oldest of the lot, had to get out and go to work and help support the family. He wanted to join the Navy, but his father wouldn't sign a release for him, so he signed on as a cabin boy on a Cunard White Star Line ship.

One of his first trips was to Halifax, Nova Scotia, where he jumped ship along with a classmate of his and bummed his way across Canada, working as a waiter, busboy, night clerk and whatnot on the Canadian Pacific Railroad and some of the hotels in Banff.

Dad had a rather checkered career. He never finished school, but, among other things, he was a semi-professional boxer in Canada. He went down to San Francisco shortly after the earthquake. Meanwhile, my grandfather had brought the rest of the family over and settled in Bridgeport, Connecticut, where some friends were living. At last count, there were some 26 first cousins, of which I am the oldest.

Now, about my mother. She was born in London, was orphaned at a very early age and was raised by an older sister. She never finished school but went to work as a nanny for a rather wealthy English family. They traveled a good deal, taking their staff with them, and for some reason they got to Bridgeport.

Dad had come East just before the war started to see the rest of his family, and that's where my mother and father met. So they were married, I guess, in 1915, and I was born a year later. My Dad became a naturalized citizen, and now, with a family, he needed a better job. He answered an ad for the Western Electric Company for "Telephone Engineers."

Well, Dad interviewed for it and lied like the dickens about his education. He never had any education-- but he got the job. When I started in high school, I had to teach my father some of the basic things of electricity and magnetism and things of that sort, science that he was supposed to know.

Dad spent a good 30 years with the company and did quite well by the time he retired. He was transferred first to Chicago, and then to Kearny, New Jersey, and we settled down in Roselle. That's really where I grew up.

"That old Navy Chief had been on my father's submarine. I walked out about two feet off the ground. I had just met my father."   *--Paul W. Rork*

I had a grandfather who fought in the Civil War. I have his rifle downstairs in the basement. My father was in the First World War. He was in the D-Class submarines, and he told my mother that he never wanted me to be in the Navy. When I graduated from Rutgers, I went down to enlist in the Navy, in spite of what my father had said. And the line was so long that I said, "I don't want to wait here all day." And someone said,

17

"Go around the corner. There's no long line at the Coast Guard." And that's how I got in the Coast Guard. (laughter)

My father saw action during World War I, but I don't know any details, only what my mother remembered. My father died when I was a baby, so I never talked to him. And the only thing my mother told me was that he always washed and darned his own socks. (laughter)

But she also told me this story. They were on a practice dive off of New Hampshire, and the submarine suddenly conked out. It just wouldn't move, and he was an engineer, and the C.O. called him in and told him that they'd have to hit the escape hatches if they couldn't get the engine started.

He went back to the engine room and took out a New Testament that my mother had given him and started to read. Where? I don't know exactly, but he read from one of the letters from the Apostle Paul and then started to look for the problem. The Lord evidently gave him the answer because the submarine was freed from the bottom and up they went, and as a result, I was named Paul.

After the war, my father was in the merchant marine for a while and then he worked at the Philadelphia Navy Yard. We lived in Paterson, and that's where I was born.

My mother was a social worker, and she worked for the B.P.O.E., the Benevolent and Protective Order of Elks. She took care of crippled children, handicapped mentally or physically or both and worked for them for almost 20 years, right through the Depression.

I was not living with my mother during those years. My father had died, and he was a Mason in a lodge in Philadelphia, and the Masons found out that my mother was widowed and having a difficult problem at home and offered to take me off her hands, so to speak, as a guest at the Masonic home in Pennsylvania. So I lived there as an orphan, or a half-orphan, from the time I was six until I was 18, when I went to Rutgers.

So I never knew my father, but years later, during World War

II, when I was on a sub chaser out of Morehead City, North Carolina, a strange thing happened.

I went into the naval base there, the section base, they called it. I went to get some supplies, and there was an old Navy chief in there, and he was wearing submarine bars. I said, "Hi, Chief. I see you were in the submarine service." He says, "Yep." I said, "My Dad was in the submarine service." He said, "No kidding, what ship?" I said, "The D-3." He said, "Say that again." "The D-3." He said, "I served on the D-3." Now remember, I never saw my father alive. He died when I was a baby. He said, "Who was your father?" I said, "My father was Rork." "You mean 'Red' was your father?" He had red hair.

This guy knew my father like a best friend. And he told me all about my father. He confirmed the story about the submarine and the name Paul. He just thought my father was the greatest, you know. And I walked out of that place about two feet off the ground. I had just met my father.

"My father got out of Russia by hiding under the seat on a train. When they got to the Polish border, he just walked across." --Irving E. Pape

Both my parents were born in Russia. They came here when they were very young. My Dad told me the story of how he came to this country. He walked across half of Europe, at the age of 15, to get out of Russia. His adventures are worthy of a novel.

He was in a small town in Russia. They didn't have paved roads in those days. They had dirt roads, and when it rained it got very muddy. So they built boardwalks about 18 inches high so the gentry in their finery could walk without getting mud on their boots.

My father was walking along and he passed by a Cossack officer wearing a white uniform. The officer took a swing at him with a riding crop simply because he was a farm boy and he was wearing farm clothes. He knocked him into the street.

My Dad said he looked up and said, "I'm not gonna stay in a country that treats their people like this," and he made up his mind that he was going. He had the equivalent of about $15 that the family gave him.

On the Russian trains, the baggage was underneath the seat. There was a sliding door in the seat. So he got on a train, went in a second-class coach and went into one of the compartments. There was a lady there. He told her he was going to hide under the seat. So he crawled in, stayed there, and the lady fed him.

When they came to the Polish border-- customs was very lax in those days-- he just walked across. Got a job in Poland. He slept in barns. Worked his way into the wine country in Germany, where he worked for a year. Saved his money and he drove the wagons with the big barrels of grapes. That was his job. He was a husky kid. He worked his way towards France. Got to France and when he had money for his passage, he got on the boat and came to Waterbury, Connecticut. For some reason that we never knew, all of our relatives had come to Waterbury, Connecticut, which is where he went.

My Mother came here when she was 12. She was a very pretty girl and there was a big Jewish community in Waterbury. She was a very popular girl. And she worked in a factory and they thought she was under age. But she said no, she was out of the eighth grade. She had done her studies and everything. And she picked up on English very quickly. And as a consequence they didn't know whether she was or she wasn't.

Waterbury was the brass center of the world and also the center of the clock industry. After these people worked for 12 hours they would run home and have a sandwich and then run downtown to study English, because the worst insult in those days was to call somebody a "greenhorn." And they didn't want to be considered greenhorns.

My mother spoke English perfectly, but had difficulty with one word. She could not say "arthritis." It always came out "arthur-itis." And my Dad had trouble transposing v's and w's. He would say he put on a "west," and went "vest," which was his only problem.

My father had two brothers in Russia with a total of nine children, all of whom were lost in the war. And his mother, who lived in a log cabin, was also lost. After the war, we never heard from any of them, so we knew they had to be dead. Because before the war my Dad would send them money, and we would send clothing and things. And they would always acknowledge the letters. But he lost his whole family in Russia, and he was never able to talk about it.

During the Depression, my father and mother moved from New England to East Orange, where my father opened a cigar and stationery store, and that's where I went to school.

"Dad wrote an essay about being in a shell hole surrounded by rotting corpses when he looked out and saw a rose blooming." --John Berglund

My dad did all kinds of things in his life. He was a man, God bless him, who saw that the grass was always greener on the other side of the fence. He was, variously, a schoolteacher in a one-room log cabin schoolhouse at 19, a surveyor, a painter, a printer, a publisher. He had a one-man newspaper in Moccasin, Wyoming, where he was a social editor, reporter, janitor, et cetera. And he became a landscape gardener through ICS courses.

He had been a cowboy in his youth, among other things. I can remember him with fur chaps and a leather vest and a Stetson and a guitar, singing western songs. He could play any musical instrument. He could play the violin left-handed.

In World War I, at the age of 30, he enlisted in the 27th Division, which was a New York Division, and my mother was in Atlantic City, this young girl who was engaged to a sailor, God forbid. She looked over a list of orphans and she picked the name of this Berglund, this harsh un-euphonious name, J. Leroy

21

Berglund, out of the list, along with a boy she knew. My Dad was not an orphan, he had a living father, he just had a dead mother, but he got on the list inadvertently.

Mother picked out two gifts, one a token gift for this Berglund fellow, and the other a nice comb and brush set. And she got the gifts mixed up and sent the nice gift to this J. Leroy Berglund. He wrote her a letter, and despite the fact that she was engaged to a sailor, he visited her before he went overseas.

He was in France for nine months in combat, came back and married her. And my grandmother always thought I would be a complete nervous wreck because I was conceived right after the war. I don't know why she thought that.

Dad would never talk about his war experiences, but he wrote an essay in which he told about being in a shell hole, surrounded by two or three rotting corpses of his own people, and he looked out and saw a rose blooming. That gave him hope and a belief that this terrible thing would soon be over. He had this profound faith that everything was going to be all right. A childlike faith. But he never talked about the war.

Swedes-- especially Swedish Lutherans-- are very dour. Yes, dour is the word. But Dad was gregarious. He loved everybody, and everybody loved him. When he died and had a memorial service, you couldn't get a midget in there with a crowbar, it was so crowded with people. He was quite a guy.

He worked for newspapers as a business manager and then he worked for a savings and loan. When I was a kid we lived, variously, in Toronto, Cincinnati, Pittsfield, Massachusetts, Camden, which was the pits, and always back to Margate.

When mother was a girl, her mother and father had a rooming house in Atlantic City, and later on, a very successful restaurant. It was where the trains came in, Tennessee Avenue. It was called the "Home Restaurant," and my grandmother did all the baking. She'd get up at two o'clock in the morning to bake, which may explain why she didn't live past her mid-sixties. They lived in Margate and so that's why, I guess, we lived in Margate.

"My mother had two sons who were 4-F, and I think she was embarrassed, so she became a WAC grandmother."   *--Crandon F. Clark*

My mother went into the Army in World War II as a WAC. She was in her 40s. She was a WAC grandmother. She had been in training as a nurse in Frost General Hospital in Chelsea, Massachusetts, and my father, who lived in East Boston, was a patient there, and that's how they met. They were married and moved to New York. She never finished her nurse's training.

Until she died, about 13 years ago, she wished she had completed her training because she did a lot of work in the health care field, but she never had that R.N. And of course that made a lot of difference financially. She didn't really work until after my father died, which was 1941, and she was a widow for about 40 years. But she didn't have that R.N., so she wasn't able to go into a hospital and get a job

When World War II came along, I think she enlisted in the WACS because she was a little embarrassed. She had three sons. My older brother in medical school at the time at Columbia had high blood pressure and was 4-F. My younger brother had a punctured ear drum, so he was sort of like a 4-F. Maybe she felt that she should do something. She was driving as a volunteer for the Red Cross in the New York area, taking people to various military stations, and she decided she wanted to get back into health care and military, and she signed up for the WACS.

She joined an organization of nurses and other medical technicians, had her training at Fort Oglethorpe, Georgia, and then came back to the Second Army area and was a nurse's aide or medical technician at Halleran General Hospital on Staten Island, New York, which was a hospital primarily for veterans who had been injured and needed special help in getting back to normal-- paraplegics I guess, but people who had something to do with their muscles and their legs and so forth. She did that for a couple of years. When I came home from the service, her

23

health wasn't good, and she had a serious operation, so she finished up her career with the Army. I think she was in for about three years, so she was a WAC grandmother by that time.

"My grandfather on my mother's side was Irish, but Orange Irish. I was sent to school with an orange tie on St. Patrick's Day."   *--C. Harrison Hill*

I'm working on a genealogy. My dad was from Highland Park, and my mother was from Milltown, and just how they met I don't know. But I found a newspaper clipping about their wedding in 1913: "Mr. Hill called at the Harkins' home with an automobile. The couple were driven to the parsonage in South Amboy, and following the ceremony, they were whirled off in the automobile to the South Amboy Railroad Station, where they boarded a train for a trip to Connecticut."

My great-grandfather Harkins (on my mother's side) came to Milltown from Ireland in the 1840s. His son, my grandfather, was the borough clerk in Milltown for 25 years and my grandchildren are now living in what was my grandfather's house, which we think is rather unusual in America.

Before they moved in, I went into the cellar to clean up after my aunt and uncle had passed away, and I found a jar in which they had stuffed all their valuable papers from the 1860s to 1970. In the bottom of this, folded up in little one-inch cubes, were my great-grandfather's citizenship papers and Civil War discharge. That's what got me started on looking into genealogy.

My father's father was a cotton carder for Johnson and Johnson, and his grandmother was probably one of the first women in the Salvation Army in the 1880s. She lived in New Brunswick and I have her picture in uniform. According to my father she was a captain and my grandfather was her lieutenant, which sounds strange in today's world. Apparently she traveled around. They went to the coal fields of Pennsylvania and lived on the collections they took up until the family became so big that they had to settle down.

My father had been comptroller at the Durant Motor Car Company in Elizabeth, and when Durant went out of business he was lucky to get a job with the Utilities Construction Company, and then ultimately he became their secretary-treasurer.

There was tragedy in my father's family. One of his sisters died of cancer, and his mother took it so hard that she felt they had to get away, so they decided to go down to the shore, and at that time they pitched tents down at Morgan. The two other sisters worked in New Brunswick and they came down on a Saturday afternoon by trolley. They went in the water and stepped in a hole, and both of them were drowned. One of the girls was pulled out, but she couldn't be saved. The other girl's body washed ashore the next day.

Now I mentioned that my grandfather on my mother's side was Irish, but he was Orange Irish. When Al Smith ran for office, my grandfather was about to die, you know: "If he had ever been elected, that would have been the worst thing that ever happened to this country." I was sent to school with an orange tie on St. Patrick's Day. But my wife's name is Patricia Kathleen Mullen, so I guess we've become integrated.

"Six years after my father arrived from Lithuania, he had served in World War I, had been around the country, and was a married man." --Andrew White

My father was born in Lithuania. His parents died at a very young age, and he doesn't remember them. He lived on the family farm, and his sister became the owner, despite the traditional ways when the son got the farm. She was older and married, and, apparently, she wasn't very nice to him. I doubt if he went to more than the third or fourth grade, if that, but he could read and write Lithuanian quite well. He could read English, but he could not write it very well.

25

At age 20 they gave him enough money to come to America through Hamburg, Germany. I have the manifest of the ship that he came on. It was the *Augusta Victoria*. I guess he came in steerage. His Lithuanian name was Jonas, which is John in English, and Vaiciulis was his surname. Immediately upon arrival, he could see the problem with his name, especially in 1914, so he changed it to White, because there is a "White" sound to it. He told me that the sound of "V" in Lithuanian had a "W" sound in English. Phonetically, it would be "Wychulis," so he made it White. So he became John White.

He landed in New York, and, according to the manifest, they asked if he had $50. He had (laughter) $25 when he came here. He was sponsored by a relative in New Britain, Connecticut, and I cannot locate the family. He stayed there for a short period to get established. He was an adventuresome sort of fellow. He then went to work in the mines in Pennsylvania. He told me that he did not like it. In fact, he said he was in a cave-in so he quit.

Then he came to New Jersey. Apparently, he had two aunts in Perth Amboy. He called them aunts, but I could never find out if they were really aunts. With Europeans, for some reason, everyone was a relative (laughter). But this one aunt was very good to him. I remember meeting both of them as a young child.

He did odd jobs around New Jersey and joined the New Jersey National Guard. Upon the start of World War I, they nationalized the Guard and he was in the United States Army at age 23 or 24.

He went into action in France. He had quite a few battles listed on his discharge papers, which I have. He was a Pfc and a machine gunner. He had been gassed. He had a wound on his face from shrapnel. He was out of the service within a year and a half. He moved to Linden, where there was a whole network of people of the same background, and a Lithuanian family said he could board with them. I knew the family. He worked at odd jobs in industry.

He met my mother in Elizabeth or Linden. She lived in Linden. They were married in 1920. So six years after he came here, he was in the service, had been around the country, and he was a married man. (laughter)

He was a very loyal American. He just loved this country. He worked very hard. In fact, he bought a house in Linden, upon his marriage. It was a two-family house. He figured he should have income, so he had a two-family house, and the original house at 1804 Clinton Street was where I was born.

He worked hard and I guess it was kind of tough after World War I. He did get a job eventually with Standard Oil Company of New Jersey, which then became Esso and is now Exxon-Mobil, and he worked as a pipe fitter out in the yard (the tank field), and worked in the mud and filth. He later became a maintenance man. He said, "Better than working out in the mud." He was a handyman and he could do a lot of things, so they liked him there.

He put in about 37 years with Standard Oil and was pensioned from there and was a very loyal Exxon man. He retired at age 62 and lived in Linden until he died. He sold the original house and moved up about eight blocks, bought another two-family house, and I lived there until I was drafted into the Army. He never got to the real nice part of Linden, although he could have. The reason he wanted to live on that street was so he could ride his bike to Exxon, about a mile away.

At that time, there was a whole swarm of men going to work on bicycles from Linden. You could see them all going to work in the morning and coming home at night. He worked long enough to be the last man to go to and from the Exxon Refinery on a bicycle.

When he retired, my parents purchased a summer home in Lavallette, and he had about 12 good years there. He enjoyed the summers in Lavallette and he loved to go crabbing in the bay. Lavallette was good for him, and my mother too. We had a lot of fun, and our children have many good memories of Lavallette and so do my wife and I. We spent part of our vacations there.

27

"When I was 10, Mother and I visited my grand-mother in Norway. She lived in utter poverty, in a shack, with hardly any light."   *--Leonard Hansen*

My parents came from two different towns in southern Nor-way, from the Bible Belt of Norway. Norwegians are not known generally among the world at large as people that are conserva-tive in their religion, but in southern Norway that was the case. One came from Grimstadt, that's my father, and my mother came from just outside of Krisiansand, a little town called Sogne. They immigrated here in the early part of this century. To this day, I don't know the exact years. But they met here.

Like so many other people, my family had found it hard to make a living in Norway. My mother and I visited my grand-mother when I was 10 years old. She lived in utter poverty, in a shack. It was almost frightening. There was hardly any light. It was kind of candlelight, in an elaborate shack of some kind. Their neighbors gave them milk, they were so poor. They had a few potatoes that they grew and some vegetables and that's all. But the air in Norway was so extraordinary. The air was clear. There were no smoke stacks anywhere.

My mother felt that there was a land of promise known as the United States and took her chance. My father, too, in Grimstadt, although it wasn't quite the same. Grimstadt is a wonderful little fishing town in southern Norway, an absolutely idyllic little town. He loved adventure, too, I think. He got on a boat and came here and never went back, whereas his brother, who got into the building business in the '20s, went back in the 1930s, just before the great upheaval of the Depression in this country. Today, they are big landowners there, my cousins. I visit them frequently.

As a matter of fact, I sent three of my four sons to Norway to live for two months or so with a family in this town of Grim-stadt. They love Norway but they love this country, too.

Norway is getting to be almost a boom country. It was always

28

very poor, struggling always, because it's rocks and it's endless waterways and islands. I've been there four times now. One time I went with the University Glee Club. I was then known as "Oh, Great Viking." We had a lot of fun.

My parents must have settled in New Jersey because they had friends here. Not to go to South Dakota or any of those places, they must have had some attachment here. My father, in one of his first jobs, worked in the clay plants in Perth Amboy. I never questioned much about it. If I had my father now, I would ask him endless details, you know, because I have a big world of history behind me now that I care very much about.

After Perth Amboy, my father moved to Hoboken, where he had a grocery store. Then his first wife died after having five children, and all the children were put in the Christian Orphan Home. My mother was working there as a cook and helper. My father met her there and married her and she brought up all of my five half brothers and sisters. I was the lowest one, the newcomer, the kid.

When we were growing up, my friends and I mimicked our parents because when they spoke they tried so hard to speak English. They would break into Norwegian and we would have both going at the same time. We all went to the Norwegian churches, which were Fundamentalist and Evangelical and Puritan. We had Norwegian sermons in the morning and in the afternoon. Occasionally, we would have an English affair at night, where we had testimonies and that sort of thing. It was very, very strict. No smoking, drinking, gambling, playing cards, going to movies. And it was very clannish.

"At 13, my father built a bicycle from scavenged parts, ran away, pedaled to a port and sold the bicycle to get his fare to America."   *--Roland Winter*

My mother was born in London while her parents were making the trip from Russia to the United States. My father had a

29

far more interesting background. He was born and raised on a farm in Germany near the Polish border, and he had a very strict father. His life was hell. When he was 13 or 14, out of scavenged parts he put together a workable bicycle. And when he was satisfied that the bicycle was capable of making a long journey, he ran away and he pedaled to a port city. He didn't even remember what port it was. When he got there, he sold the bicycle. That was his passage to the United States. He had no relatives or family friends here, no knowledge of English, either. And he was under 15. It boggles my mind today where he got the courage to do that.

But he had confidence, and he had natural mechanical skills. He boarded with a family and got a job in a machine shop. And he went to Cooper Union at night and learned English and basic engineering, and that enhanced his mechanical skills. He eventually became a tool and die maker. It was tough getting a job, but somehow he made it. Incredible story.

When the war broke out, he was working in a sophisticated machine shop in Manhattan that had a government contract to make gauges to test the accuracy and precision of gears. It was nerve-racking work for a tool and die maker because the forming of these gauges was all internal and you had to really guess at the cut and then they had to X-ray it. If you made one wrong cut, months of work were wasted. It was a terrible strain on him, but he was working six and seven days a week. And he died while I was overseas.

The last time I saw him, I was in a staging area in Fort Pickett, Virginia, and I knew I was going overseas. I wanted very badly to say good-bye to my family, but I couldn't get a pass.

There was a friend of my brother's in the same division who took a protective interest in me. He approached me one day and said, "I got a pass, I'm going home to Perth Amboy this weekend. Im gonna take you with me, with or without a pass." The train had to go through Washington, D.C., which was overrun with military police, but he says, "Don't worry. I'll save your ass." And I was frightened as hell.

When it came time to go back to the train on Sunday afternoon, my father wouldn't let other family members come along. He said, "I wanna take Roland to the train." And he took me to Newark. He was a man that didn't show much emotion, but he gave me a hug and said, "You'll make it. You're a man now." That's the last I saw him.

"The regular operator came in drunk, but my father had been studying Morse Code, so he took over, and then he got the job." *--George Reynolds*

My father was born in 1871. So he represents a link, for me, with a rather distant past. My mother was born in 1884. Her maiden name was Laura Lee, from a Trenton family, as was my father. My father's family had originally come from England and settled in farms in the Imlaystown area. Some of them, as the family got bigger and the farm didn't, moved into Trenton and became machinists.

My grandfather was a machinist and was seriously injured in a mill accident and had to stop working. As a result, my father had to leave school at the age of 13. That was the end of his education. It was a large family. He had three sisters and two brothers, and he was the oldest, and he went out to work at 13 as a messenger boy in the Pennsylvania Railroad Telegraph Offices in Trenton.

In his spare time, waiting for messages to be delivered, he learned the Morse Code. One night the regular operator came in so drunk that he couldn't function, so my father took over. Nobody knew who was tapping the key at the other end of the line, but reports came back that the transmissions that night were exceptionally good. So he got the job as telegraph operator. From there he was transferred to Jersey City, and he worked on the Pennsylvania Railroad until he retired in 1936.

My mother went to what is now Rider University, became a

first class stenographer and worked with the New Jersey Department of Geology as a secretary. She also had a couple of siblings to help support, and did not marry until 1912, at which time my father was 41 years old. I was born in 1917, in Trenton. Soon after that, I guess I was two years old, we moved to Highland Park, New Jersey, and that's where I lived my early life.

"The people in Roseto didn't have heart attacks, and a study showed that was because they were a clan, helping one another out." --Arthur Jiannine

My father was born in Roseto Valfotore in Italy. He came to this country as a babe-in-arms and his family went to Roseto, Pennsylvania, following a group of people who, a few years before, had come from this Roseto village in Italy and settled in Roseto, Pennsylvania. So his parents went there and that's where he grew up. Then his siblings were all born in Roseto.

There are some books about the fact that this was a clan of people that came to this country and kind of stuck together. There was a study, some years ago, trying to determine why the people in this little town of Roseto, Pennsylvania, even though they ate a lot of pasta, olive oil, and all that, were not subject to heart attacks, and one of the things that came out was that these people were like a clan, and, if somebody was in trouble, everybody was there to help them. There was no stress.

But when they moved, and left, and went out on their own, in other parts of the country, they didn't have the benefit of that clan, and then they start developing heart problems.

One time I went back to Roseto, Italy, with my father. It's a hill town, and we drove by this little bitty house, which was now falling apart, but he pointed out that that was his house when he was a child, and this was typical of families there. They would have a small house, and everybody, no matter how many kids there were, lived in the house.

He went to school to the fourth grade, and I don't know just how old he was then, but, at age 12, which I guess was about the time he finished the fourth grade, he left home and came to Newark, New Jersey, to apprentice as a tailor, and that was his line of work after that. Later, he was involved in manufacturing, and during World War I he moved from Newark down to Red Bank and became general manager of production for the Sigmund Eisner Company, the largest uniform manufacturing company in the United States.

We never spoke Italian at home. I wish we had, and I wish I had learned it. My mother was not Italian, and I think, back in those days, the idea was that, if you were from a foreign country, you wanted your children to become solid Americans. He didn't speak Italian in the house, but when he was with his friends and spoke Italian, I was able to understand a little bit. I have since forgotten it.

Some of the culture carried over to the extent that I think we had pasta three times a week, and we had some other Italian foods, but my mother, not being Italian, also cooked sometimes in her own style, which was mainly to boil something in water, since she was kind of English. You know, boil it in water and throw it on the table without flavor.

She came from a farm family. The homestead at the time was in Keansburg, New Jersey, and she, as a young woman, went to work at the Eisner factory, as many of them did back in those days, and she took a trolley from that area of Keansburg. She worked for Eisner, and that's where she met my father, or my father met her.

"My father's whole family were forced by the Nazis to dig their own grave. Then they were all shot and buried in that trench."   *--Herbert Gross*

My father was from Hungary. He came from a family of nine children. He was the oldest. They lived in a little village and were very poor. His father saved up enough money to send him, because he was the oldest, to America, where the streets were paved with gold. He would make all that money, and then send for the whole family.

When he was 13 years old, he arrived here and knew no one. They didn't have any relatives here, and they just had enough money to put him in steerage. He got to New York City, and a Jewish organization that took care of placing people who didn't have relatives here, put him in a boarding house in Philadelphia and got him a job in a cigar factory.

My father was never what my grandfather thought he would be. He was never a real earner. My father was more of a student and a scholar, and that's how I remember him. He was always reading and reading. He really never was interested in money, and he never brought anyone else over. That was unfortunate, because the entire family-- those children were all married with children-- were all killed in the ghetto they were in.

When the Nazis came in, they had to dig their own grave, and they were all shot in this one trench. Children three years old, four years old. The reason we know this story, three of the girls who at the time were 15 up to 19, very beautiful by the way, because we finally got them over here, the Nazis took and didn't kill them. And how they used them you could use your own imagination.

After the war, my father got them over here to this country, and they're presently living here. But that's how my father came here. And my mother came here from Hungary. She was like two years old, and she has no recollection of the old country. She came from a large family, too. They settled in Trenton. My father met my mother, and my father moved to Trenton. He then got a job as an insurance agent for Metropolitan Life Insurance Company. I was born in Trenton, and I have no brothers or sisters.

My father was very interested in history and politics. He was never interested in local politics. He loved Roosevelt. That was his God. And it turns out that Roosevelt was, as far as I'm con-

cerned, a pretty unconcerned person when it came to the Holocaust, and to Jews who were trying to flee Germany, because at
the time he refused to allow that boatload in and sent them back
to the ovens.

After that, my father was a shattered man, because Roosevelt
had always been his ideal, with the NRA and with what he did
for the poor people at the time. When I say he was scholarly, he
would read every newspaper. *The New York Times* was his Bible. This is my recollection of him. He wasn't interested in
sports or anything. It was always world affairs, national affairs.

He knew what was going on with Hitler in the 30s, and because of him and my mother, who was also very well read, I
knew what was going on. We were hoping the US would become involved. My father was pretty much of a pacifist. But I
was hoping, and I used to be angry whenever I saw anything
with Hitler or what was going on there. I used to be infuriated.
In fact, that's why I joined the Marine Corps. I thought it was a
chance to see action, and I'd get over there and get after them.

"There was a plague in Spain. His parents took him to a ship's captain and said, 'Get him out of here.' He was nine years old." --D. Robert Mojo

My father was born in Italy and came to this country when he
was 12 years old, by himself. My mother's father came to this
country when he was nine, by himself. There was a plague going through Spain, and his parents took him to a ship's captain
who was going to America, and said, "Get him out of here and
put him wherever you can when you get to America."

So he arrived at age nine in New York City. The ship's captain knew a grocer and he put him in the care of the grocer. The
grocer gave him a job, and when he realized that he could write
well, made him the bookkeeper, and that's how he started his
career in the United States.

Eventually, my father began to travel. He and his brother

formed a company, in the hosiery line, and they both traveled throughout South America and the Caribbean. My father arrived in Cuba one time, and met my mother's father, and my mother's father invited him to the house, and that's how my mother and he met. After they were married, they lived in Cuba. My father became the representative for Underwood typewriters in Cuba.

My mother's father, early in his career, had heard that there were great opportunities in Cuba and decided to pack up and move to Cuba. Before it was all over, he had amassed a pretty good fortune. He built just about every bridge and highway that there was in Cuba, and that they're still using to this day, and he also had the largest furniture store in Havana. He built the house I was born in-- it had about 30, 31 rooms.

This was in the good old days, when they had a chauffeur, a Packard and a Buick, a chief gardener and two assistants, a head cook and two assistants, a downstairs maid who never went upstairs, and an upstairs maid who never worked downstairs. I guess it was a pretty good life, but, I was too young to enjoy it.

When I was five years old, we moved to the United States, just as the Depression was starting. We were in New York City for about six months, and then we moved to northern New Jersey, West Orange, and that's where I went to school, all the way from grammar school on up through high school.

My earliest memory is, at age three, of one of the most severe hurricanes that ever hit Cuba. I still have a mental picture of looking out the front door, and seeing the water about three or four feet deep, and seeing one of our dogs trying to swim from the garage to the house.

Another memory that is very vivid, I remember that we took an automobile trip. We had a chauffeur, and the chauffeur drove us out into the country to a village. There was a traveling circus in that village, and, as we drove down to the center of the village, there was an elephant that apparently had become enraged, and he was trumpeting and walking backwards.

Our driver was transfixed by this scene, and he just kept go-

36

ing towards this elephant. I can remember the fright in every-body in that car, including myself. I was probably about four or five years old. Finally my mother screamed, and that shook the chauffeur into action, and he put on the brakes and backed up, and that little vignette is with me for the rest of my life.

"They had two brothers and two sisters marrying, so my grandfather saved money by having one wed-ding for both." --Norman Brandt

My father was born in Hrubeshow, Poland-- now, Poland, then, Russia. He was the son of a very wealthy grain merchant whose business was supplying wheat to the Russian Army. He was sent here just before World War I to, in effect, avoid the draft. Jewish men who got in the Russian Army in those days usually stayed for 30 years as an enlisted man.

He came here and was enrolled at Brooklyn Polytech, and was going there. He didn't like it after awhile, and he quit, but the checks were still coming from home. He lived on that until they stopped coming, by which time it turned out that just about everybody else in his family had been killed during the Revolution because they were wealthy.

He selected a birth date for himself-- November 11, 1885. Like so many people of his heritage, he knew his birthday only in terms of the Jewish calendar, which is a 13-month lunar calendar. As a result, he and many others had to select what they thought was an approximate date. He became a naturalized US citizen while enlisted in the US Army and serving at Camp Up-ton, New York, and he had some college.

Only one other member of my father's family left Russia be-fore the Revolution, and he went to Israel. My cousin, I met him only once, he's 10 years older than I am and he looks like my twin brother. He ended up in the Warsaw ghetto and was a member of the group that broke out of the ghetto.

He has a younger son who is almost the spitting image of my

younger son. They were born almost precisely at the same day and time, same age. The son became an officer in the Israeli Air Force, and was retired as a major general, or equivalent, in the Israeli Army. He'd been in charge of their Air Logistics Command, and, now he's working as a pilot for El Al.

My father came here as a student, primarily. He didn't come steerage, as most immigrants were coming. He came third class or second class. He became a salesman in retail situations. He worked in the garment district for awhile, as a cutter, and he owned a business during the Depression, but then there's a very interesting story about how he met my mother.

The main information we always had about my mother's father was that he was Mr. Wulf Ox. Now we researched this, and, as you know, the immigrants in Ellis Island, if the Irish agents couldn't understand it, they would assign a name. His name was William Ochs, and that came out "Wolf Ox." That's the name I knew him by, that's how his business knew him. His younger son, who was a lawyer, later took care of getting the name changed, officially, back to Ochs.

Now, how did my mother and father meet? My grandfather and mother went to New York to attend a wedding. At the wedding, they met somebody, and they got talking, and (laughter) the first people they met had four sons of marriageable age, and my grandfather and grandmother had two daughters of marriageable age. So they agreed that they'd have those sons come visit, and that's how my mother met my father in Westfield.

For a couple of years, they were courting. One of the men in the other family also married my mother's sister, so you had two brothers and two sisters marrying, and they had a double wedding. My grandfather saved money by having one wedding for both.

THE STREETS AND FIELDS OF HOME

In a state that became the most densely populated in the nation, a surprising number of us grew up on farms-- not large spreads like those of the Midwest, but manicured "truck farms" whose fresh produce could be trucked overnight to the markets of nearby New York City.

The small towns of our youth were in transition. Vestiges of the 19th century still lingered in clusters of unpaved streets, abandoned carriage factories and converted livery stables with a couple of gas pumps out front. The automobile was having a social impact everywhere, but for those who owned one it was still enough of a novelty to provide weekend entertainment in the form of a Sunday afternoon ride in the car.

There was an innocence about our childhood days that can never be recaptured in today's world. There was no television. My family, and those of many of my friends, did not own a car. My parents never had a telephone until I returned from the war. I was 24 then and wanted to be able to call my wife-to-be.

As kids, we played street games and lived mostly outdoors when we weren't in school. Summers were spent hiking, exploring the countryside, building boats and clubhouses.

Those who grew up on farms had chores. Walter Denise, in Colts Neck Township, helped his father plant rows of fruit trees and then plant vegetables between the rows while they waited for the trees to mature. There was no electricity, no water, just a hand pump in the front yard, and the outhouse was up by the barn, some 200 feet from the house.

On the other side of the state, in New Village, Joe DeMasi's father farmed and raised pigs, and Joe pitched in until Thomas A. Edison came out to the village and built a cement plant. Then Joe's father became Edison's right-hand man, and Joe went to work in the plant.

Sam Blum, in Piscataway, took care of the chickens and fed the pigeons. He lived in The Ferrer Colony, 100 families devoted to the principles of Francisco Ferrer, a martyred Spanish educator. "We were considered oddballs," says Sam.

In the towns, experiences were more varied. In Perth Amboy, Roland Winter became a river rat, building rafts, fishing and crabbing. Nathan Shoehalter helped out in his father's grocery store in Irvington. In Paterson, a tough, gritty town, William MacKenzie remembers the great silk mill strikes, when the streets were filled with screaming, rock-throwing crowds. Peter Sarraiocco, in an Italian enclave in Paulsboro, discovered at an early age the rewards of entrepreneurship, picking tomatoes for the princely sum of 75 cents an hour.

Ralph Schmidt, born in Germany and brought to this country by his parents as a child, remembered going with his father to a Newark theater to see All Quiet On the Western Front. His father had served in the German Army in World War I. "It was hard to tell what emotions it evoked in him," said Ralph, "but he always said that war was the most stupid activity humanity can participate in."

One of our number-- Fred Van Aken-- was born in Aachen, Germany, and his Jewish family suffered under the hard boot of Nazism. They finally escaped through Holland and made their way to New Jersey, forced to start a new life because they had left virtually everything they owned behind them.

40

"We had no water, no electricity, the outhouse was up the hill by the barn, but we had a grand piano and Mother sang."   *--Walter Denise*

Our family farm was started in 1712 in Monmouth County. And when Dad came along, he had kind of sought his own living and his own experience in life. He graduated from Rutgers in 1910 and worked for W.R. Grace throughout the Midwest. When his father passed on, it became incumbent upon him to come back and return to the farm operation, which he did.

I remember living on the old farm in Colts Neck Township. And also we lived up on Highway 33, right outside of Freehold; there's an old farmhouse there. And waiting for the fruit trees to mature, because we put out thousands of whips. And they had to be in perfect set rows. Dad's idea was the rows had to be set such that if you shot a rifle, you could hit every stick in a row. He was very fussy about that. (laughter) So we had to wait six to eight years before we got much of a production started. In the meantime, we grew vegetables between the trees.

Freehold was always an agricultural area. The more prosperous farmers lived in the town and had their farms on the outskirts. And that's pretty much what they do in Europe today. The farms are always outside the villages. But I remember when I was about seven to 10, we had no electricity. We had no running water, and we had a hand pump out in the front yard. And

41

the outhouse was up by the barn, which was like 200 feet up the hill from the house. And that's not very luxurious living.

Mother was a contralto in Chicago and I think she was doing some singing in different places. She and Dad met when he got the job with W.R. Grace. And they decided to marry. Mother and her mother were Christian Scientists, and they thought they could convince Dad to be a Christian Scientist. And he poo-pooed the idea, he said, "That's ridiculous." And she invited him to a lecture, and he went, and he was healed of smoking, cold turkey, no more smoking. And then he attained a respect for it, became very, very ardent, in Christian Science teachings.

Before that, my family had always been Dutch Reformed. They moved from Holland in 1638, and down to Monmouth County in 1712. So that Dutch heritage has been in the family. In fact, there are two stained glass windows in the Reformed Church in Freehold, dedicated by the Denise family. And we go there sometimes, and we just enjoy looking at them, and know that they were representative of our family. Some of the people there think that maybe some day we'll come back. (laughter)

Mother took some training at the Walter Damrosch Studios in New York. She was a soloist in our church, and she had done some musicals for the Women's Club and Sicilian Club in Freehold. She was very talented in music and had a lovely voice. We had a grand piano in our house. We have it now. They had a long, happy life. On the farm, Dad was kind of the boss and Mother took care of the social requirements.

Every summer, we would have as many as 150 migrants working on the farm. Which was one of the reasons I decided to change my occupation back in the early 60's. It was just getting too overwhelming. I wanted more of an intellectual challenge, instead of having to cope with that strain of life so much. We were good to them, but you were constantly bailing them out of jail, or getting them sobered up so they could work, or lending them money all the time. I just felt it wasn't inspiring, intellectually challenging.

"On the first day of school, I ran home and said, 'Mom, they don't speak our language.' Because I could talk only Italian." *--Joseph DeMasi*

My father was a laborer. He worked for Thomas Edison when Edison was building a cement plant out here in New Village, and Edison took a liking to him. In addition to working for Edison, my father also farmed. He had this one big pig, weighed about 800 pounds. Edison says, "I want to see it," so he put Edison in a buggy and took him to see this big pig. My father got to know him pretty well because he then started being his runner when they were building the plant.

Edison wouldn't leave the place to sleep. He used a room next to his office with a wide bench and a little mattress and he'd sleep on it. My father said, "Do you want to sleep at our house?" and Edison said, "No." He used to say, "Anytime you sleep more than two hours, it's a complete waste of time." He would take a nap for two hours and he would be all geared up to keep going.

The superintendent was very friendly with my father and he gave me a job, but he said, "Joe, a lot of men have families and you'll want to work so you can go to school." I said, "Yes, I want to go to school because of my father and my mother."

My mother was not permitted to go to school because her father, who was the mayor of Airola in Italy, said that if women got educated, they would start writing notes to their boyfriends. So women didn't go to school. That's the way it was in the country, in Italy, at the turn of the century. My father could read and write, but my mother couldn't. She always said, "I wish I could read and write." She always told me, "You gotta go to school, you gotta go."

I was a good student. In fact, I skipped the fifth grade. But on the first day I went to school, I ran out of the school and I ran home. It may have been about a block away. My mother says, "What are you doing?" I said, "Mom, they don't speak our

43

language. I don't know what they are talking about," because I could talk only Italian. My oldest sister grabbed ahold of me. She said, "You have got to come back to school."

The teacher, I will never forget, put me on her lap and she said, "Okay, you're going to be a good boy here and we are going to teach you." So I took to school and, once I start studying, why it sure came a little easier to me.

New Village was not a big place. It had maybe 1,800 people, mostly second- or third-generation farmers. My sisters, and all the daughters of immigrants, only went through eighth grade, then they went to work. Only the boys went to high school, and I was the first one who went to college.

During the Depression, when I was ready for college, there was no money. But at that time, I was a good wrestler. I was captain of the wrestling team in high school and I was winning. The coach said, "Joe, I will see what I can do." The next thing you know, I was told to take a state scholarship exam. In those days, one boy and one girl from the county got a state scholarship. Would you believe, I went down there, I took the test, and I got a state scholarship.

Then the superintendent gave me a job in the summertime working from midnight to eight in the morning. That kept me out of trouble, kept me working and I got through Rutgers.

I came back here to practice law, and I still live in the house I was born in. It's a big house with big barns. The walls are about a foot and a half of thick stone.

"Perth Amboy was unique. Between building rafts, fishing, crabbing and learning to play tennis, I had a very happy childhood." --Roland Winter

Perth Amboy was a unique community. Our Main Street was mainly supported by shoppers from Staten Island, and the ferry was the economic life blood of the town. It was also a focal point of interest for us kids. An exceptionally pleasurable experience for me was to be able to get my hands on a quarter. For a nickel, I could ride the ferry to Tottenville, which was a quaint little waterfront community with a New York flavor and also a country flavor. That was a nickel going and a nickel coming, and an ice cream cone was a nickel. They had a wonderful newspaper stand that sold ice cream in Tottenville. And that was a major outing for me, walk around the streets and go down on the Tottenville beaches.

The house where I grew up was extremely close to the Raritan River, and I'm a river rat. I've loved the water all my life and I spent most of my playtime down at the river. It was the depths of the Depression when I was a child, and I remember with great happiness some of President Roosevelt's programs that really created the Perth Amboy waterfront.

The public works projects that Roosevelt created and implemented started by bringing in huge boulders that were placed along the shoreline of the river and then they filled behind that and they built a boardwalk and eight tennis courts and a tennis house. And that was in the same area as my house.

In those days, tennis was a rich man's sport. There were very few poor industrial communities that had any tennis facilities whatever. And my friends and I took advantage of those courts. I remember the courts cost 20 cents an hour. We played doubles; it was a nickel for each to play one hour. We couldn't afford to buy tennis balls, but we used to be ball boy for the adults. When they were through with the balls, we would get them, and that's what we used all summer.

Between watching the construction and building rafts and fishing and crabbing and learning to play tennis, I really had a very happy childhood.

My family got through the Depression somehow. They chipped in and managed to buy a two-family house. And the single people and the married people, we all lived at 164 Lewis Street and pooled funds and managed to survive. We didn't have trouble buying food, but clothes, new clothes, were rare.

45

Everybody just understood there was no money! But my circumstances were no different than my friends. There were the exceptional families where money was not a problem, but my friends and I were all earth poor, just everybody struggling.

"They went into the apartments of some of my relatives and threw everything out the window into the street, even the piano." *--Fred D. Van Aken*

I was born in November, 1922, in Aachen, Germany, together with my twin brother. Aachen is right on the border of Holland and Belgium. My father had been born there, and my grandparents lived there. My mother came from a small town about 25 miles from Frankfurt, a town named Alzey, where her father had a department store and a wholesale business. We were a Jewish family, but only by designation, because nobody in the family, none of our friends, ever practiced Judaism. And we considered ourselves completely assimilated, until Hitler came along and decided that we were Jewish.

My father founded a textile mill after World War I. It was not a large factory, but he always told me he sold the most expensive men's cloth in Europe. He traveled a lot because he did the selling for his firm. And the interesting part to me was that he would not wear his own cloth. When he had a suit made, he would buy English cloth. He said it was finished better than his.

I was very fortunate that my folks were well to do, probably upper middle class. We always had servants in the house, at least two people living there with us, and additional ones coming out to help. Our favorite sports were horseback riding, tennis and swimming. This was during the Depression over here. As a child in Germany, I didn't know there was a Depression.

There were a lot of distant relatives, uncles and second cousins and cousins of my father. And I had the impression that everyone owned a textile factory. (laughter) Most of them did. My father was a bit of a snob. He'd associate only with textile manufacturers. My mother had been a teacher, so there was a lot of pedagogic theory being applied. And she watched our development very carefully. She even kept a diary on how we developed for the first 12 years, or whatever.

My father's name was Fritz Goldschmidt, and we changed the name when we left Germany, out of fear. We lived in Holland, and that was too close to Germany for comfort. The city of Aachen in Dutch is "Aken," and the word "Van" just means "from," so the new name was very appropriate. We changed it legally when we came to the United States.

My brother, sister and I attended Montessori School for four years, and then we had to transfer to the Gymnasium. That was at Easter, 1933. And by September '33, Hitler had just gotten into power, so he passed a law saying that only those Jewish children could be in class whose father had been a frontline fighter in World War I, and then only one Jewish child per class. So my brother and I were both kicked out of school. I was about 10 at the time.

My brother was transferred to another school then, and I had a private teacher, and then a year later, I was able to go into the same school my brother was in. And we were there until we were 15. Then the laws changed again. All Jews were kicked out of the school. So then we again had a private teacher. But the only thing we learned was languages; no math or physics.

Then my parents wanted to send us to the L'ecole International in Geneva, and the German government wouldn't allow us any Swiss money for that purpose. So we were sent to Berlin and we went to the American School in Berlin, which was run by an American journalist, Ziegler was his name. It was mostly for the children of the embassy and the consulates around there. Everybody had to study in English, no matter where they came from. (laughter)

Then, in 1938, they had this infamous Kristallnacht, when they attacked all the Jewish stores in Berlin and other cities, too. In Dusseldorf, I remember, they went into the apartments of some relatives, a sister of my grandmother's, her husband was a judge, and they threw everything from the apartment out the window into the street, even the piano. And my uncle's apartment in Alzey was ransacked. But my brother and I were in Berlin, and we had failed to register our presence there with the police, so nobody knew where we were.

I remember my father, who was a pretty prominent man in town-- everybody knew him-- he would lift his head to somebody in the street, and the person would look the other way. And he would say, "That scoundrel, he and his brother came to me all the time and asked for advice, and now they don't know me anymore." And on the trolley car, as children, we would get up to let a lady sit down, and the ladies would not take our seat. There was this sort of nastiness. But we never discussed it. I think it was just too painful.

My father was bringing my sister to the boat in Belgium. And when he got to the border, they arrested him and put him in prison. He managed to get out a day or two later because Mother arranged for the doctor to say he had a weak heart. But then they picked him up again and put him in a concentration camp in Oranienburg, near Berlin. The policeman who came to arrest him was wearing a suit my father had given him. (laughter)

I remember we were staying with a lady in Berlin, Frau Von Mueller. Her husband had been a famous German submarine captain during World War I. She was British. And she had a very lovely daughter, 16 years old, who did small roles in movies. And there were all kinds of people coming and going in her apartment. She had friends like General Rommel, and Knut Hamsun's son was a film director there at the time, and opera stars. And they all told their tales about Goebbels, especially about his chasing after the opera stars.

We were in school one day, and the principal, Mr. Ziegler, came and he said that he had a phone call from Frau Von Mueller, and we should not come back. She had been tipped off that

48

the Gestapo was going to raid her apartment. So he put us into the home of a well-to-do lady, a Jewish lady. And we stayed there about a week, and then found another place, with another Jewish lady.

Now my father was still in the concentration camp, and we hadn't heard from Mother, so we called her. She told us she had activated a lawyer in Berlin that was a good acquaintance of Father's. And I think he managed to bribe the chief of police in Berlin. And one night we got a phone call, we were already in bed, and the lawyer was on the phone. He said, "Why don't you come over to my apartment tonight, right now?" So we got dressed and got on the subway and went over there, and my father was there. I still have the discharge paper from the concentration camp in my file.

We made full preparation then to leave Germany. Mother had a good friend in Holland, and she did everything in her power to get us a visa to get into Holland. These things were very, very difficult in those days. And the Germans harassed us terribly. Everything was so mean-spirited that it was unreal. We had a large house, and they said we could only take with us the barest minimum. We had to itemize everything, every shoe, every piece of underwear, every piece of kitchenware to be itemized on a list.

They had two people in the house watching that we did this right. My brother and I were not involved, but my mother and the servants had to do all these things. And then they'd look at silverware and say, "Is this silver?" And the maid would say, "Of course, it's silver." And he'd say, "Can't take it with you." (laughter) Any pictures that were valuable couldn't go either. And then, when all this was inventoried and signed off, Father had to go with this official to the bank and rent a safe deposit box for about three years and pay for it in advance and put all the valuables in there. Of course, it all disappeared.

By the beginning of February 1939, my brother and I were going to Holland by ourselves to stay with people we had met in Amsterdam. And Father took us to the station because the Germans harassed everybody. Whenever a train came with Jewish people emigrating to Holland, they would delay them at the station so they would miss the train and have to stay there until the next day. But I think Father talked to these people, maybe paid them off, too. Anyway, they took us right away aside and put us in a room. We didn't have to undress or anything. They just put us right on the train. So we got to Amsterdam and stayed with this family for a couple of months until my parents got out.

Leaving was hard. When all your property is there, and you don't know the rest of the world and don't speak the language necessarily, these are tough choices. By the time we left, I think, by the time they put special taxes on us, my father may have salvaged six percent of his liquid assets. He was very happy that we were able to live a whole year in Holland for less than a thousand dollars. We really didn't have much. We looked very elegant. We had good clothing. (laughter) And he would say, "Poor, but clean."

My parents took an apartment in the Hague, and we moved over there. It didn't have a bathroom. It only had cold water. And it was on the third floor. Only one room could be heated. Bedrooms were unheated. In the wintertime, the ice would be on the inside of the window. In the daytime, the sun would shine on it and the water would melt and drip into our beds. And at night, there would be a little ice in the bed. (laughter). And we'd go to a public bathhouse to take showers once a week. We stayed there a year.

My parents were not allowed to work. My father had nightmares. He would often scream at night. I guess he had bad memories from the concentration camp. He wasn't very long in the concentration camp, but nevertheless it must have affected him.

We got sheet metal work, forging, electrical wiring, machine shop, lathe work, milling machines and bench work. Then we had sketching, mechanical drawing and some instructions on how steel was made. And all that, of course, was in Dutch. And we had to struggle, but Dutch wasn't that difficult to learn. After a year, we spoke good Dutch.

Then in 1940 we came to New York. My brother and I enrolled in a vocational school in downtown Manhattan, but after three months, we told our parents, "We can't learn anything there. They don't study. They don't do any homework. It's a waste of time." By that time I was 17, and I said, "I'm going to find myself a job." They were all short-time jobs, menial labor. I wound up in a machine shop.

It was tough to get a job in 1940. It was a terrible time. I remember taking the subway down to Sixth Avenue and going into every building, every store and asking everybody. Finally, I got a job in a machine shop. Then I was going to night school, and I was trying to become an electrician. I had all kinds of jobs. We lived with our parents, and we turned our wages over to them. They were anywhere between 12 and 16 dollars a week in those days. I gave it all to my father every week.

Those were pretty bad times. Everybody, at least in our family, was so full of fear about what was going on in the war. We all knew that America would get involved, except the Americans didn't know it at that time. My mother's brother, the uncle who had been running the department store in Alzey, decided he had to make a living. He had a small factory in New York, and that didn't work too well. So he said, "I'm going to buy a farm in New Jersey, and we're going to raise chickens." So he went down to Vineland and bought a farm. My parents decided to move with him on the farm.

"The 'tsetls' all went on a spindle, and they identified our credit customers with phrases like 'The woman with the white dog.'"   *--Nathan Shoehalter*

I was born in Newark and, when I was 18 months old, the family moved to Irvington. My father started a grocery store. I had a sister who was nine years older than me. The thing that I remember about the grocery store was that we were open seven days a week, from seven in the morning until 11 at night, and the only times we ever closed was on Rosh Hashanah and a half a day on Yom Kippur.

We had a car, my father had a car, and on those days we would drive down to Lakewood, and I remember seeing dirigibles and things like that. That's my earliest remembrance. I also remember that my father was arrested for breaking the blue laws in Irvington. When I went to research this, I found him in the *Newark Evening News*. There was his picture, smiling as he was led off by the cops for breaking the blue laws. The only reason he did that was because our competitor was open on Sundays too, and we couldn't allow that.

The other thing I remember was that we were held up in an armed robbery on a rainy Sunday night, and they got $60, which was a lot of money. It was an enormous amount of money. We lived just above the grocery store on Stuyvesant Avenue. I was upstairs, apparently asleep at the time, around nine o'clock at night. My sister and my mother and father were in the store. My father said, "Take what you want." He threw his wallet down, and they opened the cash register and escaped.

When I was going to high school, I worked for *The New York Times*. I delivered *The New York Times* at Irvington High School. It was a job that I got my Social Security card for. I would open the store, and take the rolls that had come from the baker, and carry them into the store, and put them in the front window where we kept them. Then I would trudge off to Irvington High School, which was about a mile away, and deliver papers. That was 1938, I guess, about that time.

My father had a lot of credit customers, and the only way I can say it is in Yiddish, forgive me, a tsetl. A tsetl was a note, and we used to write the name of the person or a description. We never knew the names of some of our customers. We just knew who they were and we trusted them. There was a translation, "The woman with the white dog," "The one who limps a little," those are the ones that come to mind, but, we had other ones, "The person who lives on Nesbit Terrace."

We used to have this spindle with a nail on it, and all these things would be on the spindle, and we'd go find the names, and we would write down that they owed us for a quarter of a pound of salami, or some ham, or rolls, or Jewish rye bread, or something. That's the way he carried on his business.

It wasn't until, I guess, 1939 or 1940, after being in the store since 1924, that my father and mother decided that they would sell the store, because my father had gotten a job as a wine salesman. He didn't know anything about wine at all. He just knew how to sell, and he was very good, but he was selling, traveling by car all over the state of New Jersey, and my mother, my sister and I worked in the store.

Both my parents were from Russia. My father was from Odessa, my mother from a place called Chochonov. She was born in a shtetl in Chochonov, in Russia, and she moved to Vitebsk, which was Marc Chagall's home. In the last years of my mother's life, when I guess things were just churning in her head, she said that her brothers used to play with Marc Chagall. I often thought of writing to Chagall when he was alive, but I just never got around to it.

My father was a Socialist, a Norman Thomas socialist. He used to read the *Jewish Daily Forward*, which is the Socialist paper, and he would only vote for Norman Thomas.

"Paterson was a tough town. We had blacks, Jews and Italians in our neighborhood, but it was more together than it was divided." *--William MacKenzie*

I grew up in Paterson. I was born in Paterson and I left there when I was a sophomore in high school and we moved to Little Falls. In front of the city hall in Paterson are two statues, one of Alexander Hamilton, who was one of the city's founders, and the other of Garret A. Hobart, who had been vice president of the United States.

After the war I came down to Rutgers. Freshmen were expected to go to chapel, and I was sitting there one day looking around at those pictures on the wall, and there was Garret A. Hobart. I said "Son-of-a-gun, MacKenzie, you're in pretty good company here."

It was during the Depression. It was not a good time to be around, but I guess we were poor like everybody else. My father was a treasury agent. They were sort of the forerunners of the FBI, before they had G-men, and they didn't have guns. They did the same thing as G-men. Their early job was enforcing the IRS, but they were also involved in tracking down rumrunners and that kind of stuff. It was kind of dangerous work, I suppose. Then, when FDR was elected, my father lost his job. He had made the mistake of being a Republican. He had some real problems and eventually became an alcoholic.

In Paterson, we were sort of on the cusp between the very wealthy neighborhood and the very poor. The kids I went to high school with were the children of doctors and lawyers and dentists, while other parents were just tradesmen.

I saw some of the strikes in Paterson, the great silk strikes. I saw people throwing rocks and screaming, "Bloody hicks." They were pretty vicious times. But it was all part of the growing up process at the time. It was also Prohibition, and Paterson was not the prettiest of towns.

I remember one story. My father was involved with the Veterans of Foreign Wars and the American Legion. And they used to hold occasional "rackets," which were social events. And they had beer at these events. Of course, it was quite illegal at the time. They had to buy the stuff, I guess, from bootleggers. And I remember him telling me that one of the big racketeers at the time was a guy named Waxey Gordon. And apparently Paterson was a very good market for bootleggers. So one of Waxey Gordon's henchmen came to the American Legion and said, "You're buying your beer from us." And their response

54

was "The hell we are!" But apparently there were some very sinister events. He used the term "mafia" or "black hand," and apparently there were a lot of murders.

I remember Paterson as a tough town, but it wasn't really ethnically divided. Maybe I live in a dream world, but I think it was more together than it was divided. There were neighborhoods, particularly where we lived, there were black families that lived in the neighborhood. There were Jewish and Italian families, some of whom had not been over here too long. One neighbor we called the kid "Frenchie." I think they were Algerian. Albert Alessandrino lived on the first floor and his father owned a tailor shop. And Wiech's Bakery, a Dutch family. And Gus Naundorf owned a candy store. And you went to school where you went to school.

One girl, Elinor Prell, her father owned a big paper factory. And there were black kids who were just kids. I went to school with Larry Doby, who was the first black player in American League baseball-- the Jackie Robinson of the American League.

On the Paterson East Side basketball team I remember Oliver and Hapgood, two of the guards, were black. Larry Doby played, but then Red Miller was the star really, and he was a white kid. But there was Vinnie Fuscanero, and it was a real mix. Everybody was on the team. That was the way it was. Maybe I am looking back through idealistic glasses or something, but I don't think there were problems.

"I grew up in a place called The Ferrer Colony, in Piscataway. There were about 100 families, and we were considered oddballs." --*Samuel F. Blum*

When I was a boy, we lived in the country. And although we didn't have much land, it was a farming existence. The town we lived in was self-sufficient in the sense that it relied on no support at all from the township government. The unpaved roads were our own. We had no amenities. No electricity, no city water. We got electricity in 1929, which was about a year before we moved out there permanently. We had a privy, an outhouse. It was called The Ferrer Colony, and there were about 100 families living there.

Most of them had left New York to organize a school of their own choosing called the Ferrer School, which was based on the principles of a Spanish educator named Francisco Ferrer, who was martyred in Spain in 1909. The school's principles were to allow the child to enjoy childhood; to be a child, to be anti-authoritarian; to allow the child to enjoy himself. They did not force the kids to do anything they didn't want, but they did have a kind of discipline. The discipline was to respect the other kids. You could do whatever you wanted but don't hurt or interfere or bother somebody else.

I didn't attend that school, I went to the city schools. But the community had many kids that did go to that school. Of the kids I grew up with, possibly half went to public schools and the other half went to the Ferrer School. The Ferrer School was, of course, a private school.

When I was a kid I had chores. Nobody forced me to do them, but my responsibility was to take care of the chickens, clean the roosts every Saturday morning, feed the pigeons, etc. That's what I was used to and that's how I was brought up-- to have a feeling of responsibility. But there was a great deal of freedom. Also I should say that in the sense of things religious, it was an irreligious community. We had no churches, no temples, no synagogues.

You could say they were atheists. But I'm not sure every one was. We were a non-observant home. We knew the holidays, etc., but my mother never lit candles on the Sabbath. When my grandmother would visit, she would, but my mother never did. My father was totally non-observant.

We weren't liked particularly by the rest of Piscataway. We were considered an oddball group. Around 1917 or '18, before I was born, someone raised the red flag there in sympathy with the Russian Revolution. The militia, or some group of horsemen came out from New Brunswick to tear it down.

You were really not part of the outside community and there's a great deal of animosity towards you. You felt it at school. At New Market School, some students would be rough on you. But it wasn't a dominant thing in your life. You went to school and somebody there was anti-Semitic and called you a Jew bastard, so what? Or, they'd say it in Polish. You'd come home and tell your father or your uncle and they'd say, forget about it, this is the way it is. So you glossed over it. Not that you didn't feel hurt, and not that you didn't understand it.

When I was young I didn't understand. I'd say I'm not religious so why should you pick on me for my religion, but of course they weren't picking on me for my religion, they were picking on me for what I was or had come from. And it took me years to understand that.

"I went to school in a one-room school in Marlboro. It was right next door to our house, and they had six grades in one room." --Robert I.Owen

My father was a poultry specialist and he wasn't making enough money from Rutgers to satisfy my mother. I think he would have liked to stay in teaching or county agent work, but he bought this poultry farm, in Marlboro, New Jersey, just at the wrong time-- not long before the Depression, when the bottom fell out of the egg market.

It wasn't too many years before the poultry farm wasn't paying, but my parents kept it right up until the 50s, when they couldn't stay there any more, and I helped them move out into Freehold.

I spent a good deal of my childhood working with my father maintaining those big poultry buildings, even when he no longer had any chickens. We did have the responsibility, because of the mortgage and so forth, to keep them up. So every summer I

57

worked on the roofs with him, putting hot tar and paper on the roofs, or working on the foundations. Dad figured if you did those two things, the roofs and the foundation, the rest in between you could forget about. I had happy experiences working with my father. I learned a lot.

But then, when the poultry business went down, my father went into sales work with a west coast company-- a company that had kelp products that were additives to animal and poultry feeds. He became their east coast representative and did a lot of traveling, wasn't home very much. That was a difficult period.

By then, we didn't have chickens any more. But we did have interesting times. He had fond memories of sheep as a boy on the farm he grew up on, in New York state, so we had sheep. Not exactly approved of by my mother, but we had sheep. We had them on chains eating the lawn, instead of my having to mow it by hand mower.

They all had names. The big ram was Julius Caesar. Cleopatra, naturally, had to be one of the ewes, also Helen of Troy. Eventually, Helen of Troy got loose and ran out and was hit by a car. And so, rather than waste the meat, we ate her. At Sunday dinner it was, "Pass some more Helen, please." (laughter)

Our lives weren't really isolated. We did shopping in Marlboro Village and in Freehold. One of my mother's sisters lived in Freehold. And I went to grade school in Marlboro. A school bus picked me up. Well, first, I went to school right next door. There were six grades, I think, in a one-room school. It's a house now. I started out there at four-and-a-half. Then they closed that school and then the bus would come and take me into Marlboro Elementary.

The school in Marlboro had a lot of rough kids. They were, I guess, from Estonian or Lithuanian families. A number of them had gotten together up on the next hill, (called "Big Woods"), to the east. There was a little community from the Baltic States up there. I had a feeling that the men were mostly manual laborers. Maybe some of them worked on farms, but I'm not aware of any of them having owned farms. We had a post office box in Marlboro, a general store we went to, and a fire company. We went to their firemens' fairs and suppers.

"Capitol Street was one block long, and except for maybe two families, they were all Italian. And they were all friendly."   *--Peter M. Sarraiocco*

We moved to Paulsboro because my father had a job with Mobil. He was a laborer. He did some maintenance work, pipe fitting, things like that. It was a good, steady job. We lived in a farmhouse, and then, after one year, we moved to Capitol Street, which is right next to the Paulsboro High School.

Capitol Street was one block long, and except for maybe two families, they were all Italian families, and they were all friendly. Everybody behaved themselves. We played out in the street, played all kinds of kid's games. They were only held together because they originally had all come from Italy.

As a kid, in the summertime, I thought, "Well, I have to work. I want to earn some money." So I would go out to the farms and work picking peas or beans or tomatoes. There was another fellow who lived on the same street, Joe Minniti. He ultimately became a doctor. We found a woman who had a little farm, and we agreed to pick all of her tomatoes. We'd go there at five o'clock in the morning, pick the tomatoes, and, by 12 or one o'clock, we'd be finished.

When it rained, you couldn't pick, but the next day it was almost impossible too because then there'd be too many ripened tomatoes. So, we'd hire my brother and Joe's brother. At first, we couldn't understand why they dawdled. We were paying them by the hour. That's how I learned about enterprise. When you're doing things for yourself, man, you'll work your backside off. But, if you're just working for a little pay (laughter)-- no way. We would pick twice as much as they would pick.

I remember, one time, we topped onions. There was an irrigated farm on the way to Clarksboro, and they were so profuse that you could fill a basket in no time. We made a lot of money, for those days. We might have made 75 or 80 cents an hour. And that was fantastic. The typical employee at, say, Mobil, which was known to pay pretty well, might be making 45 or 48 cents an hour. So we'd be very proud to be able to say to our parents, "Well, we did very well today." (laughter).

"My parents brought billions of marks with them, and they were absolutely worthlesss. I kept them as souvenirs for a long time." --Ralph Schmidt

I came to this country with my parents in 1928. They came basically to escape the inflation in Germany. And they brought with them billions of marks, which were absolutely worthless, but which I kept as souvenirs for some time. There was a depression along with inflation, which was kind of a strange combination. The good times were still rolling here in the United States at the time we arrived.

My father was a tool and die maker in Schweningen, the little city we came from. They considered themselves the clock center of the world. They had three different factories that manufactured all kinds of timepieces, from grandfather clocks to wristwatches. The company he worked for is still making the dashboard clocks for Mercedes. It's called Kienzle, K-I-E-N-Z-L-E. He was also a volunteer fireman.

We came to Newark because my uncle lived there, and he sort of looked after us while we were getting settled in. We lived with him for two or three months, as I recall, while my father was looking for a job, and while we were looking for a place to live. Luckily, we found both and so we set up our own homestead in Newark.

My father wouldn't tell me much about his World War I service in Germany, but I remember that he and one other man were the only ones in his unit that survived. And so he considered himself quite lucky.

He was very reticent to say anything about it. I mean, you had to get him really started before he would discuss his feelings about the war. But he called it "The equivalent of the most stupid activity humanity or human kind can participate in." If you got him interested, he would discuss some of those things. I used to wait for those moments, but there were few of them.

He fought on several fronts, but he always said the fighting was the worst in France. He was in the battle of the Somme, and I don't remember about some of the other battles, but he went up through Belgium and into France with his unit.

He said it was horrible because of the trench warfare, where people were literally buried by shellfire. He used to refer to a strong thunderstorm as a drum fire because that's what they called it in the trenches when the artillery barrages were going on, usually in anticipation of a charge out of the trenches. Those barrages might last for days before the actual charge came, and they used to huddle in their trenches and just hope that they weren't going to be the ones who would be buried. He said people just disappeared under the earth thrown up by shells. They said there was no place to go.

Then he used to talk about the machine gun nests, because they did so much damage to the opposite sides. He actually received a hernia from dragging ammunition cases around in and out of trenches, and he didn't have that hernia repaired until many years later, here in the United States. He was also wounded by shrapnel and got the equivalent of a Purple Heart.

In Newark, we lived fairly close to a cinema, and I remember going with my father to see *All Quiet on the Western Front*. Actually, my father went several times to see it. It was sort of a touching thing, and I can still see the sniper pull the trigger when the soldier was reaching for the butterfly. Things like that made an impression. Or when he was carrying a sergeant over his shoulder and the planes zoomed in.

It was hard to tell what emotions it evoked in my father. He didn't say too much about such things. But he was fascinated by the film. In many places, he'd say, "That's not accurate," but then many times he'd say, "That's exactly the way it was," with the battle scenes with all the confusion and everything. He used to marvel at the fact that he had survived.

I asked him about his friends, and I got the impression that nobody got close to other people for fear that tomorrow that other fellow wasn't going to be there. They limited their association to just one or two people. I guess it took three men to fire that machine gun and load the ammunition, and he was in charge of that squad. But he didn't want to get close to anyone because tomorrow somebody else would be there.

"Everybody wanted to get in to see the Michelin house because it had the only bidet in town, and no one had ever seen a bidet." --C. Harrison Hill

My parents settled in Milltown because my mother had grown up there, and she wouldn't leave town. My dad had bought a house in New Brunswick and she just refused to live there. She lived across the street from her mother and next door to her sister, and she and her sister spoke to each other through the window. Mother always referred to my grandmother's house as being home. So we would eat early and then I would say, "I am going over home." And my grandmother would've saved me all of the desserts from the day. We had a very close arrangement with my grandmother.

We had sort of an extended family, because my mother's two brothers and a sister never married, and they were part of our family group. My aunt was 92, and her brother was only 76, but while the minister was consoling him after my aunt's death, he had a heart attack and died, so we had two funerals together. That was a traumatic thing.

Milltown was a very close-knit community in the 1920s and 1930s. A lot of the people were related. I've always said you need to be careful in Milltown, everybody's related to every-body else. There was a German contingent that came there in the 1840s and '50s, and then they kept bringing relatives over. So they're all related to each other in some way or other. But, my family really wasn't in that group at all.

There was also a sizeable French influence because there was a Michelin plant there for many years. There was a French school, and a lot of French people. In fact, there was a certain amount of feeling in Milltown, a feeling between the French and the Germans. We had a French letter carrier who got to the point of refusing to deliver mail to one old German fellow that he had an argument with every day up until World War II, you know? (laughter)

And then Michelin left and went back to France. Mr. Michelin had a home here on College Avenue, and everybody wanted to get in to see it, because he had the only bidet in town and no-body had ever seen a bidet. We have a Michelin Field in Mill-town, with a baseball diamond. Recently someone wanted to get lights for it. And they thought "Well, we'll ask Michelin to give us some lights."

Well, Michelin had no record of having been in Milltown. So they sent somebody out, amazingly enough, and they saw the World War I monument, which was a typical French monument, and they saw we had streets named Pershing, Foch, and others from World War I, and then they decided "Gee, we must really have been in Milltown."

Michelin had these hand-made tires, and they had trains run-ning on rubber tires on the old Raritan River Railroad. I think it would have been in the early 1930s when they went back to France.

Some of the homes in Milltown were built by Michelin. My grandfather was a builder, and he built many of them. In his old barn, I found a piece of lumber labeled "Michelin house No. 4." There was a bungalow section, which was for the lower em-ployees, and more elaborate houses for their executives.

63

"My brother and I noticed that all the people who read German newspapers had 'Beware of the dog' signs on their porches."   *--Richard J. Mercer*

When I was growing up in Roselle Park, there was quite a German population there. There was a German man who lived across the way from us. He was a violinist, a very talented man. And when the Germans took Paris, we weren't in the war yet, if I remember correctly, it was 1940, this guy came over to our house. He was a very good neighbor. And he came over all excited and happy. He said, "I want you to come over and have a drink." My father threw him out of the house, and we never spoke to each other again.

Now this man had a sign on his front steps that said "Beware of the Dog." My brother Bob and I were about 16 in 1940. And we delivered papers for a Mrs. Bromberg. We delivered them early in the morning before we went to school, and then we delivered them after school. And on Sundays, we delivered them extremely early in the morning, and it took many, many trips on our bicycles because those Sunday papers were huge.

We each had a different paper route. We made 85 cents a week for this. I used to spend the whole thing on Saturday night taking Muriel Davis to the movies (laughs) and getting a cherry coke afterwards. There's the 85 cents shot. But we discovered on our paper routes that a bunch of houses had "Beware of the Dog" signs on the front steps.

Then we discovered that every one of those houses, including the guy across the street, took the *Stadt Zeitung und Herald*. That was the German language newspaper. It was printed in German, and always the people in those houses spoke German. And they all had the "Beware of the Dog" signs.

So Bob and I at age 16 called the FBI in Newark. They were very nice to us. They said, "All right. Thank you very much."

Well, Bob and I were quite excited about this. So we told my father at the dinner table. Oh- Oh. When my father heard that, he went right through the roof. Then he called the FBI, and he said, "Hey, I want you to understand that these are 16-year-old boys. They are fine young men, but they don't know any better. And these are good people." He said, "I don't like the man across the street one damned bit, he roots for Adolf Hitler, but I gotta tell you, he's a musician and a good guy," and so he sort of took the sting out of it. (laughs)

"We don't know where we are, but above the fog I can see the top of the Berkeley Carteret in Asbury Park. I take an azimuth." --David Robinson

Come January, right after Pearl Harbor, the assistant navigator was transferred to another cruiser, and Commander Becker, who was navigator, said, "Robby, I'm drafting you to be assistant navigator." I loved navigating. The next nine months, I was assistant navigator on the *Augusta*, flagship of the Atlantic Fleet. It's lovely work. It's taking sights up on the forecastle, being up on the bridge with the skipper. This is where the scuttlebutt starts, all the time. You don't have to stand watches under way. Those nine months were probably the most interesting time in the Navy. We went over to Africa twice. So that's what I was doing aboard the *Augusta*.

In January, we shifted to Casco Bay, Maine, the coldest place in the world, and then we went down to Bermuda, looking for a Nazi sub, and it was a nice deal. They had no visitors there, but they had 500 WRENs, they were women, (laughter) and we went looking for the subs in March, April, possibly, when we got word, "They have space in the Brooklyn Navy Yard. Return to the yard." So we turned around.

We're heading north for the yard and we haven't had a star sight in a day or two. We don't have a sun line, we're running on dead reckoning, and we have to pick up a buoy seven miles off Asbury Park. This is a mark for the entrance to the Swept Channel. You hit the buoy, you'd steer 2-8-6, or something, and you're in the Swept Channel.

We fix to come off the shore about daybreak. We don't know quite where we are, but there's the Jersey Shore over there, and I'm on the chart with the navigator. The quartermasters are out on the Polaris. That's the compass that you take sights on. The skipper is looking around, "Got a fix?" "No, sir, not yet." I said, "Commander Becker, let me get out there." He said, "Robby, if you can do anything, go."

I get out and I look over, and there's this fog hanging over the Jersey Shore, but above the fog I can see the top of the Berkeley Carteret Hotel in Asbury Park. I take an azimuth. Then I go down the coast and I get the Coast Guard tower at Monmouth Beach. Now we need a third one, you know, to fix it. I go down, I get the church right across the street from our house in West Long Branch.

We got a fix, we run in, we plot it. "Captain, course 2-8-9, five miles, 2-8-9, five miles," and there's the buoy. Those kids could have done it if they knew the area. It was only because I lived there, you know. The skipper turns around, Captain Wright, he says "All right, Robby, how'd you do that?" I said, "Skipper, I live there." (laughter)

HARD TIMES

When the Great Depression struck, we were approaching our teens. For those who lived on farms, there was at least food. For others, much depended on the steadiness of jobs.

Frank Kneller recalls his father's constant chase after paying work. During his youth, he attended 10 or 11 different schools in three or four different cities.

Herb Gross is still haunted by the sight, when he came home from school one day, of all his family's furniture out on the street. They had lost their house. "There was no welfare. There was no help. That's the way we lived in the Depression days."

Wages of those days seem amazingly small by today's standards. Carleton Dilatush worked 55 hours a week in a rubber factory, from the age of 15, for $7.16 a week. He took the money home to his mother, and she gave him 50 cents. Five cents of that went into his Sunday School envelope, and he'd spend the remainder on a Saturday night movie and a milk shake.

Everyone scratched for pennies. Forty cents an hour was a godsend for many. Those lucky enough to live in the country picked vegetables or berries and peddled them door to door in town. Sometimes the pay was a portion of what they picked.

Joe McCartney will never forget a touching tableau when his father, an independent printer whose work had dropped off to nothing, was able to collect an overdue bill and blew all the

67

money on food for a Thanksgiving feast: "I can still picture the two of them-- my father and mother-- at the door embracing each other and crying. To him, it was a bonanza. It was like he'd won the lottery."

My father, a railroad worker, was "bumped" out of his job by someone with greater seniority. I never felt closer to him than I did during the year he was out of work and we roamed the woods together, cutting trees and gathering dead wood to burn in the furnace because we couldn't afford coal.

Wet newspaper, rolled up and dried out, made papier-mache logs. Cardboard was saved to put in our shoes when the soles wore through. There was nothing fancy to eat.

Even so, my mother shared the food we had. Hoboes came to the door, she fed them and they marked an "x" on the sidewalk out front, so the next brother-in-want who came by would know a handout could be had there.

My uncle's family had a farm that bordered on the Lehigh Valley Railroad. When I was 11 or 12, Uncle Charlie led me across the corn field and down the embankment to the tracks. It was the first time I'd seen a hobo jungle. Fifteen or 20 men were milling about, and a Mulligan stew was simmering over an open fire.

Uncle Charlie introduced me around, and I noted that many of those men didn't talk like bums. On the way back, I asked about that. "That last man you talked to," said Uncle Charlie, "was a bank president in Iowa. The tall man with the grizzled beard was a railroad executive in Chicago. They're all on the road, looking for food, for work, for anything." Then he took me up in the haymow and showed me the indentations in the hay where the visitors slept before they hopped the next freight.

68

"My father's life was spent trying to find a job, or going from one thing to another. We must have moved 10 or 11 times."   *--Franklin J. Kneller*

The Great Depression affected my family pretty horribly. I can remember the banks closing, and they were trying to sell their Public Service stock. When my grandparents came to this country, they worked for Consolidated Edison in New York, or Public Service, because that was an obtainable job for immigrants, lifting and doing manual work. So they had some shares of stock.

They didn't have much money in the bank, and they sold some of their stock so we could eat. I can remember the depth of the bleakness, particularly when the banks closed down. They lost some money.

My father was a veteran of the Spanish-American War and Pershing's visit to Mexico. He had one job after another, or else he was trying to get jobs. He was a salesman, he worked in banks, in roofing, roofing materials, roofing services, and most of his life was spent that way-- going from one thing to another. He finally joined the CCC, (Civilian Conservation Corps) because at least then he had $15 dollars a month or whatever it was, but it was something he could depend on.

I guess we moved from Orange to Irvington two times, then to New York, back to East Orange, back to New York, back to

East Orange, back to Irvington, back to New York, and then East Orange again. I went to 10 or 11 different grammar schools in Orange, East Orange, Irvington, and New York.

In those days, when you were 18 you got a little invitation to take a blood test. Then they'd let you stay in school to finish. I finished school and the day before we were going to graduate, they wanted us to go down to be sworn in. But the draft board said, (laughter) "Let them have graduation," so, they took us a month later, in July instead of June. One month after we graduated from high school, we went in the Army, Navy or Marines.

"I remember going to a house with two old people and bringing them a five-pound bag of potatoes, and they kissed me in joy." --Edwin Kolodziej

I grew up in the Parlin section of Sayreville. Parlin is where DuPont and Hercules had built munitions factories in World War I. In those days, if you worked for a company, they built a company village. If you were an executive, they provided a house for you to live in. Well, Hercules and DuPont had built two large sections of houses.

My Dad, he'd go around selling meat. It dawned on him that these engineers were a very fine clientele, so he built his new store where those people lived. With the help of my mother and the horse and wagon-- and later a truck-- he became a successful businessman.

In the summertime and on Saturdays, I would always go with him. I went to work when I was six or seven years old and the whole family worked in the business. I got to know everybody in town, and many years later, when I went into politics, I was extremely well-known, because my father was very well-liked, and so was my mother.

During the Depression days, nobody who wasn't an executive or an engineer at one of the plants had a job and nobody had food, so that when the programs came out-- the NRA--

where people were given food, my father's shop became a depot. We would receive the food and deliver it. I remember going to a house with two old people and bringing them a five-pound bag of potatoes and they kissed me in joy, because they had something to eat, so my views about government and what it should do are a bit colored by what I saw back then.

People would come into my father's store and say, "I'll do anything for food, any job you want done here." People were picking berries in the woods to eat. That was the Depression. This country hasn't known a depression like that since then. I was around 11, 12 years old and I was very conscious of it all, because of my father's business.

The Hercules executives were customers of his. When the young engineer would come in with his young wife, my mother would teach her how to cook, and what to buy, so we ended up being friendly with all of these people. In fact, they formed a part of my education. My mother was very conscious of the fact that she had a sixth grade education and my father had a third grade education in Poland.

As I grew up and it became obvious to them that I was going to move ahead in the world, those college graduates across the street in the Hercules Village became my tutors, my mentors, who, when I needed a tuxedo, they provided a tuxedo. When it was a question of what manners to use at the dance, they taught me that, so I had a lot of teachers.

You see, on the north side of Washington Road, where we lived, there were a lot of Polish people. On the south side were all the executives and supervisory personnel and foremen, and stuff like that. Those people on the south side sort of looked down on us on the north side, but eventually, as you got into school, you formed friendships and that all dissipated itself and became a non-factor. I was the president of my grammar school graduating class, I was the president of my high school graduating class, etc.

Hercules Village-- the executive area-- is composed of about

71

35 or 40 houses. One of my childhood ideals was to someday live in one of them. I mean, that was the top of the mountain. One of them in particular intrigued me.

A friend of mine, who worked in Hercules, one of my mentors, called me one day-- by now, I'm a lawyer and practicing law in my father's old butcher shop, which I'd taken over and converted into a law office-- and he said "There's a house for sale back here. It's Chrisfield's." I said, "That's the house I always wanted." Within an hour, I had bought the house, and I still live there today, almost 40 years later.

"They reduced my father's pay to 25, 30 cents an hour. My mother must have had a hell of a time trying to make it do." --Peter M. Sarraiocco

Most of the men on our street worked at Dupont or at Mobil. I remember that during the Depression they reduced my father's pay to some minimal level, I forget what it might have been, maybe 25 cents an hour, 30 cents an hour, something like that. But he still worked. I seem to remember that there was a period there when he got either $16 a week or $16 for two weeks. God rest her soul, my mother must have had a hell of a time trying to make it do. He would give her the money and she would dole it out.

I know that there was a widow, Midilli the name was. She had lost her husband and she had two boys and a girl. What kind of help she got, I don't know, but, you know, they struggled but they lived good lives.

I had a garden, and we always had food, and there were other things you could do, too. There was a railroad that goes through the town, and just before it crossed Mantua Creek there was a place where the locomotives would stay, maybe change a freight car. And I had noticed that they would drop coal. It was bituminous coal, and some coals didn't burn through, so it was coke. I said to my mother, you know, "I'm going to bring my wagon over there. I'm going to get as much of that coke as I can. We can use it." Because at that time we had a coal stove. And that's what I did. It wasn't a big deal, and I don't know what coal cost in those days, but I suppose it was an expensive item.

"We'd buy cans of stuff where the label had come off for a nickel a can. You didn't know what it was until you cooked it up." --Frederick Wesche II

In high school, we had a dance band, so-called, and I think the first job I played was at Upsala College. I played the trumpet, and we got a dollar and a half and all the soda pop you could drink. That was my first job.

When I came down to Rutgers, it was a matter of living from week to week. Everybody was scratching for a nickel, believe me. So I was waiting on tables in Winants Hall there. I had a job at one of the apartment buildings. On Sunday mornings, I had to go and shake down the ashes in the furnace and, you know, little odd jobs like that, plus, of course, playing, usually Saturday nights, in almost any gin mill around New Brunswick.

The things we did to save money. At NJC they had a pay telephone, and since most of us were scratching for nickels, if you wanted a date over at NJC, you made an arrangement with the girl, "I'm going to call you at exactly seven minutes after seven" or something like that. So you dial the number, let it ring once. That meant, "I'll pick you up at so and so." If you let it ring twice, it meant, "I can't make it tonight." We had a way of communicating without completing the call.

One of the guys had a more sophisticated system. He took two pieces of plywood about the thickness of a nickel from a cigar box or something, and he drilled holes in them the size of a nickel and then nailed them together. Then during the winter, you'd fill these little spaces with water, put it on the windowsill and it would freeze, and so what you really had was an ice nickel and you could stick that in the machine. Of course, that didn't last long, because the telephone company, when they came to collect the money, saw nothing but a bunch of water, so they put the freeze on that pretty quick.

Our housemother was a Mrs. Stone, who was a kindly old lady. Cooking was prohibited in the dormitories at that time, but what we used to do was a few of us would go down to the local supermarket, and you could buy cans of stuff where the label had come off, or you could buy a two- or three-day-old loaf of bread. You'd get a can-- of something-- literally for a nickel. You didn't know what it was but one of the guys brought a little electric hot plate and we'd cook up a meal for ourselves. Mrs. Stone would come around sniffing, and say, "If I didn't know better, I thought one of you boys might be cooking." "Oh, no, Mrs. Stone." Well, we weren't out to break the rules. It was literally a case of getting through the day.

Those were the things that sustained me through college, that helped me meet day-to-day expenses. I would make a few bucks on the weekend playing in a band and whatever else I could get out of it, plus all these other things that got me through.

"I cut grass, I delivered magazines. The big break was the bankers' meetings, when Virginia got 45 cents an hour as a waitress." --George Reynolds

I was very lucky, in the following sense. My father was a long-time railroad employee. He had to work very hard. The railroad was cutting back drastically. He never lost his job. That's a big thing. Neighbors? One was vice president of Carrier, or something, another one was big in public service. They went to poverty. But we always had that few hundred dollars coming in. Never more than $200, but that was enough.

And I was lucky in that I had a job all the time. I cut grass, for example. I delivered magazines. I'm no hero. Everybody did this sort of thing, anything they could. I was just lucky all the way through. I had this job, and then I was getting thirty cents an hour as a field hand in the Rutgers Experiment Station, and glad to get it.

Also, the big break of the year was the bankers' meetings at Rutgers, where Virginia got to be a waitress. I didn't know her then. But I was in the mailroom. It was big pay. It must have been forty-five cents, or so, an hour. And then, when I was a junior, majoring in physics, two graduate students flunked out. So they had no student assistant for the sophomore lab, which I had just taken.

Professor Winchester called me into his office and said, "We need somebody to take two or so afternoons of laboratory as a teaching assistant. We can only pay you seventy-five cents an hour if you're willing?" I thought, "Boy, I'm more than willing. (Laughter) I was in the field all day for thirty cents an hour.

So it was just plain luck. Certainly the Depression affected us. What we ate, what we could afford to do. I got out of going to the movies, and I still don't like to go to the movies. I talked my family into getting a radio, and they did. I was an only child who had a job. We were better off than most people. So, yes, it affected you. In fact, one of my colleagues here came to me the other day, and he has a son in high school. And he said, "My son has an assignment. Would you be willing to be interviewed by him? He has to interview somebody who's had a tough life." (Laughs) So, that's the reputation I've got, I guess, having come up through the Depression.

But it was terribly tough. My father had a pass on the railroad because of his work, and once in a while he'd get a Saturday off and he'd take me, as a school kid, to New York. And we'd see people selling apples. He made sure that I saw that. He'd take me to the Bowery where he once worked as a ticket agent for the Coney Island Railroad, and he showed me that side of life. We would go to the Automat, and for five cents you got a cup of coffee, and for fifteen cents you got a beef pie, and that was a good lunch.

People would beg you on the street for five cents to get a cup of coffee. And they didn't use it for alcohol, or drugs. They used it for coffee. And on a good day, we could spend a dime and get a cinnamon roll at the Automat. That was a big day. But you didn't feel bad about it. You felt good! But it was a desperate time. People suffered.

"We didn't know we were poor until some visitors came from Princeton High School and said, 'Oh, my God, you live in a shack.' " *--Charles Mickett Jr.*

My father came from somewhere near the Hungarian-Czech border. He was five foot two. He never had any formal education here in the US, so whatever he learned, he learned by himself. He would dedicatedly read *The New York Times* everyday, when we could afford it. It was just amazing that he was such a good, honest man. My mother learned to read in this country.

When my father retired from the railroad-- he didn't retire, he had to quit for health reasons-- they bought a little store in Little Rocky Hill, which is out on Route 27, a mom and pop store, which they operated for pretty close to 60 years. He was just so proud that he could do things by himself. He did not go on welfare, in those days, they called it "relief," because he said it was the responsibility of every family to take care of themselves.

We were poor, gosh, were we poor. We were proud, I guess you could say. (laughter) I looked at my father, and he said, "We gotta do it. Chuck, you gotta do it." He told each one of us we have to do it by ourselves. But you couldn't believe how poor we were. We lived in a house which had a store in the front, my mother, my father, my brothers, George, Mike, and myself. We had three rooms. All three rooms measured nine foot wide by 27 foot long. We had no heat except for a little coal stove. We had no plumbing, really. When we washed to go to school, we'd break the ice in the basin and wash. That's the way it was. It's surprising though, I don't think we considered ourselves poor.

We had the store and an acre of land, and we would plant tomatoes, corn, you name it. Then, my younger brother and I,
George, we built this wagon with two great big boxes, one in the
front, one in the back. We would take the wagon and go into
Kingston loaded with tomatoes and vegetables. We would go
door to door, selling all of our vegetables. Then, when the
huckleberry season would come up, we'd go out, pick huckle-
berries, and sell them from house to house. That supplemented
our income and we managed.

I don't think we realized we were poor until I went to Princeton High School and some visitors came and said, "Oh, my
God, you live in a shack." We didn't have any money, our
neighbors didn't have any money. That's the way it was.

The store closed in 1995. When my father died, in 1982, my
mother maintained it. She was in that store by herself for 13
years. She had problems with her legs. She was not a very
good disciple of medical care, and her legs swelled up and she
ended up in the hospital. After the hospital stay, we brought her
home and closed the store down.

Now the problem was having my mother at our house. She's
in her eighties. She had nothing in common with anybody, no
friends here. When she was at the store, she saw many people
whom she knew, so she said, one day, "I'm going home."
"Hey, Mom, you can't go home." She says, "Yes, I'm going
home." I said, "No way, Mom." But she packed her clothes,
opened the door, and said, "I'm going to walk 18 miles." So,
we said, "Okay," so we took her home.

At least when she was home, she opened the store, she had
somebody. She knew all the neighborhood. She felt important,
that she was doing something.

I think the Great Depression in many ways was very good for
us. We would have one pound of meat a week. My mother
would cook it in stuffed cabbage, two pounds of rice, one pound
of meat, and we would have a whole pot that lasted three or four

77

days. Because of the fact that we did not eat too much meat and too much fat, my father lived to be 97, and the only reason he died, he had a double hernia that strangulated his intestines. He was climbing trees at 95. My mother lived to 100 and I hope maybe I'll do the same. We didn't eat rich foods, never ate any dessert. (laughter) When I went into the Army, the guys would complain about the food. I thought I was living like a king. I'd never had dessert and all those good things like bacon and eggs for breakfast.

That time when she moved in with us, after my father died, I had started to play golf. So I was telling Mom, "Boy, Mom, this is great, I can play golf for $5." What a lecture I got. "How could I?" Now I also like to go fishing, and I caught some fluke. They were a nice size, and I put ice in the water, so when I get home to filet them, they're still alive. My wife Fran said, "Why don't you show these to your mother?" So I showed Mom. First thing out of her mouth was, "See, when you go fishing, you bring food home. When you play golf, you spend money."

"We would pick beans from morning to night, and then they would say, 'Well, you picked 10 bushels, so you can keep two.' "   *--Forrest S. Clark*

My father lost his job in New York during the Depression, so what we didn't have from then on was a steady income. My father's main hobby was art. I still have a lot of his paintings hanging in my house; he had a lifetime interest in oil painting. Because of that, he got a job with the Federal Arts Project in Newark. A lot of artists and theater people got jobs doing scenery, working in the theater, doing art work for posters, work like that, and that's what he did during the hardest years of the Depression.

We were living in Roseland. It was very rural country, all farms, big dairy farms. You may have heard of Becker's Dairy

Farm. Anybody who lived in that part of New Jersey would know Becker's. It was a huge dairy farm, like Borden's, practically, and it covered a large area of the town.

My brother and I had a country, rural boyhood, because we had these open fields, a lot of fruit orchards, a lot of farms, a lot of produce farms, and we worked on some of those farms, picking beans in the summertime. You've got to remember that during the Great Depression it was almost taken for granted that, in order for you to live you had to grow a lot of your own vegetables. We did that, and we also had to pick vegetables on various farms in the area around where we lived, and that was a big occupation for my brother and me during those years.

My father admired Roosevelt because Roosevelt pulled a lot of people out of the Depression. When the New Deal came in, there was all kinds of things, and then shortly after that, Social Security and all those Roosevelt programs came in, the New Deal programs.

We had a lot of unemployed people in Roseland, a lot of welfare people. A lot of people owned small farms and made a living off of them. They either sold produce or they picked it for their own table, and a lot of times we would share. We often shared with other people in Roseland. I remember that many times my brother and I would work from morning until night picking beans-- we were just young kids, of course-- and then, at the end of the day, when we thought we were going to be paid, they'd say, "Well, you picked 10 bushels today, so you can keep two," and that was your pay for eight or 10 hours work.

"In the summer, I'd work 55 hours a week at the rubber factory, and I'd get $7.16, and I took it home to my mother."   *--Carlton C. Dilatush*

My father died in the great influenza epidemic of 1919, and I almost did, too. I was one year old. Both the minister and the doctor stayed overnight with my mother. Thank God I made it.

My father was 26 years of age. My mother was left with two children. My brother was 17 months older than I, so my maternal grandparents, Daniel and Elizabeth Cook, gave up their farm and came to live with us so my mother could go to work in Trenton. She used to ride the trolley from Hamilton Square into Trenton, and she worked in various department stores. My grandfather, in many ways, took the role of my father as I was growing up, but then he died when I was only 12.

Before I was 10, I started to pick strawberries on the farms below where we lived, and the money I earned I brought home and gave to my mother. I went to the Mercer Rubber Company in Hamilton Square, and the owner knew that I was not 15. I told him I was 15 and I needed a job, so he gave me a job in the rubber factory feeding the tubing machine with rubber stock. So I worked there from the time I was 12 until between my junior and senior years at Rutgers.

I worked every Christmas, every spring and every summer vacation. I don't remember having any vacation, to be honest with you. My mother needed all the help I could give her. So I'm used to work, but it was a good experience. From the moment I started there, I knew I wanted to go to college, because I saw how dirty it was, and how hard the work was, and the owner knew that, too.

My grandfather Dilatush worked there for years and years. He was working there when I applied. I guess he was also a father image to me, because after my grandfather Cook died, when I was 12, my grandfather Dilatush was there. He worked his entire career there. He used to run a huge press where they'd make these heavy, wide conveyor belts for conveying coal at coal mines. He retired when he was 85 and lived to be about 95.

There were times when I wouldn't even sign out. I would work seven days of the week, because the factory owner asked me, "Do you want to be night watchman? The regular night watchman is going on vacation." So my card would be in all week and then for the next two weeks, because I'd be there as a night watchman. Our home wasn't too far from the factory, about a quarter of a mile, so my brother, or my mother, or someone would get my lunch to me, or my dinner.

I worked hard, and they knew I was ambitious and didn't loaf on the job. If there was something I could help people out with I'd go over and give them a hand. It worked out okay.

I worked 55 hours a week in the summer, and as soon as I was finished with school I'd go to the rubber factory, and I think I earned $7.16 a week, or something like that for 55 hours. And I used to take that home and give it to my mother.

I also had two lawns that I mowed after hours, after I finished at the factory, and I received a dollar from each of those, so I had about $9.16 a week that I would give to my mother. She in turn would give me 50 cents. Five cents of that went into my Sunday School envelope, so I had 45 cents and I thought I was loaded. On Saturday night, I'd go to the movies, and afterwards have enough money to buy a sundae or a milk shake.

My grandfather and my grandmother lived with us, and I remember my brother and I, and my grandfather Dilatush, used to go to the woods and cut trees in the winter. We would cut up the trees and limbs for firewood, and haul it home, and that was our fuel. Because in those days, in the Depression years, we didn't buy coal, we were burning wood in the furnace.

I guess I learned early that it was necessary to work. Even later, when I was in college, I was given a job in the fraternity dusting, mopping and making the beds. I did that for three years, and that's how I earned my room.

"I can still picture my father and mother embracing each other and crying because he had $27 and we could have Thanksgiving."   *--Joseph B. McCartney*

The Depression was very, very difficult for us. My father was a printer, a sole proprietor printer with his printing business in the basement of the house. There were stretches when I can re-

81

call him sitting on the front porch and not having any work to do. Sometimes as long as two months. Throughout that period, he had many customers who were unable to pay their debts.

I recall, when I was about 10 or 11, he had spent the day out to collect on jobs that he had done and finally, in the late afternoon, he visited a doctor, Dr. Peters, who paid a bill of $27. And my father went out and he just blew the whole payment and came in with five or six bags of food. This was around Thanksgiving. He had a turkey and all kinds of vegetables and fruit and God knows what. He just went berserk.

And I can still picture the two of them-- my father and mother-- at the door embracing each other and crying. To him it was a bonanza. It was like he'd won the lotto.

Through that period of time, we had tried to buy our home but all he could pay was $10 interest per month. Just the interest, and $10 was about the going rate at that time, which sounds almost unbelievable today. But never putting anything on the principal, not being able to do it.

Basically, the way we got through the Depression was that he was fortunate enough to do printing for a butcher, and a small grocery shop owner. And that's the way we lived. Instead of taking money, he took food. And for maybe a stretch of at least one and a half years, that's the way we existed. And it just was an awful experience.

Thank God that I had the opportunity to work for the press, the little printing section of Publications, when I was in school. It was a Godsend. All day Saturday, all through high school, I worked in supermarkets, and sometimes I had some odd hours during the week.

I wanted to go to Fordham, but we couldn't afford it. I received a general scholarship from Rutgers, which was a special grant from President Clothier in view of my financial situation, plus the fact that I was valedictorian in high school. But after two years, I went to the dean and I said, "I have no money to go any further and I hate to drop it right now, after two years," and

I said, "I'd appreciate it if you could give some consideration to my background, plus the fact," I said, "that I know of some people who are here on full state scholarships." And I said, "I know they've done no better than I have. It would be a different thing if I couldn't validate this situation." So I guess I sparked a little interest and they were taken aback.

But I couldn't help it. It's the way I felt. And I guess it made quite an impression because he went to the president. It was President Clothier at that time. In those days, the tuition was only about $400 a semester, so they gave me $200. I made the other half up by working in the print shop and on Saturdays in a supermarket.

Every time I had a free period, I was either in the library or in the print shop. Either place. And getting in a car and scooting home about four o'clock in the afternoon to work. And then on weekends I worked at the supermarket. There wasn't much time for anything else.

"We lost our house in 1933. I came home from school, and all our furniture was out on the street. There was no welfare, no help."   *--Herbert Gross*

My whole recollection of my father was, and it used to annoy me, why didn't he get out and try to make some money? Because in the Depression we lost our house. Our furniture was out in the street when I came home from school. It was a terrible time.

Now that I look back, I'm sorry that I felt that way. I used to say, why don't you get out and do like other people? But he was mostly interested in reading, reading, and I always remember him in that light. My mother always catered to that with him and that's the way it was, but they were very rough times. Not only for my parents and myself, but for other people we knew. It was a bad, deep Depression.

I remember we lost our house in '33. In those days they just put your furniture on the street. I came home from school, and that's what I saw-- all of our furniture out there. There was no welfare. There was no help. There were no laws that said you can't put anybody on the street, you've got to give me three months or something. And that was the way we mostly existed in those Depression days.

My father was never out of work. He worked for the Metropolitan Life Insurance Company. He had a debit that he would collect 10 cents a week, those kind of policies they had, and it was drudging to go because the people who had 10 cents a week never had any money. We also had a tough time because my father was always lending out 10 cents when he couldn't afford it. I remember my mother would get so upset with him because he would get his salary and then this would happen. "They're going to pay me, they'll pay me." It's not that they wouldn't, most of them couldn't. He made very little money.

So when it came time to go to college, my folks were caring enough to tell me that I should go and not have to worry about taking care of them. So in that way, they released me. Friends of mine from high school had obligations to their parents to help them. That's how rugged it was in those days. Anyway, in the class that I associated with, we were, I guess, pretty much lower strata financially. And my friends were the same way.

Rutgers was a state institution. I think it cost something like $400, and I got some kind of help or aid. It cost me about $150. There was a Sigma Alpha Mu fraternity on campus. And someone from Trenton that I knew was a junior there. He was from a very well-to-do family, and he got me a job at the Sammy House waiting on tables and cleaning up, That's how I went through Rutgers.

And then my uncle had a butcher store when I was a kid and I used to work in it. I was a half-ass butcher, and I got a job at what in those days was a supermarket. While all the other guys were working at drug stores and shoe clerks and all, I was making more money because butchers were making more. So I more or less had a good life at Rutgers, because I had free room and board, and I made enough money to take care of my clothes and my books.

"I didn't know the Depression. Our house had six bedrooms, we had five acres, Grandpa had two cars, we had horses." --*Norman Brandt*

I didn't feel any effects of the Depression at all, as many others did. We lived well. The house that I spent most of the time living in, where my mother grew up with her brothers and sisters, is now a Charlie Brown's Restaurant on the edge of Westfield. The house had six bedrooms, and the property was about five acres.

We had a stable and horses. Once my mother and Aunt Min were sitting on the bench of a buggy with Frank and me in their arms. Aunt Min was driving, and the horse was a pinto named Buck. This was a one-horse shay which could be used to carry passengers. Aunt Min had forgotten to secure the tailgate properly. Consequently, when Buck started forward, the tailgate fell down and the bench that we were on fell back. Although we landed on the ground and there was no unfortunate consequence, I used to tease Frank that he had fallen on his head at an early age and that accounted for his erratic action ever after.

Later, there was a beautiful brown horse named Penny that Grandpa had bought to replace Buck. Aunt Min and Uncle Ben used to ride her. I first lived at Grandpa's when I was about two years old. During that time, whenever Uncle Ben went down to the stable to saddle up Penny before his ride, my mother would sit me on the backstairs post. Uncle Ben would come up from the stable, pick me up from the post, and sit me in front of him on the horse. He would then trot all around and bring me back to the backstairs post before he went off for his canter.

My grandfather still had a decent income. He had two cars. Before that, when we moved to Orange, we had a nice apartment on Main Street, near High Street. My father had a business. We didn't know what "Depression" meant, basically. I never felt it.

Now I would have the feeling that money meant something. It would have cost money to send me to another town for instruction if I were going to have a bar mitzvah, and I wasn't sent. Actually, my family could have afforded the dough to send me there, but religion never meant anything to my father. My mother grew up that way, but she was not particularly religious.

So the Depression, per se, I was not ignorant of some of the things. Reading *The Grapes of Wrath* really was an eye-opener, and then, the movie, fantastic, but I didn't see any of that. There were, obviously, people on relief, but I didn't know what that was, I didn't know who they were, and so, really, in those terms, the only effect may have been a little less funding.

But, gee, I remember, when I was about five or six, my grandfather was religious, but he couldn't live in a circumstance where he'd be closed on Saturday, because that's when all his customers came, because they were Wall Street people, and Saturday night he'd bring home all the proceeds that he'd collected during the week, and my grandmother would count the bills while my grandfather was eating dinner, and I would pile up the silver dollars and all the coins, and there were times when they had $50 worth of silver alone.

So, as I said, he had two cars. Only one son went to college, went to law school, Newark Law, his others didn't, but I think they could have. I don't think the Depression prevented them. And from my point of view, I just didn't know the Depression.

COLLEGE DAYS

Before the war, Rutgers College had a student body of about 1,500. It was small, intimate and almost like family. Many still remember being invited to a professor's home on a Sunday evening for an informal seminar complete with cider and cookies served by the professor's wife.

When students needed encouragement-- or financial help-- they were usually able to get it. "They knew what I was going through," says one. "You could sense the empathy."

Robert Clothier, a stately Princetonian, was president, and Fraser Metzger, a craggy man with a shock of white hair, was Dean of Men. Dean Metzger "somehow or other knew everybody's grades and whether anybody had done anything, good or bad." He seemed always to be walking up or down College Avenue and "he'd stop you and say, 'I hear you got a good grade in economics,' or 'How'd you do on the math exam?'"

Tuition was $400, and one former student recalls the Dean asking, "How much can you afford?" "$200." "Then you can have a $200 scholarship," said the Dean.

Another student of those days recalls how, when he told the Dean he'd have to leave school because his funds had run out, the Dean reached into his own wallet and lent him the money, which he repaid over a period of time.

"Kindly, but strict" is how we remember Dean Metzger. Cutting a class or missing compulsory Sunday chapel got you a summons to his office for an explanation or a lecture.

There was hazing, but it was mild. Freshmen were required to wear name tags and small hats, called "dinks," carry shopping bags and tuck their trousers into their socks. Saying "Hello" to everyone you passed was mandatory, and at first a nuisance, but in a few weeks it got you acquainted with a surprising number of people.

Fraternities had their hazing, too, but it was circumscribed by rules-- no alcohol, and a housemother in each fraternity house to keep a motherly eye on dating couples.

"Rutgers became your life," says Robert Ochs. "You didn't shove off and go other places; you just did things there." NJC, the New Jersey College for Women, was across town and the obvious venue for Rutgers men looking to date. And you couldn't get into too much trouble; the girls had an 11 PM curfew.

Activities were curtailed by available cash, too; pre-war was still pretty much Depression. Peter Sarriaocco remembers looking longingly at the cafeteria's 35-cent meals, while he could afford only the 20- or 25-cent versions.

After the war, things were quite different. Nathan Shoehalter, who returned to Rutgers under the GI Bill in 1946, recalls that "we were mature, and we traveled in our own age group. I'd missed everything. I'd lost my youth, 18 to 24, whatever it was. Those years were just gone. The younger students were just kids. I didn't know anything about them.

"It was so exciting, so different from what I remember when I was an undergraduate before the war. Really, we talked like adults. When something was bullshit, we'd tell the professor, we'd let him know it was bullshit. It was very exciting."

"Rutgers was a tiny little school. You'd meet Dean Metzger on College Avenue and he'd say, 'How'd you do on the math exam?' " --*Lewis M. Bloom*

I walked over the bridge from Highland Park to the Rutgers campus, brown-bagged it at lunch time or had a sandwich some-where nearby. Later, a group of us would go have dinner, and then came back again and work in the library.

Remember, Rutgers was a tiny little school and if you didn't know everybody, you could recognize a face at least. It was a to-tally different school. Dean Metzger somehow or other knew everybody's grades and whether or not anybody had done any-thing, good or bad. You'd walk up College Avenue from Van Nest up to Bishop or the gym and if he'd be walking there-- he was always coming or going-- he'd stop you and say, "Hey, I hear you got a good grade in economics" or "How'd you do on that math examination?" He was strict, but he was very fair.

The administration at that time was a different kind of animal, but I loved them. They were very good to me, because I was having a rough time. I had a loan, but the school gave me addi-tional funds, which I paid back. I still have a beautiful letter that I received from the Treasurer of the University after I paid back the loan, wishing me well. It wasn't only the money, but they gave me a sense of encouragement. The school was so small that I knew they knew what I was going through. And you could

89

sense the empathy. We were almost like part of a family.

Sunday chapel was required, and I knew the University made a conscious effort to have a nondenominational service, but some students tried to get out on religious grounds. I came from a very orthodox background-- my grandfather was a rabbi-- but we were more adventuresome. I liked the architecture. More than anything, I loved the music. I loved the Bach and the Handel. It was good for me too, because it got me down on campus at nine on Sunday morning. Then I'd walk home quickly, have a bite, and be back when the library opened. It was a good discipline.

I started out as an engineer, but Dean Marvin had spoken to my father, in my presence, and said very candidly, "Don't let your son take engineering because Jewish boys are not hired in the field of engineering, and you are wasting your time." He said, "He's going to end up selling insurance or being a salesman. The chances of him succeeding in engineering are minimal." Of course, when the war broke out, they needed engineers. They didn't care what the color of your skin or your background was.

"Tuition was $400. The Dean asked, 'How much can you afford?' I said, '$200.' 'Then you'll have a $200 scholarship,' he said." --C. Harrison Hill

I had thought of going to Princeton, but it was just too expensive. No, Rutgers was my choice. My uncle had gone here and everything was wrapped around Rutgers. I used to come here on the campus and be impressed with the fact that everybody would say, "Hello." And I would go home and say, "Boy, I must look like somebody on the campus," you know, "who do they think I am?" And then I read the freshman handbook which said it's customary to say "hello" to anybody on the campus.

I went to see Dean Metzger about applying for a scholarship.

Tuition was $400, and he said, "Well, how much do you think you can afford to spend?" And, I said, "$200." And he said, "Well, you'll have a $200 scholarship." That was it. There were three people who controlled the college community in those days: President Clothier; Cy Johnson, who was the comptroller; and Dean Metzger.

I remember President Clothier saying that his classmate was president of Princeton and the one thing that he envied Clothier for was his home here. The Princeton president's home was in the center of the campus and it wasn't as nice.

A neighbor was secretary of the chairman of the Ceramics Department, so she was always promoting ceramics when I was trying to make up my mind what I wanted to do. I thought I wanted to be an engineer, but I was working with engineers who were talking me out of being a civil engineer. They didn't think that was a good way to make a living.

I was convinced there was gonna be a good future in ceramics, and most likely I made a big mistake later because when I got out of the service I went back to Yale to study architecture.

There were nine ceramists in our class, and the fellows that stayed in ceramics did very, very well. One of them became president of Carborundum, and others did very well. So there was a great possibility. There were 20 jobs for every one of us when we graduated in 1940.

In those days there weren't very many professionally-trained ceramists. Most of the people were craft-trained. I had a job selling clay and ceramic raw materials. My job was really to go into a plant if they had a problem and work with them to resolve the problem using my materials, and then, as long as the batch worked, nobody thought of changing it.

There were not many schools of ceramics at that time. Ohio State had one, which sort of took care of the Middle West, and Rutgers was the East. And in the summer of '39, Rutgers got the idea with DuPont that we would sell ceramics by having an exhibit at the New York World's Fair. So Otto Stach and I

91

worked for DuPont at the New York World's Fair, really promoting Rutgers ceramics. We started April 1 and went to November 1. We took our lectures in the morning, and then they rearranged our labs. We did a lot of commuting. We got $35 a week there, which was one of the high-paid jobs.

I was on the crew at Rutgers. That was the one sport that you could start on an equal basis with everyone else because nobody else had any crew in high school either. So you were starting out on a level playing field and competing. I rowed freshman and sophomore year, but then our labs were just too much.

Those early years were interesting. Rutgers crew started in '33, and I started in '36. We had a floating boathouse. We'd come in and would put the boat up over our head and get soaking wet. But that river water was a different color every day because of the dyes from Calco Chemical. That was foul.

"The cafeteria had meals for 20 cents, 25 cents and 35 cents. The 35-cent meals looked wonderful, but I couldn't buy them." --Peter Sarraiocco

I guess my parents realized that I wanted to educate myself, but one of my biggest lacks was the lack of a mentor. My parents couldn't really be my mentors. They had a limited education. They never stood in my way, but they had no way of guiding me. I said to them, "I want to go to college," and they said, "Well, you're going to have to do it on your own."

I came to Rutgers because I took a competitive examination for a scholarship, full tuition and fees for four years, and I was fortunate enough to win. I don't know how many they had in those days, they didn't have very many throughout the state. All right, so now here I was going to go to college; I didn't have any money. So I had to go to the bank, and the doctor, our family physician, had to co-sign a note for $250. So I had $250 to pay my expenses. And that doesn't sound like much, but remember, I would buy a $5 meal ticket at the cafeteria, and the

92

idea was that you got $5.50 worth of meals. And I would try to make that last for the whole week.

They'd have 20-cent meals, 25-cent meals, and 35-cent meals. I never bought a 35-cent meal. I'd look at it, and it would be wonderful, but I couldn't buy it. It wasn't in the budget. I'd buy 20- and 25-cent meals and stretch the money out. But we didn't only do that. For a variety, we'd go to various places.

Three or four of us would go to a little restaurant. The waitresses would know what we were doing. We'd sit down and eat the bread, before we even ordered. Then, we'd say, "Well, we need some more bread." (laughter) We were so damned hungry. You're 18, 19 years old, and you're hungry all the time. Then we'd go through another idea: We'd say, "Well, maybe we could save some money if we bought the bread and the ingredients ourselves," and, we'd try that for a few days to see how we could stretch our funds.

"You couldn't have a girl to the fraternity house for dinner unless the housemother came out and sat there during the meal."   *--Raymond Mortensen*

I lived off-campus when I first came to Rutgers. I didn't know how early you had to apply, and all the dormitories were booked. I lived at 10 Bartlett Street, right off College Avenue. I'd guess there were five or six of us in that house. You see, in the early '40s, Rutgers was a small place. The whole college went from Queens Campus to the gym and from George Street to College Avenue. Except for the Ag School, that was it. I never felt that I was different from somebody who lived in the dorms. I was friends with the people that lived in that house. We were good friends. So I never had a feeling of being strange.

Then I was rushed by the Zeta Psi fraternity. All of a sudden, somebody says, "Come around for dinner." I was rushed by Chi Psi and I forget who else, but those two I remember distinctly. I joined Zeta Psi because I liked the people, and they had

93

a great location.

Some fraternities were associated with a particular sport or activity, and I suppose you'd say Zeta Psi was oriented toward *Targum*, the campus newspaper. The circulation manager was a Zeta, the editor was a Zeta. A lot of us were in the *Targum* and the Glee Club.

We had a housemother. She had an apartment in the house, right off the kitchen, a two-room apartment with a bath, and you could not have someone of the opposite sex for dinner or lunch unless she came out and sat during the meal. So that imposed a certain damper on any kind of activity that was (laughter) untoward. And there were rules. For example, we dressed for dinner, not dinner jackets, but you had to come to dinner in a coat and a tie. Otherwise, you couldn't eat.

There was no raucous behavior. In the years that I was there, we never had any drunken nonsense, windows being broken and all that stuff. I found that behavior when I went back. I said to my wife, "I'm never going back there again." (laughter) There was a respect for the property. I remember one spring break, three of us went back and spent two days sanding the floor on the second floor and painting it, because it needed it.

I always felt it was a beautiful house, with a huge room on the right hand side that we called the "Bum Room," and it had nice leather furniture and a big center library table. When you brought a gal there for a dance weekend, you were proud.

The NJC campus was right across town, and I thoroughly enjoyed it. I went out with my fair share of girls when I was at Rutgers, and it was so easy, because they had a curfew. By the time you had dinner and got over to NJC, you've got to take the bus, and walk to someplace where you could have a drink or something, and then it was time to take her back. At 11 o'clock, she had to be in, and only one hour later on weekends.

The big events on campus were the Soph Hop, the Junior Prom and the Military Ball, and they were very festive occasions, full dress affairs, and usually a three-day event. Ladies usually arrived on Friday and left on Sunday. When they arrived, if you were in the fraternity, you had to move out. You went over to a dormitory and bunked with a friend of yours, or if he had gone home, he let you stay in his dorm room. I enjoyed the ones I went to, and of course NJC had similar events. I remember going to a couple of their Christmas Balls.

I didn't get into any trouble at Rutgers, except once with Dean Metzger. He was a dignified man with snow white hair, and very fair. I cut a class once, and it was a class that I should not have cut, not only because it was against the law but it was a Military Science class, ROTC class, and I got caught, obviously, and I had forged a medical excuse. (laughter) I got caught at that too, and got called to the Dean's Office, and went in to see Fraser Metzger, and he confronted me with all this.

It was a Monday morning after one of those long weekends, and I just didn't want to get up, and I figured, "This is easy," and I told him the whole story, just like I told you. "This is what I did, this is what I thought I could get away with, and I apologize." The fact that I graduated from Rutgers proves the fact that he didn't have me expelled. (laughter) Well, I have a nice letter from him, handwritten, I still have it, congratulating me on being truthful.

It was so much simpler in those days, because there were so few of us.

"I walked into the hall of the brand new gym at Rutgers, and I thought it was the most beautiful building I'd ever seen." --Vincent Kramer

The way I got to Rutgers was through a man named Les Wilding, who was a teacher of mine in grammar school in Paterson. He started teaching manual training when I was probably in the seventh or eighth grade. He was from Paterson, and he came back there to teach. He was going to Rutgers at that time to get his teaching degree. He was an extremely active person with the students, and he still is today. He just received the award for being the outstanding volunteer in Bergen County.

Les took those of us in the High Y to Rutgers for a prep school weekend. And we had to take a transcript of our high school work.

When I walked into the hall of the brand new gym, I thought it was the most beautiful building I'd ever seen, I couldn't get over how beautiful that foyer was, with the display cases, and the beautiful swimming pool. They had that open for us.

As I walked in with these others, someone took a hold of me and said, "We want to talk to you over here." I said, "Okay, I got nothing to do all day anyway." So I went in and it was the football coach. And he said, "Could we see your transcript." And I said, "Yes," because I'd been playing football in high school and I was quite a big boy. And he took my transcript and he said, "Good." He said, "We'll see you a little later."

Well, he sent for me a little later and he said, "You're short half a credit." That's how tough it was to get into college in those days. I lacked one half a semester of Spanish. He said, "You know you can't be admitted?" I said, "Oh. Well, I really just came down for the weekend." (laughter)

He said, "Well, I'll tell you what we'll do. We'll send you to prep school. We have someone who'll pay for you to go to prep school. We'll send you to Bordentown." I said, "I'm not sure." I said, "I may have to go to work." I said, "My family expects me to start being productive."

So I went home and told my mother about it, and she said, "Well, you know it is bad times now for your Daddy," because she was running the business, although we never suffered, but to put up $400 or $500 was a little out of their reach at that point. But we never really hurt. She said, "You know you're going to have to start contributing to the family." And I said, "Well, they told me it wouldn't cost anything to go to prep school." She said, "I'll talk to your Daddy." They ended up by agreeing that I could go.

Bordentown was a very fine experience. It was my first introduction to boys that had been sent there by Penn State, Cornell,
Fordham-- football players. Two of them later made first string
All-American. In our first game, we came in at half-time and the
score was 33-0 in our favor. I think we played seven or eight
games, we scored 218 points against seven or so. And everyone
of us went away to a college with a full scholarship.

After Bordentown, I thought about possibly going somewhere else than Rutgers, but I felt a loyalty to Rutgers; they had
sent me here. I was offered a scholarship to Penn State, which
had a great football team, and they invited me out there.

I went, and one of the football players took me aside and he
told me, "Look, if you are in good shape, that's fine, but if you
get injured, (finger snap) you're off your scholarship just like
that." He said, "You better think about it before you come." I
said, "I've thought about it already," (laughter) because I had an
Upson Scholarship at Rutgers, and Rutgers was not that way.
Rutgers, once they took you in, they took care of you.

*"When I came to college, I had never really trav-
eled. New Brunswick was as far north as I'd been. I
had never seen New York City."* --W. Wallace Kaenzig

I was from South Jersey, and when I came to Rutgers I was
very much aware of the split between North and South. Atlantic
City was our only big city. The seashore towns were very
small. Cape May, Stone Harbor, Wildwood-- they were much
smaller than they are today. A lot of what's there now was wil-
derness in the '30s. The state's population was mostly in the
north.

When you got to college, you were in competition with some
pretty sharp kids. You didn't have that competition in your own
high schools in the south. Some of the top students would go
away to medical school, law school, and so forth. But you're
talking about one or two out of each class.

97

It was a very different lifestyle. They lived a much faster life-style than we did. We were still low and laid back in the south and when you came up here and got into the rat race, you found yourself not only trotting but sometimes running to keep up.

Economically people up here were better off than they were in South Jersey. We were strictly a rural farming area and the money just wasn't there. When I came to Rutgers, I lived in the Phelps House, on the Ag Campus, and one guy's father was a bank president, another was a vice president of Esso. That's how it was in those days. It was a lot different. You weren't talking lower class, middle class, upper class. You were talking lower middle-class and lower upper class, really.

Some of these guys were poor-mouthing everything, and they had more money than I thought I would ever see in my lifetime. And I said to myself, "I can't stand this. I've got to get out of here." So I came down with two other fellows in the Ag School, and we found a place on Patterson Street by the church, and we lived on the third floor of the manse where the caretaker lived. We had a little apartment up there. Three and a half dollars a week for each of us and we did our own cooking, brought food from home. We would bring potatoes and canned goods, be-cause everyone canned.

I came to college from an Ag background. So the place to go was to Rutgers. I envisioned going into some type of commer-cial agricultural. Either into sales or into some type of market-ing or something like that.

Professor Schermerhorn was my favorite prof. He was one of the nicest people that you could ever run into. Very dedicated, very knowledgeable, a real teacher. Had the patience of Job. Would work with you. Would share things with you such as his work that he was doing in research. He developed the Rut-gers Tomato. That was one of his things. And he would talk to you about his experiences in traveling through the country, like trips to California viewing the growing of lettuce. He always had time for any student, and was just a great teacher.

Remember, up till then I had never traveled anywhere. I had crossed the Delaware River into Philadelphia to see baseball games and the farthest north I'd ever been was New Brunswick. I had never been to New York City or anywhere.

"I worked hard in college. I thought the draft board might be looking at me, and five days before I turned 21 I was told to report." --*John L. Archibald*

I was just an average student, and I wanted to be an athlete, but I was too small. I did play 150-pound football and lacrosse my freshman year and realized that I couldn't cope with both athletics and studies. I worked hard in college. I thought, when I didn't get in the Advanced ROTC, that the draft might be looking at me. I tried to get into another branch. I thought I might get into Naval Meteorology or something like that, but I had no luck because of a congenital condition in the left eye, just couldn't pass an eye test. So they had a summer school, and I accelerated so that I actually finished up in college in September of '42, and got my degree on three-and-a-half years of school.

Everybody was concerned about when his number would be called up. Just five days before I turned 21, I was told to report to the draft board. I think you were supposed to be allowed two weeks or 15 days, something like that. There was obviously something fishy about it. (laughter)

My father, having knowledge of the draft procedures because of his work with students, immediately appealed to the Somerset County Draft Board, stating that his son needed six weeks to finish his degree, and that it would be in conjunction with such-and-such War Department protocol that was automatically granted, and he couldn't understand why I was being drafted.

Just a day or two before I was to report, he went up to the draft board, and he said that this was one of the most unique experiences he ever had. This sort of tough sergeant major-type guy, a civilian, an older man, was just browbeating these young

99

kids, saying, "You're in the Army now, kid. Get lost," and my father stood in line, patiently. When his turn came, he explained the situation, and this guy, very briskly, said, "Well, we never got that letter," and my father said, "Well, what is your name?" and he said, "My name is," we'll say, "Mr. Smith." My father pulled out the return address card, Mr. Smith had signed the card, and then, of course, he was very upset, and he started eating humble pie. It was an oversight and a mistake, he said, but I would have to go to Fort Dix on the 31st, which I did. In the meantime, my father got off a telegram to Secretary of War Stimson.

When I got to Fort Dix, they issued uniforms, and the guy said, "Is your name Archibald?" I said, "Yeah," and he said, "Everybody would like to be in your shoes right now. You're being given a furlough," and I was given a furlough for six weeks, so I could finish college.

My father always suspected that this man had some friend who had put influence on him and that my name was just drawn out at the last second, and I was slated to go so this other person's friend wouldn't have to.

"In your third year of ROTC you began to get paid-- $21 every three months. That was big money-- almost a month's worth of meals." --Edward Bautz

This was in the Depression, and all of us were on a shoestring. A number of students at the Raritan Club were commuters and they would have lunch there. We fed the people that lived in the house on a dollar a day. Everything was a lot cheaper. We took turns waiting on tables and washing the dishes and that kind of stuff, and when we did that we got our meals free.

In my junior year, I was the treasurer of the house. So I got my room free, and in my senior year, I was a steward, so I got my meals free, although I had to wait on tables every noontime.

But it was a penny-pinching kind of operation, and it had been nip-and-tuck as to whether I was going to go to college at all. At the last minute, we decided I was going, and I just had my fingers crossed. I did see Dean Metzger when I first got down there, because I didn't have a scholarship. He said, "Well, you know, would this make the difference between your coming or not coming?" I said, "Well, it may well. I don't know," and so he took some action and got me that first half tuition scholarship, which was $100.

A full tuition was $200. The fees, with everything, were about $160, and then, of course, as time went on, I also got into the advanced course of the ROTC, which most all the senior people on the campus did, because Rutgers was a land-grant college, and everyone took ROTC, unless they were physically unqualified or a conscientious objector, and then they took it for just the first two years. In your third year, you began to get some pay-- $21 every three months, which was big money in those days. That was almost a month's worth of meals. Although you also had to pay for your uniforms.

"The prof would invite us to his home on Sunday nights, and his wife would serve cocoa and cookies, and we'd have a bull session."   *--Robert Ochs*

When I was a freshman, they had a freshman reception in the College Avenue gymnasium. And you lined up, and the girls at NJC came into town by bus. Hats on, and white gloves. And the two lines would meet. And so you had a partner, and you'd go through a reception line. First one I went through in my life. And you actually got to meet the President of the University and his wife. I used to think, "Ah, this is terrible." But it wasn't till you got older that you'd say, "Hey, Rutgers was teaching me something there, and I wasn't smart enough to recognize it at the time." Those things don't happen anymore.

You got associated with a fraternity if they wanted you, and in

101

my case it was the DU house, and you know, alcohol wasn't allowed in those days. But when I was a pledge they had a fraternity party, and they were going to serve alcohol. So the pledges were lined up on College Avenue-- we didn't have radios in those days-- and if the Dean was coming down the street, we were the relay system. And one time, the Dean actually came down the street, and I put the system into effect so the guys could hide the stuff before the Dean walked in.

Rutgers became your life. You didn't shove off and go other places; you just did things there. And there was a lot going on in those days. You didn't have the number of automobiles that you have now, you didn't try to drift as far away, and if you went over to "The Coop," as we called NJC, they blew a whistle at 11 o'clock, and you were off the campus anyway. And it was tough to try to buy illegal beer. You had to prove you were 21 to get a beer in those days.

Every freshman wore that little hat-- the dink-- first with a little bit of fear and trepidation, but after that, with pride. The Dean of Students in those days also used to lecture us about how you said "Hello" to everybody on the campus. I thought to myself, "Now what the devil is this guy talking about?" But you did it, because you were told to. And again, it's a tradition that was so meaningful, because you actually got to know everybody's name, and the next thing you know, by the time you're a freshman for six weeks, guys are saying, "Hey, hi, Ochsie, how are you?" I wore my dink with pride the whole time. In fact, it was the only hat I owned, I think.

There were so few students that they could really give you hands-on treatment in those days. And they did. And they were more than fair with you. But they also represented what my father was with me. Firm. If my dad said, "You will cut the grass tomorrow morning," you would cut the grass tomorrow morning. And so there was a father figure, and a great deal of respect for him.

But the profs were that way, too. I took an economics course once, with a guy named Agger. Great economics man. And on Sunday nights he used to invite us to his home. Not every Sunday, but maybe four times a semester. We'd sit on the floor, Mrs. Agger would serve hot cocoa, or cookies, and he'd lecture us. Well, in those days, it was, "Well, yeah, I'm going to the prof's house, have cookies tonight." But you didn't know how important that was until just a few years of your life went by.

I recognize it can't be done today, but the place was so small in those days, it was so intimate, that that was part of your education. And like most things in life, years go along before you recognize what that man really did for you.

" 'Ma'am, can you keep a secret?' he asked. 'That's a new weapon the military has developed. It's called a grenade catcher.' " --Livy Goodman

I played four years of lacrosse. I was a good lacrosse player. I played inside attack in my freshman year, and we were undefeated, which was quite an accomplishment for a freshman team. Nobody had ever seen a lacrosse stick, let alone what the sport was when they came to Rutgers. There was no high school lacrosse. For a bunch of guys who didn't ever play the game to go undefeated! You got numerals as a freshman, instead of a letter, on a white sweater. You don't think that was something! We put those letters on a white sweater and wore it morning, noon, and night. In '43 we had a good team, a very good team.

Now at that time we were in the the first year of advanced ROTC. You had to have two years of ROTC, mandatory. And then it was optional to go into the advanced ROTC.

None of us ever thought about military careers. Advanced ROTC was just another activity. We had a drill team called the Scabbard and Blade, an excellent drill team. We had a good army cadre here, and they taught us, and that was a competitive thing to do. Plus there were nice uniforms, and we had a military ball. And you did some training. I don't remember the training really, but it was something to do. So we all signed up.

There were 50 of us that were juniors when the war broke out. The Army didn't know what to do with these fellows all over the country. In normal course, you'd graduate from college, and if you chose to, you went for officer training or you went to your local reserves.

Finally the order came down: Seniors in ROTC will finish their current year-- this is '43-- and then go to their officer training. Rutgers was infantry so they went to Fort Benning. Juniors will stay, get inducted, and then finish their junior year, period. They didn't say what you would do after that.

So we all went down to Fort Dix, and were inducted in March of '43. We came back, and we were now in the Army and in uniform, finishing our junior year. That's the time I was playing lacrosse. Three-quarters of the team was in uniform. The senior members as well as the junior members who were in ROTC were in uniform.

So we played the University of Maryland, and after the game we were coming home, we were standing on the train platform in Baltimore with our duffel bags and our lacrosse sticks sticking out of the duffel bags. And these two little ladies were standing over here and they kept looking at us and looking at us, because we're all GIs.

Finally one lady says, pointing to our lacrosse sticks, "I just can't help asking you, what are those?" Well the co-captain of the team was an All-American defenseman by the name of Bill Newman. Without batting an eye and without any expression, he said, "Ma'am, can you keep a secret?" He said, "That's a new weapon that the military has just developed, it's called a grenade catcher. When the enemy throws the grenades we throw them back." (laughter) We were all standing around, and we tried our best not to laugh.

She bought it, she went back and told her friend, and I'll bet any number of people in her circle of friends heard about the new grenade catcher.

We were a group, we were together, we had done a lot of things together in school, we'd gone in the ROTC together. So we were Scabbard and Blade and all that kind of stuff together. So we stayed together, and in June of '43, we were shipped down as a group to Fort McClellan in Alabama to do our basic training

We went on an old Pennsylvania Railroad troop train and it was sooty and hot. It took about three days to get down there, and we were pretty crummy when we got off the train. We got off that train, and this one little sergeant called us the dirtiest, blackest bunch of white men he'd ever seen, and that's the origin of our name, the Black Fifty.

"They took my clothes and left me stark-ass naked on the NJC campus. A girl came to the door, and I said, 'Don't look . I'm naked.' "   *-- Roland Winter*

When I got to Rutgers, I was shell-shocked, overwhelmed and too young. First of all, I turned 17 in June of '41; in September, I started Rutgers. I was 4 feet, 11 inches tall and I weighed about 87 pounds. I was a freak on the campus. I was underage and undersized. And the work. The professors expected you to come prepared. I tried, but I had never done that much work every night. By today's standards, it wasn't difficult, but to me it was.

How did I get to Rutgers? I had two uncles that were making a living. One was in insurance, the other was a lawyer, and I had an aunt who was in the Perth Amboy school system. The three of them contributed thirds to establish a college fund for me. The family had made up their minds that I was going to practice law with the uncle who was a lawyer.

A family friend I admired had gone to Cornell, so I applied to Cornell. I never heard from Cornell and the summer ran out. I had friends going to Rutgers, so I borrowed my father's 1930 Model A coupe and drove to New Brunswick. I found the office of admissions. They said, "Well, you need a transcript from high school." I drove back to Perth Amboy High. They gave me a transcript for a dollar. I went back to Rutgers and they said, "Well, these are the only courses that are open now, but okay." That's how I got to Rutgers.

Of course Rutgers was an ROTC school. I didn't want to put on a brown uniform and march with the infantry. I despised the infantry! I hated camping. One summer my family sent me to a YMHA camp in Pennsylvania and on the first visiting day I just ran to the car and locked myself in and wouldn't let them leave without me. And ROTC, marching with a 12-pound rifle. Uhhh! My God, the rifle hurt my shoulder.

Parties were a problem. I was as big as a midget. Even the smallest girl at NJC was taller than I. One of the early things that happened after I moved into the frat house, some guys from the Sammy house kidnapped me. I wasn't hard to pick up. I could run fast, but they got me and they drove me to the NJC campus at the other end of town. They took off all my clothes and left me there stark-ass naked. They took my clothes back to the Phi Ep house, opened the door, and threw them in. So the guys there knew whose tiny little clothes they were.

First person I saw on campus-- this was 11 o'clock at night- - was a guard. I didn't want to meet him. What the hell am I gonna do? This is early October, pretty cold, too. I went up to one of the dormitory houses, and I rang the bell, and I kept myself off to the side. One of the college girls answered the door, and I told her my predicament.

I said, "Don't look around. I'm naked." She didn't giggle. She said, "That's terrible." She said, "First of all, we'll get you some stuff to put on and wrap around yourself. And then I'll call the Phi Ep house. Somebody there has a car, right?" I said, "Yeah." She didn't call the police. She did exactly what she said. She brought me some clothes, then somebody from the house picked me up.

106

"The comptroller took my $30, put the bill in his desk, and said, 'Young man, as far as the University is concerned, this bill is paid.' "--John Dowling Jr.

I graduated from high school in 1937. It was my mother's desire that I go to college, and it was mine also, but there certainly was no money in the family because my father had just recently gotten a job, and we had so many debts that had to be taken care of, so I couldn't go to college. I didn't go to college until September of 1938.

I didn't get a job until, I think, February or March. So I only worked for about three months before I left my job and came to college. I was working at the DuPont Film Plant when I came to Rutgers. It was a hard start, because I came up here with no money. They wouldn't let me in.

I knew I could pay my term bill payments, and so I came over to New Brunswick with $30, and I went to the cashier and presented him with my $30, and I said, "There, there's my first payment," and he said, "No, that's not enough money. You need $38." Well, I couldn't get $38 and I said, "Well, there's no way I can get $38."

He said, "Take your term bill across the hallway here, and go in and talk to the Dean." I went in, and I talked to the Dean, and the Dean listened to me, and he said, "Young man, if you can't get $38 by five o'clock this afternoon, you might as well go home and forget college, because college is not for you."

I went back to the cashier, and told him what had been said, and he said, "I'll tell you what you do. Go down to the end of the hall, in that door, he's the comptroller of the university. Don't even knock, walk right in. He's there.

I did, and I told him my story, and he took my $30 and took the bill, and he said, "Young man, as far as the university is concerned, this bill is paid," and he shoved it in the back of his desk, and he said, "I don't care when you get the money, but when you get it, come in here, and take it out of my desk, and go

107

pay it. This bill is paid."

It was several months before I took that bill out of his desk, and he left his desk open, he left his door open, and when I went in and took it out, he wasn't even there. I left a note on his desk thanking him, and I went and I paid my bill.

The first class I had was in Van Dyck Hall, in the Physics building. Professor Helyar was the professor, and at the end of the hour, Dr. Lippman, who was the dean of the college, came in to welcome us. After class, he stood at the door and shook hands with everyone, and said, "Welcome, have a good career," and then I knew I belonged.

I commuted to college from South Amboy. We had an old car by that time, and when we didn't have the old car, we came by bus, and we could ride from South Amboy to New Brunswick for ten cents. I had to live at home.

My father was working, my mother was working, our chickens were laying eggs in the backyard, and I was peddling eggs every day, and I was setting up pins in the bowling alleys to make 50 or 60 cents at nighttime. We scraped enough money to keep going.

I had a good deal at the DuPont Film plant and I'm very thankful for them. When I left DuPont to come to college, I had only worked there for three or four months. The plant supervisor was a golfer and he played golf with Professor Keller, who taught economics. So the plant supervisor knew that this young guy quit his job to go to Rutgers to get an education, and he thought that was a noble venture, and lo and behold, in my second term, I took a course in economics, and I was assigned to Professor Keller's class.

The first day, I walked in and he called roll, and he read off my name and he says, "Dowling, are you the Dowling who worked at the DuPont Film Plant and quit to come to college?" and I said, "Yeah, that was me," and then, he told me the story about how he knew about it, because he played with the plant supervisor out at the Metuchen Country Club.

He said, "Let me tell you something. When this term is over and you want that job back at DuPont for the summer, you tell me and the job is yours." So, when it came to the end of the term, I spoke to Professor Keller, and I said, "You told me that you would speak on my behalf for a job." He said, "Okay, I'll take care of that." Within a week, I got a telephone call to come to work, anytime I was ready, just come to work.

That's the way it was every summer after that. I just had an inside track. I just would call the personnel manager and say, "I'm ready to come to work, is there work for me?" and I got a job every time. That's how I got through college.

"I figured the doctor would be too lazy to go past the first three lines on the eye chart, so I memorized the first three. I passed."   *--John Berglund*

I was no Communist, but I remember going to a couple of Communist rallies. There was one right here on campus on May Day, '39 or '40. There were two groups, the Stalinist, whatever they were called, and the Socialists, the Fourth International. They were competing and fighting, not fist fighting, but fighting with propaganda. And they passed out a piece of paper that said that guns from the ROTC were diverted for some capitalists' purpose. I knew the guns from the ROTC didn't have firing pins in them, because I had carried one for two years.

I was interested in a young lady at the time, and because of her, I went to a communist rally in Jersey City. The theme was "Get Earl Browder out of jail." Then I decided to run away and go fight in Spain, but I didn't get very far. I think I was flunking a course, and I packed my things, and I guess I was going to go out and hitchhike, but I didn't do it.

I went to as many dances as I could swing. And I was madly in love with a girl named Bernice. I remember washing dishes in the cafeteria. I'm washing dishes and looking across at the Zeta Psi House. I knew Bernice was over there, up for the weekend.

And this is like a Steinbeck play, here I'm working, doing dirty dishes, and the girl I love was over there. And I saw her later that night in some nightspot around here somewhere.

It was quite an effort for me to go to a dance. I did go to a dance or two. But I had to squirrel money away. I worked, I did all kinds of jobs. What'd they call it? NYA. Yeah, 35 cents an hour. Oh, taking the finish off a floor in somebody's home with steel wool. I was a kitchen scullion in Woodlawn. And I tended bar at The Corner Tavern for a dollar a night and all I wanted to eat or drink.

When Pearl Harbor happened. I was in Winants Hall, and guys started yelling up and down the stairwell. And that night, The Corner Tavern was very busy. We were singing, "It's a long way to Yokohama," and "It's a long way to go, where the yellow bastards grow," etc. I went over to see Dad in Newark and said that I wanted to enlist, and he asked me to wait until the semester finished. Well, at Christmas time, in spite of that, I tried to enlist in the Navy as a hospital corpsman. And fortunately, they turned me down. I failed the eye test.

Then the Marine Corps came around the college and solicited people to apply for OCS. And I memorized eye charts to get into the Marine Corps. If I'd been killed, it would have been my own damn fault. Right there, in the Rutgers Quad, I took the first physical. I'd gotten letters from my clergyman, my doctor, this and that businessman, the whole bit, but when I took the exam, I failed. My right eye was 15/20 instead of 18/20.

The doctor was a kind man, a Navy doctor, he saw how crushed I was and he said, "Go home and don't wear your glasses for the rest of the day and try it again tomorrow. We'll be here tomorrow." Well, if you don't wear your glasses for a week, you can strengthen your eyes, but if you don't wear them for 24 hours, that weakens them. And the next day, when I came in, it was worse than ever.

But the eye chart was in the room where you took your clothes off, and I did a sort of "Gypsy Rose Lee." I took my

110

clothes off slowly all the way around the room and walked past the eye chart until I got D-E-F-P-O-T-E-C. I read it backwards and forwards with both eyes. And today, when I'm in the hospital or someplace, the same eye chart is still there. And I tell the nurse, "You know, I can read that with my back to it."

Then I got down to Quantico and into OCS, and I was there a few days and there was a notice on the blackboard that said "Complete Form Y tomorrow." I didn't know what a Form Y was. I asked one of the old salts who had been in the Marine Corps for a while and he said, "It's a physical."

I had visions that night of my being put on the train under armed guard for fraudulent enlistment. But when I took the physical, the EENT room was the last thing on the list, and I looked through a half-inch crack in the door and there were 10 half-inch lines on the eye chart. I figured the doctor would be too lazy to go past the first three and I memorized the first three.

I can't remember them now, but I bet under hypnosis, I could recall them. But the doctor didn't ask me anything past the first three. So I was home free. I didn't wear my glasses for two years. I fired the M1 rifle, for the record, and made expert rifleman, which was a triumph of faith. I imagined where the bullseye was at 500 yards.

As I stepped up off the final course, I had counted in my head, and I stood up and I said, "Shit." And the coach said, "What do you mean, 'Shit?' You made it." I had miscounted. I was three points over. So at least once in my life, I was an expert rifleman.

"About 10 of us drove to Washington. War had been declared, and here the Congress was arguing about some farm subsidy bill." --William Gutter

Worrying about the war was not really high on the agenda of our problems. We were more worried about the freshmen getting paddled or something like that. There were some students

111

who were concerned about our keeping out of war, and others who were just gung-ho to go-- small groups on campus, but nothing extreme.

But then, when the war broke out, we were all anxious to go. I can remember that Sunday night of December 7 very well. Nothing was doing on campus that weekend, so I think everybody had headed to the hills, and I took the train home. And on the train back, on Monday morning, of course, this was the big excitement. We're at war. And Monday morning, everybody was crowding near the radio to hear President Roosevelt declare that we were at war.

So several of us at the fraternity house decided, "Well, let's go down to Washington and see for ourselves what's going on." We knew a few of the boys down at Penn who had started at Rutgers and some of them were very close friends of ours, so we called them and said, "Hey, we're coming down."

I think we ended up with about 10 of us piled into this car, and we drove down to Philly, spent the night there, and Tuesday morning we're in the halls of Congress very early. War has been declared, and you'd think it'd be frenetic in the Congress. But no, they're arguing about whether the Conservation and Domestic Allotment Plan should be extended or not. This is some farm thing for subsidized farms in the far west. And nothing about the war. Nothing. Didn't even look like anybody gave a damn. Of course, it was too early for the bills to filter down from committee to take action. But what a disillusionment that was.

We stopped at the office of the congressman from New Jersey, and he came out to say hello to his good constituents and told us the best thing we could do for the war effort was go back to school and finish. This was in December, and we did finish in May, a little earlier than usual.

Actually, a few of the guys skipped out and went in right away. But most of us waited until graduation in May. And then the day after graduation, I went looking to see if the Navy would take me in. They turned me down for the Navy Air Corps, but they did take me for the V-7 program.

"The younger students were just kids. I didn't know anything about them. I'd lost my youth. Those years were just gone."   *--Nathan Shoehalter*

January 29th, 1946. I'll never forget that. That was the day I was discharged from Camp Kilmer. I had to do something. I had no idea what I wanted to do. I had had dreams of being a veterinarian. I had to finish school and wanted to be a teacher.

When we were in the Army, we would talk about the stupidity of war, what we would do when it was all over. We wanted to be teachers. How could you not? How could you possibly condone the stuff that we were going through? We thought education could help. That stuck in my mind, "Maybe I'll be a teacher."

I don't remember which offices I visited at Rutgers, but I remember I got 18 credits for being in the Army. I'd left when I was a junior, I guess, so I got a couple of credits for being a soldier. I remember taking an education course which was just dreadful. We were treated so differently. All the men who came back were mature. We never talked about our experiences, never talked about them at all.

Most of the guys who were there were under the GI Bill, as I was. We tended to travel together by age groups. I don't remember any younger people. I'd missed everything. I'd lost my youth, 18 to 24, whatever it was. Those years were just gone. The younger students were just kids. I didn't know anything about them.

I do remember I had an English class with Professor Donald McGinn, and we studied Shakespeare. I'll never forget that. It was so great. I knew what he was talking about. I was so mature at that time. I think we all were. It was so exciting, so much different from what I remember when I was an undergraduate before the war. Really, we talked like adults. When something was bullshit, we let him know it was bullshit. Forgive me, it was very exciting. I remember, I just had a couple of credits to go before I would get my degree, but I got it, and at the same time I got the degree, we had to do a thing called student teaching. My job was at Irvington High School teaching biology and chemistry

There was a big building on Neilson Campus-- we called it the barn. It was a mess hall during World War II, and after the war it was also a cafeteria, and I worked in the basement there with a guy named Bob Bell. We never talked about our war experiences. We washed dishes and we wiped trays

At that time, the radio station WCTC was being formed. It was September of 1946. It went on the air in December. Bob Bell and I got jobs as announcers. We were the first people on the station. I wanted to teach, but at the time I got my teaching job at Irvington High School, WCTC was coming on the air. I used to teach from eight o'clock in the morning until 12:30 in Irvington, and then drive down to New Brunswick.

When the station went on the air, I was hired, and I did a disk jockey show beginning at three o'clock in the afternoon, and I worked until 11 o'clock at night, and then I'd drive back to Irvington and start all over again, but I couldn't keep that up.

The radio was much more exciting than the high school stuff. All those things you talk about doing, I thought I could do it in radio. I thought, "Radio, by God, we're talking to hundreds of thousands of people." It's much more than a classroom, and you could change people's minds. So I started in radio.

Then they asked me to join the staff at the university, to moderate this program called the Rutgers University Forum. It was on WAAT in Newark, and a station in Trenton, WTNJ, and an Asbury Park station. Anyhow, it was three or four stations live, none of this wire recorder or tape stuff. I ran the Rutgers University Forum for many years. I was behind the scenes as executive producer for decades. That was my association with the University. I loved the University. I really was so proud of it.

AND ALONG CAME LOVE

What causes the spark of love to ignite is still a mystery. In wartime, when there may be no tomorrows, it often bursts into flame quickly. Bob King, on leave from the military for his father's funeral, was walking through the Suburban Station in Philadelphia when he saw her. She was working at the counter of a newsstand, and "she was the most beautiful thing I've ever seen." He asked her to dinner, and 50 years later, with her at his side, he could still say, "It was the best move I ever made."

It was an old-fashioned time, the early 20th century, a time when lasting relationships blossomed from chance encounters. Some came early in life. Dick Mercer was only 16 and a sports nut when his older brother pushed him into a dance date. Dick botched the date, but when he grabbed the girl in front of him in the conga line and she turned around, "I looked at those blue eyes and that pretty face, and who cared about baseball?" She was "the only girl friend I've ever had in my entire life."

Rutgers was the meeting place for others. George Claflen met Cecilia at a Newman Club dance. He didn't have any money so he took her to a swimming meet, walking all the way there and back. George Reynolds, on his way to dinner at the Dean's house, saw a girl on the bus and mused, "If I ever pick up a girl, that's the girl I'd pick up." She turned out to be a

115

friend of the Dean's family and a fellow dinner guest. My own late wife, Inez, virtually twirled into my arms at a folk dance on the campus of NJC, the cross-town girls' college that later became Douglass College.

But it was the chance wartime meetings that match most closely the romantic fantasies of our era. Mark Addison finally found a New York City canteen he'd been looking for. "I walked in, and right opposite the door was a long serving bar, and there she was." The rules for canteens were "No liquor, no dates," but if a suitor proved persistent, a girl was supposed to take him home to mother, and she did. "We saw each other maybe four times before we were married," says Mark. "You didn't know if there would be tomorrow," says Mrs. Addison, "so you took today." At the time of the interview, they'd been married 52 years.

Courtship and marriage often had to fit into the chinks. William Godfrey met his wife Karen in Manitowoc, Wisconsin, where his new submarine was being built. When it was finished, they married, and the submarine's 10-day trip down the Mississippi on a barge gave them time for a honeymoon. Then he and the submarine were off to the Pacific for 15 months.

Fred Wesche, in Australia, delivered a letter to a friend's girl friend and met her friend, Maureen. They were engaged before he left for home at war's end, but there was no civilian transport to get her to the US. Fred got back to Australia as an airline pilot and they were married there. Their 55th anniversary was celebrated about the time of the interview.

Sometimes the roadblocks were formidable. Lyman Avery saw the face of a shy waif behind the bar of an English pub and so met Edith. Her mother and father had been killed iu the blitz of Sheffield. They were soon in love, but getting married in the military, overseas, wasn't easy. His request had to go from company to division to theater commander to SHAEF, where General Eisenhower's signature was needed on a special order. It took six weeks.

116

"She probably didn't even know where New Jersey was. I asked her for a date, and she took me home to meet her mother."   *--Mark Addison*

I was at Fort Monmouth, in radio repair school. My best friend, my bunkmate, had been going into New York every weekend, because he knew New York. He refused to tell me where all these beautiful girls were that he was meeting in some canteen. And it wasn't the famous Stage Door canteen. But he wouldn't tell me. Then he became ill and went to the hospital. I had snagged what was a rare item in those days: a portable radio, battery operated. I went to see him with the radio and I said, "Newt," (he was bored to death) "this is a radio. You know where these girls are. No girls, no radio." (laughter) So he said, "Okay." He told me he couldn't remember the name, but he said, "It's on lower 5th Avenue."

Well, I couldn't find it. I wound up at a canteen operated by the National Women's Republican Club. You can't imagine a canteen any more dull than that. And I couldn't stand that. So there was somebody there, and I said, "I gotta get out of here." He said, "Well I know there's a canteen down on lower 5th Avenue around 15th, or 10th, or somewhere in that neighborhood." I said, "I'll try anything."

Well, I found it. And I walked in and right opposite the door was a long serving bar where they had cookies and milk and

117

soda and whatever. And this young lady was behind the bar. And that's how we met at the Music Box Canteen.

(**Mrs. Addison,** *who was present during the interview*: "As a matter of fact, my reaction to him was a very funny one. He introduced himself with his full name, and he said he was from Barnegat. And I looked at him and I was going to ask him if he was serious. I'd never heard of Barnegat in my life. The whole thing just sounded completely incredible to me. But something told me I had better just accept what he said.")

She probably didn't even know where New Jersey was. Anyway, I asked her for a date. And like most girls then who were cautious, she said, "All right." But she took me home to her mother. Apparently she'd been taking these street sweepings home and giving people a decent meal. And so that's how we met, really.

(**Mrs. Addison:** "Dinner went well. He didn't pay for it and didn't pay for anything else. He never took me anywhere, he just came up and ate my mother's cooking, that's all.")

I might have been stupid, but I wasn't crazy. (laughter)

I was in Signal Corps OCS, and we were laying wire. Laying the wire was easy. Picking it up was murder. Not only was it raining, but it was sleeting and it was snowing and you're soaked to the skin and cold. That field problem took 36 hours. Finally I managed to get into some dry clothes and I had the weekend, and I went to New York and got in touch with her. And she said, "I'm sorry, I have a date." I said, "Well, you may have a date, but I don't." She said, "Why don't you come back next weekend?" I said, "You take what you can get and this is what I got, and here I am."

(**Mrs. Addison:** "They were both at the house. Each tried to outstay the other.")

The worst part of it was that he was already commissioned in chemical warfare and I had the rank of corporal. Do you know the vast difference between those two? It was quite an evening. Then he left early, and I fell asleep, and her father came and ordered me out of the house. So I went downtown and got a place to sleep.

I think we saw each other maybe four times, tops, before we were married, if that. Everything was accelerated. Everybody was under tremendous pressure. You never knew what was going to happen to you. What would normally have taken six months to a year could be accomplished in three months.

(**Mrs. Addison:** "You made the most of it. You didn't know if there would be tomorrow, so you took today. And we happened to be particularly fortunate that we had 15 months together before he went overseas. See, I traveled with him. Many people only had the one night, and then . . .")

And then if they came back, it was a whole bad scene, because they were two strangers, had to start all over again. We didn't. We had to start over, of course, but we had a basis of a relationship, so we were fortunate. Maybe that's why it's lasted 52-plus years.

"'Do you know your own mind?' he asked. 'You're a military man, with a college education, and you want to marry some slut.' " --Lyman Avery

I was married in Mansfield, England. I met Edith in a pub-- the Sir John Cockle. My friend T-4 sergeant Tom Donahue and I got on to Sir John Cockle because they always put up a bottle of scotch at six o'clock when they opened. And if we got there early we'd be able to get a few drinks out of it. So it had become quite a thing for us.

Whenever we were free, we'd trot down to the Sir John and have our couple of drinks and come 10 o'clock we'd go back to the barracks. And I don't ever remember getting drunk there. There was a husband, wife and daughter who ran this place. One night I looked behind the bar and there's a door in back of the bar that leads to their living quarters and there's this new girl. A real attractive woman. "Where'd she come from?" I asked.

119

One thing led to another and the bartender told her there was an American soldier sitting out at the bar and he looked lonely. "Why don't you go out and talk to him?" Well, Edie is so shy she wouldn't talk to her mother, I think, unless she got an invitation. So she just stood there in the door and the bartender came over to me and he said, "Have you met Edith?" And I said, "No." And that's how we met. I took her to the movies about a week later, and we dated and talked and I found that she liked what I stood for and I liked what she stood for.

She'd come from Sheffield, where she'd lost both her mother and father in the blitz of Sheffield, and she was working on her own. She was living in a boarding home just down the street from Sir John Cockle.

Some nights she still wakes up screaming because she still remembers walking through Sheffield and seeing the bodies lying in the street from the bombing the night before. They hadn't been able to clean everything up. And she's said, many times since then, "If I hadn't been so lonely and desolate, we'd never been married." (laughter) And I've said, "If I hadn't been so lonely, and had nothing else to do, we never would've been married." But we were. We were married in a church.

When you got married in the military, it wasn't like getting married any place else. The military has a lot of protocol, a lot of administrative regulations you've got to go through. If you were overseas it was even worse. Would you believe I have 10 copies of our marriage certificate, our original passports, original certificates from the Church of England, I've forgotten what else. I've got a special order signed by General Eisenhower giving me permission to marry.

My company commander was the first I had to go see. He forwarded it to the colonel, the colonel forwarded it to the commanding general of England's theater. From him it went over to SHAEF, which was Eisenhower's command force in Europe. And finally, after six weeks, I got permission. But the first step was the hardest. My company commander was a 22-year-old from Long Island who was a captain because he had gone in early, out of high school, and they'd moved him right on up. I was 26, with four years of college education.

Before I could get to him I had to ask the first sergeant's permission. And the first sergeant said, "For what?" I said, "I want to seek permission to get married." And he said, "You're out of your fucking mind!" I said, "That's not for you to say, Sergeant!" And he went to the company commander's door, went in and shut the door behind him. So I don't know what the hell's going on. Then he comes out and says, "Captain Heally will see you."

So I walked in, saluted like I was supposed to, and the captain said, "What can I do for you?" I said, "I'd like permission to marry Edith Henry, a spinster." Because that's what you had to say. He looked at me, he said, "Avery, do you know your own mind? Here you are a military man, with a college education, and you want to marry some slut." I said, "Sir, she's no slut. This is the woman I want to be my wife." And he said, "I want you to take some time to think this over." And I said, "I've thought it over." He said, "Take some more time." I said, "I'll be in tomorrow morning." I was. I came in the next morning. So he finally realized that I was serious. But what was really bugging me, here's this 22-year-old kid asking me, with my age and my experience and my education, if I knew my own mind.

Well, he finally gave permission and after six weeks and all the paperwork, we got married.

The rest of the story is really a strange twist of fate. Later on I was shifted out of 184th General Hospital and assigned to the UK Medical Center in London, Grosvenor Square. My responsibility was to work with a lieutenant and clear out all the medical troops in England. This was 1945, and we had to clear them out either to the European theater or to the Pacific theater, because the Japanese war had not yet ended.

Well, one day I was sitting in the office. I've moved up in rank. I'm now a master sergeant. And my buck sergeant said,

"Sergeant, there's a captain out here to see you." And who comes in but Captain Heally, my old company commander. And I said, "What can I do for you?" "Well," he said, "I've got my orders here. I've been assigned to San Diego and I gather from there I'm going to the Pacific Theater." And he said, "Sergeant, is there anything you could do?" And I said, "What do you mean?" "Well," he said, "I'd just as soon either stay here or go to France." I said, "You can't stay here, but if you want to go to France, maybe I can do it."

"I've become very friendly with a young lady in the south of England," he said. And I said, under my breath, "You son of a . . . " Because I knew he was married and had two kids back in the States. And I said, "Okay, Captain, I'll see what I can do." You know what I did? I sent him to San Diego.

"I went in this restaurant and there was Maureen. She was a flaming redhead. We'll celebrate our 55th anniversary this October." *--Frederick Wesche III*

Most of the young men from Australia were in the First and Second Army Brigades over in North Africa. So there was a dearth of young eligible men in Australia. People went overboard to be friendly and helpful to us when we were there. Local churches would run parties for us and have us come over.

I remember going to one church affair-- a little get-together for the American troops-- and one of the soldiers went over to one of the young ladies sitting there and said, "Would you like to dance?" She said, "Oh, I'm all knocked up. Why don't you go ask my sister?" In American, that means something quite different. To them it meant, "I'm tired."

The Australians were very friendly. Among other things, I met my future wife there. Maureen, that's my wife, was working for the American Navy. She was a switchboard operator in the Navy office there in Sydney, and at noontime she and a couple of her co-workers used to go down to the local restaurant. One

122

of my buddies up in New Guinea, when I went down on leave to Sydney, gave me a letter to deliver. He didn't want it to go through censors, so he asked me if I'd hand deliver it to his girl friend in Sydney.

We agreed to meet, and it happened to be one of Maureen's co-workers in the Navy Department. So I went down to meet her at the restaurant, and I met Maureen. She was a flaming redhead. I got to talking with her and set up a date. "What are you doing tonight?" At first, I didn't get very far. But I was a little insistent, and, sure enough, we went out a few times, and then every time I got back to Sydney, and we'd stay overnight, we'd meet. So we met quite often and corresponded all the time.

It was almost a year later, I guess, when I was scheduled to come home. She said, "You're gonna be leaving soon." Then I decided, "Gee, I don't know if I want to go." So I called her, or rather, I sent a telegram. I said, "Will you marry me?" When I got home, there was an answer, a "Yes" telegram.

That was our courtship, such as it was, and of course she couldn't come immediately, because there was no transport. Transport was strictly for military or military married personnel. But when I came out of the military, I went directly with Eastern Airlines, and I had pass privileges, so I went over there on a pass and we were married over there in 1946.

We'll be celebrating our 55th wedding anniversary this coming October. We've had a good life together, believe me.

"Once I had $3 saved up, we'd go to New York, to the Paramount, and see a stage show and movie for a quarter before 12 o'clock." --Morton Kernis

I met my future wife on the beach at Belmar, when I was working as a bingo boy-- working to go to Rutgers, actually. It wasn't the most lucrative way to earn money. However, its chief attribute was the part it played in meeting my wife.

I wasn't very wealthy, so I couldn't see her very often. I used

123

to be able to save maybe a dollar a week because the rest I gave to my mother. I used to work in supermarkets on Saturday until 11 o'clock at night. After that I worked with the newspaper agency. Once I had $3 saved up, I would visit my future wife.

She lived in Jersey City. I used to hitchhike into Jersey City on a Saturday morning, very often in a rumble seat, so I would be pretty wind-blown by the time I got there. We'd go into New York and go to the Paramount. In those days you could see a stage show and a movie for a quarter, up to 12 o'clock. We saw Frank Sinatra there. We'd bring our own lunch.

We'd buy balcony seats, which cost a half a buck. Then we'd eat at a place called The Champlain, a little French restaurant that gave you filet mignon for a dollar and a quarter. So that was two-fifty. So that would eat up the three dollars and change, and then I'd go back to Jersey City and I had enough money left to take the train home. And that's how I courted my wife.

We were very close. We were in love in Belmar, but we didn't get married before I went in service. Nobody would let us. I didn't think it was a good idea either, for her sake or for mine. But she saw other guys. I was jealous, at the time, because she used to go out with other guys, but it was during the war and I guess it was unreasonable to think that she shouldn't.

And that's the way it went, and when I came home she was ill with influenza and I guess I got her at a weak moment, and we got married. We just had our 50th anniversary.

"At the next stop, this girl got on. I thought, "My gosh, I've never picked up a girl, but if I ever do, that's the girl I'd pick up." --George Reynolds

Unbeknownst to me, Virginia was a friend of Dean Read's daughter. In fact, I think she was her junior sister at NJC. I was a friend of the Dean's son, Thornton Read. The Dean's son was an unusual person, in the sense that he was mostly self-educated. Very, very bright. First degree he ever got, I think, was a master's in math, from Brown. Anyway, I liked boxing a lot, and had been a fairly serious boxer in high school. In fact, I got to the end of the tournament, the final in the heavyweight class, and got knocked out. But even so, I liked boxing, and so did Thornton Read. We boxed together quite a lot. He became rather good. He went into the Newark Golden Gloves tournament. He did very well in that.

Well, one night I was invited, because of Thornton, to Dean Read's house for dinner. Unbeknownst to me, Virginia had been invited also, because of her friendship with the daughter. It was wartime, and we had very little gas, so we used the bus. I got on at one stop, and at the next stop this girl got on. I thought, "My gosh, I've never picked up a girl, but if I ever do, that's the girl I'd pick up."

She went behind me in the bus, sat down, and I kept thinking, "Shall I go back there or not? What'll I do?" Well, time ran out, finally, while I was still debating. I got out of the bus, and there was Thornton Read, apparently overjoyed to see me. And I thought, "Why in the world was he so pleased to see me, for goodness sake?" But he was looking past me, and he stepped around me and was welcoming Virginia.

There I was, to spend an evening at a dinner party with this girl. I really saw nothing else from the time she got on that bus. So we had dinner together. Then, because it was war, and no gas, the Dean's wife said, "Well, Virginia lives near you. Would you see her home so she doesn't have to go alone on the bus?" I said, "Well, I guess I can manage that." (Laughter)

We got off at her stop, and it turned out she lived only about two blocks from me in Highland Park. But because our ages were different, we'd never been in the same school system together. I had never seen her until that night.

On the way home, somehow or other, I managed to get hold of her left hand, and did a survey. I said, "I notice you're not wearing a ring." Now the only reason I said that was I wanted to know if I could date her or not. She claims it was a proposal.

However, it did result in a proposal. So that's the way we met.

Our wedding was scheduled around the fact that people were working all the time. I was determined to be a Navy officer during the war, and that led to a relatively early marriage. Everybody was getting married. It had to be on a Friday night because everybody worked, and it was a brief honeymoon in the Poconos. In that sense, it was affected by the war. Then we had an apartment in Trenton, and she was a librarian in Trenton, at the Public Library, until we were ordered to go to Los Alamos.

"She was the most beautiful thing I've ever seen. I asked her if she'd like to go out for dinner. The best move I ever made." *--Robert C. King*

She worked in the Suburban Station in Philadelphia behind the counter of a newsstand. And I was home for my father's funeral. And you know it's one of those things, I saw her and thought that's the most beautiful thing I've ever seen. And so I went up and introduced myself and asked her if she'd like to go down to have dinner and have a couple of drinks with me that night, and she said she would, foolishly.

So I met her around seven o'clock that night back in the train station. We had no other place to meet. So I went home and she went home and we met back at the train station that evening. And we went out for dinner and had a few drinks. And that was the beginning of that. The best move I ever made.

"Do you believe in fate? I kept running into her at USO dances. I said, 'This must mean something,' and I invited her to dinner." *--Morton Burke*

I met my wife when I was in training in the Navy in Chicago. The area was very friendly, Milwaukee, Chicago, very friendly to servicemen, really wonderful. What they used to do is, all the girls who were old enough used to volunteer to go to the USOs.

126

They'd dance and talk, but they were not supposed to date any of the soldiers or sailors.

I met her, I think it was at the Washington Street USO, in Chicago. I talked with her, I danced with her, and that was the end of it, because she couldn't date me, and this is an interesting thing. Do you believe in fate? I don't know. (laughter) About a week or so later, I go to a dance at another USO, way the heck out of town, I look up, there she is. So we talked and danced again. This happened on three or four different occasions over a three-month period. I kept running into her, for no reason, at different places around Chicago. So I said to her, "Look, this must mean something. Can I take you out to dinner?" So she said, "Well, you've got to come home and meet my mother first." (laughter) She was all of 17. I was about 19, so I had to meet her mother.

I didn't know this when I met her, but she was an actress, going to dramatic school. We kept in touch while I was in the service, and then, after I was discharged, I come back home. I used to call her up once in a while. All of a sudden, she's coming to New York. She's trying to make it big on Broadway. She lived in a women's club in New York City and I used to date her every week, so that's how we got to know each other very well.

We were married I guess about four years after the time we first met.

"Shirley and I were married on Friday night. We spent two days in New York and came back on Sunday afternoon." *--Carleton C. Dilatush*

Shirley and I had planned to be married when I was one year out of Rutgers, and we did. My papers came back in September of 1941 advising that I would have to go to OCS for commissioning as second lieutenant. I was then a staff sergeant. Originally, we had wanted to wait until I was a lieutenant, but we decided we would be married then, as I would get quarters and al-

127

lowance as a staff sergeant.

We were married in the Episcopal Church on a Friday night, in Mount Holly, New Jersey. My wife was from Mount Holly. Her dad was chief of Burlington County detectives. His name was Clifford Cain. He relieved Ellis Parker when Ellis Parker became involved with the Lindbergh case.

Shirley and I were married on Friday night, September 26, 1941, and we spent two days in New York, came back on Sunday afternoon. We were living with her parents and her grandmother. I would drive her to the railroad station in Mount Holly. She would go to by train to Philadelphia, where she had a job as a secretary. I went over to Fort Dix and worked there with the Station Veterinarian. I'd pick her up in the evening, take her home. And that's the way it worked out until I was finally ordered to OCS at Fort Lee, Virginia.

"I didn't have any money, so I took her to a swimming meet. We walked over and back, all the way to the end of Highland Park."   -- *George L. Claflen*

I met Cecilia in November of 1941. I was in my Ford Hall dormitory, and it was my senior year, and my two roommates were electrical engineers. One night, this fellow came in, his name was Jimmy Roets, and he got to talk to us, and he said, "Why don't we go out and do something?" He had a car, which was nice.

Well, my two electrical engineer roommates couldn't go. They had too much to do, so I went, and he said, "Why don't we go up to the Newman Club?" which was the Catholic club. I said, "Fine."

When we got there, there was a dance going on in the basement of the Sacred Heart School. And Jimmy introduced me to a girl named Cynthia, and he didn't say any last name, so we had this dance, and we danced a couple of times, and then I knew that she was going home with a big fellow that was a foot-

128

ball player, Sy Klosky his name was.

At any rate, I thought, "She's pretty nice. I ought to date her, but I don't know her name." I asked Jimmy Roets, "What's her last name and how can I meet her?" He said, "Well, she goes out with a fellow name Jack Ambos," who was in our class, another engineer, "and you could ask him."

So I got in touch with Jack. I said, "Jack, I met a girl named Cynthia while we were at the Newman Club, and she lives in Highland Park, and I hear you go out with her, or went out with her." "No," he said, "I don't go out with any Cynthia. Describe her a little bit," and I did. He says, "Oh, yes, you must mean Cecilia Blundell. She lives at 22 Riverview Avenue, Highland Park." I said, "Oh, thanks, Jack. I'll give her a call."

I didn't know what to take her to. I didn't have any money or anything. So I took her to a swimming meet (laughter) and we walked over and back, all the way to the end of First Avenue in Highland Park. It was quite a walk, and later she invited me to the Christmas Dance. We walked there. I walked over to her house from Ford Hall. Then we walked across the bridge, and up Burnett Street, and over to Douglass, where the dance was, and then, when it was over, we walked back again. (laughter).

It was a good thing I was a walker. I loved to walk, and just never thought much about it and she didn't either. But that's how we met, and it wasn't too long after that that the war started.

Before that, I had tried to get an appointment to Annapolis. My father wanted me to do that. I had no real desire to get into the Navy, but I took the test, and I wrote some papers. I was a freshman when that happened.

Well, as it turned out, I did pretty well on the test, and I got the appointment, but we knew I was in trouble. One thing we knew and one thing we didn't know. We knew that my teeth were not perfect. I had a maloclusion. Well, my father immediately got me going to an orthodontist. That was in February, and I didn't have to go down there until almost summertime, and by then, some work had been done.

129

I went down to the Academy and they said I'd passed everything but two things. They said, "You have a maloclusion and we can't take you if you have a maloclusion." I said, "Well, you don't have to worry." I said, "My father's paying for that." But that wasn't all. I also had a deviated septum, and they said, "We can't have anybody with a deviated septum." I had just about enough money to hitchhike home with (laughter) and I didn't feel too badly about it. My father did. He thought that would have been a great opportunity, but that was before I had met Cecilia. So I don't feel badly about it at all now, because I never would have met her if I had gone there.

Cecilia and I talked about the war, and I was sure I was going to be in it. We figured everybody would be in it and she would do the same. Some of her friends went into the WAVES, but she didn't. She did her thing and got a job.

I don't know when we decided to get married. It wasn't immediately, but it was pretty soon. We always felt that we were going to, but we didn't put it into words right away, but eventually we did.

Later, when I finished my Air Corps meteorology course and got my commission, I had to go to an air base in Dover, Delaware, and then to Aberdeen Proving Ground. We'd set our wedding date for April 15th, 1944, but it turned out that I couldn't make that because I was sent to a staff weather school in Florida for a month, and they just said, "You've got to go. That's it." So we had to call the wedding off.

I wrote a letter to the commanding officer of the weather school, and I said to him, "I was supposed to get married on the 15th of April, and you transferred me, and I had to miss the wedding, but\ it's now scheduled for May 13, and I want to know if you can just let me stay there until I'm married. Then I don't care. Do anything you want."

I got a letter back from him. He said, "I'm sorry to hear about the terrible mistake you're about to make, but if you want to go ahead with it, we don't have any objections. However, if at any time before May 13 you change your mind, just let me know and I'll have you out of the country in 24 hours."

Well, I came back from Florida and we got married on May the 13th, and we went into New York. We had a short honeymoon, and I had just enough money to get back to the base, and Cecilia went home.

"I gave her my fraternity pin, and she said, 'Do you know what this means? It means that we will be forever together.' And I said, 'Fine.'" *--Paul W. Rork*

My first wife was a little girl genius. She finished Newark State Teacher's College. Her name was Ruth Buller, and we met at Camp Hope, where she was a counselor, and I was a latrine digger, or whatever. I had to make up the camp, get the camp ready and close up the camp, and we met there. She had just finished college, and I was just going into my sophomore year. But I fell madly in love with her. And fortunately, she reciprocated.

So from then on, she was my Kappa Sigma sweetheart. She came down to the Soph Hop that year, and I took her over to the School of Education porch. We sat on the steps, and I took my fraternity pin, and I said, "Sweetheart, I'd like you to wear my fraternity pin."

And she really called my bluff. She said, "Do you know what this means?" I said, "Yes, you're my girl." And she said, "No, that's not what it means. This is a substitution for an engagement ring, because you're still in school and you can't afford an engagement ring. But the giving of a fraternity pin is a pledge that we will be forever together." And I said, "That's fine with me. Will you please wear my fraternity pin?" She said, "It would be a pleasure."

And from then on, we were literally engaged. She came down to every Rutgers function for three years, and then after, when I went to the Coast Guard Academy, she would visit me up there. I got my first Coast Guard command at Moorhead City, North

131

Carolina. We had planned to be married as soon as we could, and we were married that April. I received my commission in 1942 and in April 1943 we were married.

We had a cottage on the beach, at Atlantic Beach, and it was terrific. Great honeymoon. And it was pretty. It was kind of expensive, but it was nice. Now Vance, my old buddy Vance Kniffin, was quite wealthy. His father was the president of a bank on Long Island, and Vance said, "If you want me to rent one of your rooms, I'll be glad to, if it'll help you out." Ruthie says, "Fine." We knew Vance from way back. So that helped.

"There was a slippery floor. When I saw her there, I'd slide across it and say, 'I'm going to make you the mother of my children.' " — *John Berglund*

I guess a lot of us met our wives through Rutgers, but my story may be a little different. My classmate Bill Lewis and I were on terminal leave at the same time, he from the Air Force and I from the Marine Corps. And, in our youthful arrogance, we decided to go to New York and see which medical school we were deigned to honor with our presence as students.

We didn't know how bad it was. I had applied to four medical schools and only Temple sent for an interview. And the dean looked at my transcript, and he said, "You couldn't get into medical school with these grades. You wouldn't last if you did." He wanted to know what I'd done for the last four years. When I said "I was in the Marine Corps," he snorted.

Well, if I had wanted to go to medical school badly enough, I would have managed it. But, anyway, Bill Lewis and I were broke after a night in New York. And we got off the train in New Brunswick, because he had a checking account and we wanted to cash a check. And going across the campus, we met a guy we both loved, Bill Lamont. He was a wonderful professor, wonderful. He could make you love the subject. And we had an Old Home Week, and he said, "Have you registered at the employment office?" We said we didn't know the college had one.

So we both went over and registered at the employment office. And in less than two weeks, I got a postcard telling me to go to Sharp and Dohme in Glenolden, Pennsylvania, and see William A. Feirer, who was a Rutgers graduate. And Dr. Feirer was Lynne's boss's boss, he was head of research. And he hired me. And that's how I met Lynne.

She had graduated from Temple as a medical technologist, a microbiologist, and she was doing research in bacteriology at Sharp and Dohme. She had been there about a year and a half when I came along.

At first, she wouldn't go out with me. Wouldn't think of it. Maybe I scared her. There was a slippery floor at the time clock, and I'd get up a head of steam and slide across the floor when she was punching the time clock. I'd slide up to her and I'd say, "I'm gonna make you the mother of my children."

She was living with two other girls in an apartment in Glenolden, and she was pretty skeptical at first, but I was persistent. We started going out at the end of January, we were engaged in April and married in June.

Her mother said I was too fast a worker. And every time we went and told her mother she was pregnant, she said the same thing. Thirty years later, when I decided to become a minister and entered the seminary, we had three kids in college, and Lynne went back to work after a 23-year absence. She went back to work with Merck, which is Sharp and Dohme, and stayed there for 17 years.

"And she turned around, and I looked at those blue eyes and that pretty face, and all of a sudden, who cared about baseball?"   *--Richard J. Mercer*

I wouldn't have met my wife except for Olga Bensik. No, it was because of my brother Donald. Donald was eight years older than my twin brother Bob and me, and he had a profound

133

influence on us. He was a pageboy at NBC. He would get sent out to get a cheeseburger for Toscanini when he was rehearsing and all sorts of fascinating things.

At night he would read to us. The three of us would go to bed and he would read to us from the *New Yorker*. He read S.J. Perelman and Robert Benchley. And anybody who came to our house, if they ever asked Bob or me, "Did anybody call?" they got an answer like, "Yes, a Mr. Bleevy, Peavy, or Rasmussen," (laughs) because that's a line straight out of Benchley.

When Bob and I were 16, he made us get dates. He said he and our mother thought the pair of us were going to be homosexuals, because all we gave a damn about was baseball. And he said, "Isn't the Thanksgiving Dance coming up?" And I said "Yeah." And he said, "Well, you guys have to get dates for this." And we said, "What?"

My folks would buy us nice clothes, and we wore baseball caps with them. We would never take off our baseball caps, that's all we thought of. So I think my mother thought, my God, they don't even look at girls. And she was right.

So Donald said, "You guys are going to get dates." He said, "When is the dance?" And we told him, so he gave us a deadline. He said, "All right, you have to have dates by next Thursday."

By the day of the deadline, my brother had gotten a date. God, she was a cute little girl, a little Italian girl. And I didn't have a date yet. So I'm in chemistry class, and I'm sitting on a high stool at this slate-top table. And we're doing experiments, and across the way from me is Olga Bensik. I knew Olga Bensik from kindergarten, and we're both sitting on these high stools, and I looked over and I suddenly thought, "Gee, Olga's kinda cute, she's pretty." So I said, "Hey Olga," and she said "Yeah?" I said, "Are you going to the Thanksgiving Dance?" She said, "No." I said "You want to go with me?" And she said "With you?" (laughs) And I said, "Yeah." And she said "Well, I don't know, I'll have to ask my mother."

134

Next day, here we are sitting on these high stools, and she says, "Dick." And I said, "Yeah." She said, "You still want to go to the dance?" and I said, "Yeah." And she said, "Okay, I'll go with you." So that was great, now we're all set.

Well, about two days before the dance, Donald tells us at the dinner table, "You have to call up the girl and ask her what color dress she's wearing, because you have to get her a corsage to go with her dress." I'm ready to die now, and my brother Bob is ready to die. It's bad enough we had to get dates, you know. So we each make the telephone call, and we find out. And now we order the flowers. At least Donald paid for the flowers. And he said he would drive us, so we had a chauffeur.

And so I get to Olga Bensik's house, and I knock at the door, and the door opens and no light comes through, because Olga fills the doorway. I had forgotten sitting on this high stool, that Olga was like six feet, and 160 pounds. I was five feet, and 110 pounds. (laughs) So all night long it was painful for both of us. "Hey, Mercer, you got a heavy date there, huh? Heh! Heh! Heh!" See, I mean it was dreadful.

And we got on a conga line. I think Olga picked me up and put me on the conga line. And so I grabbed the girl in front of me, and the girl was blond and she was wearing a silk jersey dress with a basque top and a pleated skirt. And that girl's name was Muriel Davis. And she turned around and I looked at those blue eyes and that pretty face and all of a sudden, who cared about baseball?

And that was the beginning of the end. Now I was raised to be polite and decent, but you're allowed to change partners once in a while, so that night I danced with her a couple of times, and I asked her would she go to the Christmas Dance with me. And she didn't have to ask her mother, she said, "Yes, I'd love to. And that was the end of that, and she was the only girl friend I've ever had in my entire life, including three years in the Navy.

When I was in Navy boot camp, all the guys would disappear on weekends. I didn't want to go anywhere. All I did was, I wrote letters to Muriel Davis every single day that I was in the United States Navy, that's two years and eight months, right up until the time when we got married. Every single day I wrote Muriel Davis a letter, and she wrote me a letter every single day.

She was very proud of me. And I was very proud of me. God, I was so excited. I'll never forget, coming back on leave from boot camp, that's when Muriel and I got engaged, and my mother and father didn't want us to get engaged. They kept saying to me, you have to go to college, you have to go to college. But I said, "Well, I just want to get engaged."

Then when I came back from Europe, we got married. And my mother, I remember her saying to me "You know, Dicky dear, when two people get married pretty soon there are three people, and you have to go to the Pacific now." And I said, "I know all about that, Mom." She didn't like that too much. (laughs) I wasn't supposed to know all about that at age 21, whatever we were then. (laughs)

That dress that Muriel was wearing at the Thanksgiving Dance still hangs in our attic, and I'll never let her get rid of it.

"While they took the submarine down the Mississippi, we had a 10-day honeymoon in New Orleans. Then I was gone for 15 months." --William J. Godfrey

One week before I was to depart the Midshipmen School, I got orders sending me direct to Manitowoc, Wisconsin, on Lake Michigan, where the Manitowoc Ship Building Company built 28 fleet-type submarines under license from Electric Boat Company in Groton, Connecticut. These were full-size, fleet-type submarines. I was ordered there for new construction, fitting out, and commissioning. I watched the submarine being built.

And that's where I met my first and only wife, Karen Dean. Karen was from Chicago but her cousin lived in Manitowoc, and her cousin Dorothy and I were on a blind date, and Dorothy introduced me to Karen. And after that, I made a trip to Chicago, and she made a trip to Manitowoc, and finally, after five or six visits, we decided to get married.

So when the submarine was taken down the Mississippi River from Manitowoc to New Orleans, I asked the captain for permission to get off and get married. Back in those days, you asked the captain for everything. And I think the captain liked all his officers to be married, because they'd be more concerned about coming back. (laughter)

So we were married in Chicago. And while they were taking the submarine, on a dry dock, down the Mississippi River, we spent about 10 days in New Orleans. That was our honeymoon. Then I left and didn't come back for 15 or 16 months. (laughter) And by that time, Karen had moved down to Miami, and she had a job with the *Miami News*. When she met me at the airport, there were about four lieutenant JGs coming off the plane. Karen had rented a convertible automobile! And, coming off, I said, "Which one is she?" She saw the four JGs all dressed alike, and she said, "I wonder which one is he."

We went up the coast by train, after a week or so in Miami. She had a little apartment right on the beach. We had a great time being reunited. And we went up the coast by train to New Jersey and met my folks. That's the first time they'd seen her.

Then we took the train, and we shared an upper berth from there to Chicago, went to Manitowoc, and went through the same routine, new construction with my second submarine, the *Kraken*. And then, when the *Kraken* went down the river, Karen was pregnant with our first child. And I didn't know I had a daughter until I arrived in Fremantle, Australia, about two months after Anne was born. The division commander received a little message they tacked on to another message, and it said, "Advise Lieutenant Godfrey that daughter born, wife and daughter doing very well." And that's when I knew I was a father. (laughter)

I was still out there for another full year. I came back to port after those last two patrols on the *Lamprey*, and by golly, I was

137

lucky enough to have the con coming up through the Golden Gate. I had the 12 to four watch. And I navigated the ship under the Golden Gate Bridge and up through the real strong currents in San Francisco Bay; up to Tiburon Bay, where we anchored the ship. And then I was approached by the Captain, he says, "Bill, I'd like to think you might want to augment into the regular Navy." But I was gung-ho. I wanted to get home. And I didn't think I'd like the peacetime Navy. So I passed that up.

I was released from active duty in San Francisco, processed, and then went back to Great Lakes, the big Navy base at the Great Lakes Training Center. I was released from there and went back to Manitowoc, where Karen and the baby were residing. I had about 30 days of terminal leave. I looked for a job in Wisconsin, but I didn't think I liked the climate. I didn't think Karen would like living in such a cold climate for the rest of our lives.

By then, my dad was in charge of refrigeration on all the ships being built in Wilmington, North Carolina, for the Maritime Commission. He phoned, "Bill, come on down. You can work for me for a year. And then we'll go down to Florida and start our own business." So I went to Wilmington and gained a tremendous amount of experience. Very soon I was his right-hand man, conducting tests and taking the ships out for trial runs. After completing all the contracts in about a year, we moved to St. Petersburg, Florida.

"Beverly's wearing her new outfit, with rice in her hair, I have my new 2nd lieutenant's bars, and everybody is giving us a knowing look." --Russell Cloer

Beverly and I lived on the same block, and there was an empty lot on the block. We were both in junior high school and we had a science project. We had to make an insect collection, and I met Beverly on the empty lot where we were both chasing the same butterfly. It's true.

138

Then we had an "on again, off again" relationship all through high school, but getting my degree was so important that we agreed we wouldn't get married until after I got out of college. And, of course, when I got out of college, I went right into the Army, and we decided we wouldn't get married until after the war, but we did.

My first assignment after OCS was in a cadre unit of the 13th Airborne Division. I was down at Fort Bragg, and there was nothing to do. We had no enlisted men, and the word was that it would be at least a year before we would be up to strength and able to go overseas.

I decided, "I'm going to get married. I am not going to wait any longer. This Division isn't going any place soon." So I called Beverly, we agreed, and she made the arrangements. I got a five-day leave, which was as much as I could get, because I had only been in the Army five months, and you accrue one day for each month.

I went up to New Jersey on the train, and we were married. She had made the necessary arrangements up there, and we had a nice church wedding in the Presbyterian Church. Beverly made a first night reservation for us at the Waldorf, over in New York City; it was a short hop over there. After the wedding ceremony, we get on the Jersey Central Railroad, and the only seat available in our car was flipped backward. We were sitting there facing the rear of the car. She's wearing her new outfit, with rice in her hair, and I'm in my second lieutenant's bars, and everybody is giving us a knowing look. (laughter)

Anyway, we go over to New York and we went to the desk at the Waldorf, and the clerk said, "I don't have any reservation in that name," he said, "And the hotel is full." So I lost my temper, and I got pretty loud in the crowded lobby there, in uniform, you know, and so he found us a room.

Then we had to go back to Fort Bragg. I had a car, a very, very used old car, a 1934 Chevy that I had used at Rutgers. I needed it while I worked the summer job at the bookstore to get back and forth from Roselle Park. That car was still running. We drove down to Fort Bragg, and we made two stops.

Two friends of mine, from before the war, had asked us to stop and see them enroute. One of them was in the Navy aviation cadet program at Chapel Hill, North Carolina. We stopped to see him for the day and saw the Carolina-Carolina State football game, but we didn't stay overnight.

The other friend was Howie Alberts from Rutgers, a close buddy of mine from the Class of '43. He was a physics major, and he was in the Marine Corps, was now a second lieutenant. He had told us he'd put us up for the night, which was important to us. We wouldn't have to spend the little bit of money we had, and they did.

This was the second night of our marriage, and we spent it in separate cots on the second floor of a Marine Corps barracks in Quantico, Va. There was no one else on the floor, but we had separate cots in this big barracks. Some of those things you don't forget. (laughter)

We went on to Fayetteville, North Carolina, and there was no housing to be had, because Ft. Bragg was full of people. There was no housing available on the base nor in town, but we found a second-rate motel. We stayed there for one night and then Beverly dropped me off the next day at Ft. Bragg. She would spend the rest of the day looking for a place for us to live.

She found this wonderful place, on a tobacco and cotton farm. An elderly couple owned it, and he had been an infantryman in World War I. They treated us just like their own kids.

There was no central heating in the farmhouse and when it got cold, Mr. Elliot would come into our room in the morning, before we got up, to light our fireplace. But anyway, we stayed there at the Elliots, and I was gone all day, of course. I gave Beverly the car about half the time. She'd drop me off and then she drove around seeing the South.

Those were some of the happiest days of my life.

TRAINING CAMPS

After Pearl Harbor, almost all of us expected to go into service. For some, it promised gung-ho adventure. Righteous anger against the Japanese or concern about Hitler propelled others. Still others did what was expected of them. Who wanted to look like a draft dodger? Tom LaCosta, in the Counter Intelligence Corps, wore civvies on the train, and when he got dirty looks he opened his jacket to let them see his .38 police special in its holster.

First stop after enlistment, or draft, or commissioning, was probably a basic training camp, followed in many cases by a confusing array of specialized camps.

Some were by choice ("I knew from the outset I wanted the Navy"), others by shifting priorities or administrative foul-up ("For some reason, they thought they needed us more in artillery") and still others by the toss of Fate's coin ("The adjutant said, 'I have five for Motor Maintenance School. Let's see-- you, you, you, you and you'").

Some of us accepted casually what we got. Paul Rork went to New York to enlist in the Navy, but the waiting line was too long, so he went around the corner and signed up for the Coast Guard. Others strove hopelessly against the system. I craved the Air Corps, but because I already had my 2nd Lt. commis-

141

sion in Infantry through ROTC, I could not transfer in grade.

Early in the war, training was thorough and well organized. Later, as the need for manpower rose, there were short cuts. Crandon Clark went through basic training twice, once at Fort McClellan, Alabama, and again at Fort Benning, Georgia, and found it excellent. "There was never any question in my mind when I arrived at the 69th Division," he says, "that I knew how to do all the things that we were going to train people to do."

If the training was too difficult, there was frequently a strong motivation to accept it. Frank Kneller, with the 101st Airborne in England, was inspired by the paratroopers who refused to jump on D-Day. They were in the stockade, and that convinced Frank that he'd jump when the time came.

Roland Winter insists that Jungle School in Hawaii saved his life in the Pacific. Determination drove him to practice until he could go hand-over-hand on a rope with 100 pounds of equipment on his back. His instructor's theme helped, too: "When your mind tells you you can't take another step, your mind is lying. You can do 10 times more than you think you can do."

Accidents happened in training, and many men died before they ever saw action. At Fort Benning, where the airborne trained, I remember watching, fascinated, as an occasional trooper hurtled to the ground, an unopened parachute trailing behind him. And in Virginia, Dick Mercer had the terrible duty of retrieving the burned bodies of fellow Air Corps trainees from the swamp where their B-24 had crashed.

Southern camps, of which there were many, were often foreign places to northern boys. Herb Gross, a Marine officer, cringed when a black Marine was forced to the back of the bus in North Carolina, and many others had similar experiences. It was a problem that persisted through the war, despite efforts to overcome it.

142

"The old sergeant said, 'I've never seen a blacker bunch of white men arrive at this camp.' So we've always been 'the Black Fifty.'" --Crandon F. Clark

The Black Fifty is a unique group among Rutgers World War II veterans. There were 50 of us from Rutgers, new second lieutenants, and we were on our way to Fort McClellan, Alabama, for infantry basic training. We'd been on the train for two-and-a-half days. It was a steam engine, the windows were open and there was lots of soot.

We just had K-rations. There really wasn't much in the way of water facilities. There was some running water, but it was an old southern railroad car, probably 40 or 50 years old, and when we arrived at the camp, we were met by an old sergeant by the name of Sergeant Greenway from Alma, Georgia, a guy probably just tall enough to qualify (laughs) for the Army.

He had a red face and was kind of bald, and he was probably 40 years old, and he stood there and said, "I've never seen a blacker bunch of white men arrive at this camp than you fellows." And he knew why, because we had ridden on this train. So for some reason we remembered that, and we became known as the Black Fifty.

The basic training then was 16 or 17 weeks, and you made your beds. You had inspection every day. You scrubbed floors. You cleaned latrines. You pulled KP, not for discipline reasons.

143

We used to run at night. We'd go out and run three or four miles at night, for conditioning. We had obstacle courses. We used to help some of the guys over them.

We used to stand at attention for weekly regimental parades under the hot Alabama sun of June, July and August. Many guys fainted from the heat. We had rifle target practice. We used to pull the targets and shoot, hiking, construction of bridges and things like that, tactics, fire and maneuver, long marches, 30-hour problems.

You know, when the regiment was going to do something together at say, eight o'clock, in the platoons we got up at five and then the companies had to be ready at five-thirty and the battalions ready at six. We'd all get ready and wait. You learned how to take orders, and if you had a speck of sand in your bayonet at an inspection, you didn't get off that weekend. It was good, very good training, and we went through it twice. We were in two different companies, 16 weeks and then another 16 weeks.

When we went to Benning, they had basically the same thing, but there we had to learn how to operate the machine guns and take them apart and put them back together and instruct people on how to do it. We had very good training at Benning; they had mortar groups and map reading groups, and I always liked map reading. We knew the subject. We knew about night compass courses and how to set them up, and how to run them, and how to do them.

There was never a question in my mind as an officer when I arrived at the 69th Division and we were assigned to a platoon that I knew how to do all these things that we were going to train these people to do. In combat it was much like maneuvers, but more fouled up, but all the things that we learned in basic and at Benning we put to use.

Benning was like a Hollywood movie lot, you know. When they wanted tanks to come out of the woods, they came out, and when they wanted some planes to fly over, they flew over. That's good training. That's realistic.

"We decided on a belly landing. We skidded across the field, over a ditch and into the woods. One wing almost snapped off." *--Frederick Wesche III*

We were the first class at the Army Air Corps flight school at Gunter Field in Montgomery, Alabama. This was when you first started to get into the military aspects of flying an airplane, and that involves such things as gunnery, formation practice and so-called "mock combat."

They didn't have to teach us how to fly. We'd already learned that. It's now how to use the airplane as a weapon, and that lasted for six weeks and it was quite rigorous. I mean, they were trying to emulate West Point strictness with cadets. You got up at five-thirty, and 15 minutes later, you're out in front of your barracks doing calisthenics, then you had another 15 minutes to shave and make your bed and get dressed and then in formation. Then you march into the mess hall.

When we first got there, the barracks were not complete, so they put us up in the local prison. We occupied regular jail cells. Of course, we weren't locked in. Then after six weeks, no, almost eight weeks of that, we went on to advanced flight training. A few got washed out along the line.

We went on to Barksdale Field in Shreveport, Louisiana, and there we were flying the AT-6, which was a more advanced trainer, and then you really got into military maneuvers. We're shooting at ground targets. We had a session where we flew down to Eglin Field off the Gulf in Florida and did gunnery in the Gulf, shooting at a towed target. After the session was over, they'd come back, drop the target and you could go and see how many of your hits were made. Not very many, I might add.

Now, something happened there at Eglin Field, or rather on the way home. We'd gone down in formation from Barksdale Field, making one stop at New Orleans and then on to Eglin Field. I think we were there for three days. Then we came back to Barksdale, on the same route, in formation. I think there were something like 18 airplanes. They had two cadets in each plane, except the lead plane had a second lieutenant, a rated pilot. None of us were rated yet.

As we left New Orleans, there was a strong weather front between us and Barksdale. None of us had any instrument training, or any training in severe weather. Only the second lieutenant had-- but he led the whole 18 ships into this, figuring he was going to climb over it. Well, he never got over it, and at the last minute, he decided to turn around. But when you have 18 airplanes and you try to make a turn, the guy on the end gets whipped around and the guy in the middle is not moving at all.

Well, that's what happened. We were about half-way down and all of a sudden we were into clouds and lightning, rain, hail and very severe turbulence, and we were scared out of our wits. None of us had been in a situation like that. I was flying from the rear seat and in the front seat was my associate, a fellow by the name of Leonard Gindrick.

We milled around in that for about 10 minutes or so. We didn't know which way was up, down, or sideways, and we lost the rest of the formation. What I was afraid of was we were going to run into one another, because we weren't that far apart. We finally broke out at a very low altitude, it was still raining and we were over a farmer's field.

We didn't know it at that time, but we were only a few miles east of Baton Rouge, Louisiana, where we could have landed at the airport, but this situation we were in was such that we decided to get it on the ground as fast as we could. We made a couple of passes at this field to size it up. It was all muddy, so we decided to land with wheels up.

A belly landing is better than with gear down, because the gear sticks in the ground and the airplane turns over. Otherwise, it just skids along on its belly. So we finally landed it, or actually Leonard did, near the edge of the field, skidded all the way across the field, across a ditch and on into the woods. One wing almost snapped off. When it hit the trees, it came to a stop. All

146

was quiet except for a klaxon warning horn. It sounds if the gear is not down, which it wasn't, and the horn is blatting away there.

About that time, here comes the farmer, running up with his son. I think he expected to pull out a couple of dead bodies, but both of us were in good shape. So he took us into his cabin nearby and sent his son down to the general store to call the police or somebody. In the meantime, he reaches under the table and pulls out a jug, and pours us a stiff drink of what they called "Louisiana Lightning."

That put us on our feet. On the other hand, when the police showed up, both of us sure smelled of this, and I think that the cops thought, "Oh, boy, here we got a couple of drunken cadets." But it wasn't that, and so we got back to Barksdale Field. This was just before graduation.

Then we learned that two of our buddies-- one was a barracksmate of mine-- didn't make it. They lost control and the plane went straight in, and they found the two bodies in it. So later on we had to go to the funeral.

The lieutenant was court-martialed for that. We had to attend his court-martial. They absolved the students; we weren't rated pilots. We were depending on the lieutenant and he let us down. I never knew what his penalty was.

"The guys who wouldn't jump on June 6 were in the stockade. When I saw them, I said 'Goddamn, I'm gonna jump.' " --Franklin J. Kneller

I joined the 101st Airborne in October, 1944, in England. I volunteered because I was eager to get out of the replacement depot. I really shouldn't have been in the airborne, but they took me. I was heavier than the usual paratrooper, and when I jumped, I went down fast, so sometimes I would land on another chute. So I had to walk off a chute, yes, walk out into the air. You just walk fast, the air hits you and your chute opens. They

147

trained you to do that. It's a funny feeling, walking in air, trying to get off another chute. It's not that difficult, you just gotta remember to walk fast.

On my first jump, I passed out, like most of them did, but after that it was OK. It was probably fear. It's something so different. You have no history of jumping into air. From a baby on, you're taught not to jump, or if you jumped as a baby you learned the hard way why not to jump. (laughter) So you generally pass out. Then your chute opens and you come back again.

This was a crash course, and if they started out with 100, they were lucky to end up with 40. Some washouts were officers, including chaplains. You hope for them but some don't make it because they just couldn't keep up.

No one I know refused to jump, but we saw a lot that didn't jump on June 6, they were pointed out to us by the jumpmaster, and they were in the stockade. You didn't hear about those guys. I haven't heard about them since, but I remember passing the stockade. I said to myself, "They didn't jump and, goddamn, I'm gonna jump."

"They told me I was to be an instructor in electronics intelligence. I said 'You're crazy. I don't know anything about it.'" --Lewis M. Bloom

I was sent to the Military Intelligence Training Center in Camp Ritchie, Maryland, for a three-month course. I was told a new brigade was being formed, and when I came back from the training, I would be an assistant S-2.

When I got to Camp Ritchie, I found a whole bunch of guys there-- a couple of hundred of us-- all assigned to engineer units, infantry regiments and so on. It was all phony. What they were doing was planning-- personnel and specialist-- for the invasion of Europe. And they were securing people of specialized backgrounds to be part of the Military Intelligence Service in their specialties. I had left all my personal equipment back at

Camp Edwards, which eventually had to be sent down to me.

They put me in aerial photo interpretation. Everyone took a basic course in intelligence and then you specialized-- aerial photo interpretation, interrogation, electronics, etc. And a lot of men were pulled out in the middle of things for secret missions in Anzio and various other places.

When I finished the courses, I was to be assigned overseas. And everybody left, and I was alone. Well, eventually, after I raised a lot of hell, they told me I was going to be an instructor in electronics intelligence.

And I told them they were crazy. I said, "I know absolutely nothing about electronics whatsoever." And they accused me of trying to get out of it.

Earlier, when I had organized my anti-aircraft platoon at Camp Edwards, we got new radios on our half-tracks. I know very little about electronics so I called the guys out and I said, "Hey, we got any radio nuts here?" And I got four of them and I said, "Look, I don't know the first goddamn thing about these radios. Put them in the half-tracks and have fun." I got them out of KP. I got them weekend passes, and they developed a net that was terrific. I got the credit for it, and my battalion commander put a letter in my file, telling me what a great electronics genius I was. That plus my A in the Camp Ritchie radio course, convinced them that I was a radio whiz.

Finally, they pulled me out, and they sent me to Order of Battle Analysis School, and that's what I became, an order of battle analyst. There were very few men trained in this. I don't think there were 200 in the Army in order of battle analysis. Sometimes we were attached to the divisions, and sometimes to corps and armies.

This was an open door to a new field where I could apply a lot of what I knew. I was a military buff. I mean, I read all kinds of things. I had a pretty good idea of how the German army and other foreign armies functioned, and that's what order of battle is. It's the analysis of military structure, equipment, logistics, personnel. I knew what I was doing.

I followed German army personnel on almost a personal basis. If you showed me a pistol, or what a man was wearing, I could give you a picture of the unit.

The German leadership was very impressive. That's what held them together. Whatever the unit, say a "panzerabteilung," or tank battalion-- and its commander was someone named Franz. If that unit was destroyed, and if Franz was alive, Franz would stand on a highway and pick up as many troops as he could and organize a "kampfgruppe Franz," a battle group Franz. And he'd immediately make contact with people on his right and his left, and he'd give you resistance.

They believed in the "einheit prinzip," or unit principle. This not only could be done on a combat level, but also on an administrative level. Every soldier carried in his coat jacket, on the right side, a booklet called a "soldbuch," which had his whole history in it, including the number of his rifle, where he had trained, everything.

"At four o'clock in the morning we're all awakened by this moaning. It's the atheist, he's saying, 'God help me, God help me.'"   *--Edwin Kolodziej*

I would say that the lowest IQ in that company must have been around 116, 120, or something like that. We had guys with 180 IQs. We had guys that were so smart I couldn't believe it. It made the training kind of difficult, because a lot of them rebelled against the training, and, of course, they were a hell of a lot brighter than the people who were training them. They rebelled against authority. They're so super-intelligent, who the hell's going to tell them what to do?

They spent a lot of time in the kitchen until they learned that, eventually, the Army subordinates your personality to it. It's a disciplinary tactic. You're going to wear a necktie when it's hot as hell whether you want to or not. You're going to tuck it in

150

here, like this, it's going to be the second button, and when you stand, you're going to have your thumbs along the seams of your trousers. Discipline, it's all discipline. These bright guys rebelled against that completely.

Plus some of the brighter guys did not have personal beliefs that were like everybody else's. In the barracks, in the evening, there would be discussions at a high intellectual level. (laughter) They got into a discussion one night about, "Is there a God or not?" We had these 18-year-old intellectuals, and one was a pure atheist who took the attitude that there absolutely is no God, and this argument went on until two in the morning, until everybody was hollering, "For Christ's sake, shut up."

At four o'clock in the morning, we're all awakened by this moaning. So we all jump up to see what it is, and it's this atheist, and he's laying there, moaning and groaning. Something's in his ear. A bug had crawled into his ear and was crawling around on his eardrum. Guess what he was saying: "God, help me. God, help me." We went and got some warm water, put it in his ear, and we flooded the bug out. He never said anything about being an atheist again.

We had gone out to our first bivouac, where you stay out over night and you set up pup tents. For your personal use, there are slit trenches. So if you wanted to go have a bowel movement, you go to the slit trench and you straddle it. Well, apparently some of these people didn't want to walk that far.

Well, at the morning inspection, we're all standing in front of our pup tents, and they found that somebody had had a bowel movement and it was laying there. They formed us into a company and the first sergeant says, and I'll never forget this, "Someone has defecated in the area." (laughter) You know, that was the first time I'd heard that word. What the hell? "Defecated?" And a friend of mine says, "He means, 'shit.'"

And the sergeant says, "So, we are not going to do anything until that man stands up and says who he is." That man never said who he was, and we went through about a week of hell, un-

151

til they finally gave up. They were punishing us to make him reveal himself. He never revealed himself. I'm convinced it was one of the super-intellects we had there, one of these 180 IQ guys that always violated the rules.

"My wife was used to a New York apartment. Now we had a kitchen with no running water and a shared bathroom down the hall."   *--Mark Addison*

The evening of the day we were married we went to Lexington, Kentucky, to my first post as an officer. We thought we were in the south. But we found out that in the wintertime it's the boundary line between heat and cold, which meant snow, sleet, and rain, and low temperatures. So that was a surprise. But other than that, it wasn't a bad deal; we were there for six weeks. After that, I was assigned to the Dayton Signal Depot, in Dayton, Ohio.

We had to find our own quarters in Lexington. Mrs. Addison had always lived in an apartment house in New York City. If there was some problem with the heat, you banged on the radiator pipes and sent a nasty note to the superintendent. But in Lexington we had only a small part of an apartment. It was a living room and a kitchen with no running water. The bathroom was down the hall, and we had to share it with the others. To get water, to wash a dish, we had to go to the bathroom.

There was no heat in the so-called kitchen. But in our living/ bedroom, we had a fireplace. It burned soft coal that we had to bring up in a bucket from the first floor. I was accustomed to lighting a fire and having wood to burn, not soft coal. It was an awful job to learn how to have a soft coal fire and to bank it so it was still alive in the morning, so you could get some heat out of it for the rest of the day.

Later, in Dayton, we had ration books for sugar, and ration books for coffee. But at one point we couldn't find my ration book, so I went to the ration board and signed a statement that it was lost and was probably burned in the furnace. They believed me. I was an officer in uniform.

(**Mrs. Addison:** "So they gave him another book. A few days later I found the original ration book. Our landlady's mother was going to do some canning, and she knew I had found the book, so she asked me for the stamps. I couldn't find it anywhere. When he came home that night, I said, 'that book has disappeared again.' He said, 'It didn't disappear. I burned it.' I said, 'What do you mean you burned it?' He said, 'Well, I signed a statement that it was burned, didn't I?' (laughter) So he burned it.")

"We're wading through swamp water, picking up bodies of fellows we knew. And some of them had no heads, no arms, no legs. --Richard J. Mercer

When I was training at Chincoteague, on Mother's Day, on Memorial Day, and on Father's Day-- on each of those three weekends-- we lost one four-engine B-24 bomber and 11 men. And every single one of those things happened on a Saturday night. And they all happened within a space of a month. And it just so happened that my crew and I had the duty on every one of those weekends.

In the Navy, the duty means that you're not assigned to your normal activities. You are assigned to administrative activities. You stay on the base and you're now doing staff work instead of line work. So there we were.

Each one of those planes went in just short of the main runway in the terrible woods and swamps of Virginia. Chincoteague is an island, and it's famous for wild ponies. We used to buzz them. The locals didn't like us for doing it. But here we were, at that time I guess I was 19 years old, and we find ourselves out there wading through this swamp water, which we didn't realize, and should have, was full of gasoline and terrible fire. And we're picking up bodies of fellows that we knew.

153

And some of them had no heads, no arms, no legs, so we couldn't tell. The dog tags were gone because the dog tags are on your neck and if you lose your head, that's it.

I remember that it was a long time before I could eat meat after that. Because these dead bodies that had been consumed in these flames, they smelled just like roast beef, you know. It was just terrible, terrible.

I have a friend, still a great friend of mine, he lives in Morristown, and we keep in touch all the time, Jimmy Mooney. He was a kid from the Bronx. And there was a body, a guy we knew and we could recognize him, and his foot was under one of the engines. Those engines weigh a couple of tons. And they couldn't get the body out of there, and somebody said leave it. And Jimmy said, "Get me an ax." And somebody produced an ax and Jimmy just chopped his leg off at the ankle and then we were able to get the body out of there. I could not have done that, but he did it.

"I carried a back pack and four boxes of machine gun ammo. I was 4 feet 11, about 90 pounds. My gear weighed more than I did." --Roland Winter

I liked training, but there was also a lot you could learn from special people. There was a guy in my platoon who'd had a hard life in Pennsylvania. He had difficulty expressing himself, and he'd ask me to write letters for him. But I admired him for the way he adapted to living in the field. He was never hungry, dirty or thirsty. He never looked cold or wet. He was an outdoorsman.

We were actually hungry at one point on Okinawa, and he said to me, "You and I are gonna eat. I'll be back in half an hour. You find an onion." Well, I found one, and by this time my friend had a fire going and he'd taken his steel helmet and he was boiling water and he had other vegetables and a small animal, skinned and cut into pieces. I don't know what the hell it was, but it smelled pretty good.We boiled it up into a stew, and it was absolutely delicious.

Also in my outfit there was a group of Oklahoma Indians and one guy was their chief. One day he was talking to his friends, and to pass the time, he would reach down in his crotch and pull out a homemade stiletto and throw it at a palm tree about 20, 25 feet away. He'd hit insects or miss them by a hair. He could throw that knife like I could shoot a gun. I said, "Teach me how to throw a knife." "Okay, Ill teach you." He showed me the technique. And we became friends.

When I first got in the Army, I had prayed to God for two things. I said, "First, don't let me stay in the infantry. And second, don't let me go to the Pacific." Afraid of snakes, crocodiles, jungles, living in a hole. I wanted to fight in civilization. But they needed infantry for the Pacific, and I wound up in the 77th Division-- in the Pacific.

What saved my life in the Pacific was the Jungle School in Hawaii. The 77th were a highly trained outfit because the Army used them as training guinea pigs. I went in as a cold recruit, so I missed all their US training. The Jungle School was only two weeks, but it taught me everything.

Jungle School was conducted on the island of Oahu. The man who ran it was a major who was as wide as he was tall and hard as a rock. And the two-week training they gave us was beyond intense. They taught us how to ford streams, how to live off food in the jungle, how to catch water that ran off a palm tree, how to make things out of bamboo, how to survive on the ground. Except for at night, when we went back to a tent dead tired, you were in the jungle all day. You didn't see skylight, it was thick jungle.

The major would speak to us every night after dinner. He would always finish by making a fist and holding it here (midsection) and saying, "If you don't learn anything else, right here in the pit of your stomach there's a ball of guts. When your mind tells you that you can't take another step, that your

155

fingers can't hold on for another minute, that you can't hold your head up any more, your mind is lying. You got a ball of guts here, that's a reserve tank. You can do 10 times more than you think you can do. And that's what I'm here to teach you."

So for our final test, he had constructed two small platforms with steps going up 20 feet in the air. These platforms are 40 feet apart, there's a thick piece of rope stretching overhead from one platform to the other, and underneath them were balls of barbed wire. If you fell, you'd fall on the barbed wire.

You had to go hand over hand for 40 feet with your full combat pack on. Let me describe what a jungle combat pack was. Everybody carried two full canteens, their sidearm, four hand grenades and ammunition for their sidearm. Everybody carried a field pack, with a blanket, half of a tent, a shovel or a pick, a full canteen, and your personal hygiene things.

In my case, I was an ammo bearer. In addition to my personal gear, I had to carry a backpack to which was tied four boxes of machine gun ammunition. They weighed 22 pounds each. Remember, I was 4 feet 11, and I weighed about 87 or 90 pounds. My gear weighed more than I did.

I'm looking up at that rope, and I am thinking, "How am I going to go 40 feet with over 100 pounds of weight on me?" Every night I'm looking at that thing and I said, "Not only am I gonna get cut by the barbed wire, but when the ammo lands on my back, I'm going to break my back."

I said, "There has to be a trick to that." So when everybody else went off to rest or bullshit, I got up on that thing and I started to practice. First I took a couple of swings, then I'd hustle back, and the first thing I learned was that the rope is springy and that you don't have to keep tension on your hands all the time. Let your weight go down, pop up, let go, and just keep doing that. Wasn't long before I could go across like a monkey. I developed a rhythm. Then each night I added some weight. Finally I did it with the full pack.

Now comes graduation. Everybody has to do it. Oh Jesus,

guys were falling off. I would say only half made it. I get up there. I went across in a zip. I breathed a sigh of relief. The major says to me, "Come here, you. You've been practicing. Get up there and do it again." By this time my hands were a little tired. Wasn't so easy the second time, but I did it. God first, and the Jungle School second, is why I'm here.

"I used to give prophylactic treatments. The guys always came back drunk, and they'd say, 'Want a drink, Doc?'" --*Nathan Shoehalter*

They shipped us off, and I went down to Camp Blanding in Florida, outside of St. Augustine. They were starting a new division, the 66th Infantry Division, so we were cadre. I didn't know what the hell a cadre was. I remember building boardwalks, and one of the kids in my tent was from Lima, Ohio, and he couldn't read or write. I remember reading letters from his wife to him and writing back to her.

My first job in the Army was, when we got to Camp Blanding, I was put into the medics, in this infantry division. It was called the medical detachment, I believe, and my first job was shaving assholes of men who had pubic lice.

I was very young, and very naive, and I had never heard of anything like this, but that was my first job. My officer was an obstetrician from Brookline, Massachusetts. He was the worst soldier I have ever seen in my life, a disgrace to the uniform, but what a wonderful man. "Shoehalter," he'd say, "get out there and shave those guys' assholes," (laughter) and we'd lather them up. They would do the front, but I had to do the rear.

I was in the medics all the time, and that's not all I had to do. I used to give prophylactic treatments. I didn't know what I was doing, really. The guys coming back were always drunk, you know: "She didn't want any money, but I gave her money, and she always . . .want a drink, Doc?"

I used to be under the green light. The sign of the green light,

157

that's where we had our prophylactic stations. I used to brag that I gave 114 prophylactics one night at the municipal stadium in St. Augustine. I was a virgin at the time and I didn't know what the hell these guys were talking about-- "Short arm inspections," "fall out with your raincoat and socks." "if you're drippin,' you ain't shippin,'"-- stuff like that, all new to a lot of us. I learned very rapidly, of course. I learned what condoms were. We never called them condoms, rubbers. I was extraordinarily innocent.

An interesting thing happened at Camp Blanding. My sergeant said, "Shoehalter, when you go into town, and go to the bars, and hear anybody talking about what's going on at camp, I want you to write it down and send it to this address." He gave me an address of a bank in St. Augustine. Well, I never went into town. I didn't drink. I wasn't interested in the women. And it was a pain in the ass to get into town from Camp Blanding. You'd get on these huge cattle-car buses, you had to stand up for God knows how many miles, and it was hot and muggy.

Then the sergeant said, "And if you have nothing to report, I want you to write it down anyhow." I wanted to get out of whatever it was. So I used to write in, "I have nothing to report." Finally, they told me my services were no longer needed as a spy. They never said this was spying, but that's what it was. I don't know who they chose for this, and I have no idea why they picked me-- unless it was because I was a college person and could write.

"The bus driver wouldn't move. One white Marine yelled, 'No Marine goes to the back of the bus; I don't care what color he is.' " --Herbert Gross

It was near Jacksonville, North Carolina, when we were at Camp Lejeune. They had a country club there, and they would invite the officers from our battalion to a country club dance, and they'd have all these southern belles there whose fathers

158

were members.

We'd get on a bus to go there. One time we got on a bus, and there was this Marine, a black Marine. That's when they had just come in. This black Marine was dressed beautifully, starched and everything. He got on the bus, and we were ready to go, and the bus driver got up and said to him, "Get to the back of the bus." And I think this Marine was from up north. He said, "What are you talking about?" The driver said, "You're black. Get to the back of the bus."

The back of the bus was pretty well filled, there were just a few seats that weren't filled and he said, "Get back there. I'm not taking off, and you guys are not going anywhere until he gets to the back of the bus."

Things were beginning to heat up. One white marine yelled, "No Marine goes to the back of the bus. I don't care what color he is." Well, the black Marine was getting up when two or three white Marines got up first and took those empty seats. They were enlisted men.

As an officer, I was concerned about taking a stand, but I was glad they did what they did. And the driver said to the enlisted men, "Get up. I saw what you did." And they said to him, "You know what we are going to do to you if you make us get up and give a seat to a black man? No way."

And I thought, Boy, I'm sorry I'm here. I was an officer, and I didn't want to interfere. Then the driver got out and he came back with a cop. And the cop said, "Now look, this is our rules down here. This is the way we do things. If you don't like it, get off the bus." And they wouldn't. They wouldn't get up. They said, "You can't make me give up my seat."

It was sad, because the black guy said, "Wait a minute, hold it, thanks anyway." And he got off the bus. It was an experience that I wasn't used to, being from New Jersey. But that bus driver would not move. They would not move the bus.

I remember my first experience with the Marines. I couldn't wait to get to Quantico. And when we got off the train, they lined us up. We had a sergeant that made me say to myself, What the hell am I doing here? This is wild. He talked to us like we were the worst dirt that ever lived, and he'd come up and put his nose right in your face, and he'd practically spit when he spoke to you.

They marched us to get our clothes and everything else. And it was a hassle. And they degraded you. And they belittled you. And they abused you. This was my first experience. And they shaved my head. And I thought, Oh, boy, this isn't what I thought. I thought we were going to go to war and not do this.

It was 10 weeks of the most fierce abuse of your body. But it wasn't abuse. It was really building you up that we went through for that 10 weeks. And as a result, what's interesting, everybody got very close. We all became close. And everything was alphabetical. Griffith, Gold, Haley. Haley was an All-American tackle at U.C.L.A. Big Irishman. And a fantastic Marine, too.

And this Griffith, did you ever hear of Griffith's Shoe Polish? Well, that's who he was, and he was absolutely unbelievable. Griffith the III he was. And he was Gri and I was Gro so that's why we got friendly. And when we arrived there, everybody came in the train except him. He was late. And he pulled up in front of the barracks in a big Pierce Arrow.

We had a sergeant by the name of Dumbrowski who I don't think went to sixth grade. He always would say, "youse" guys. And this Griffith used to say to him, "Sergeant, 'you' guys, not 'youse.'" Well, he used to steam this guy up. And nobody ever talked back to a drill sergeant. I think he was intent on getting thrown out of the Marine Corps, which he did. It was an interesting 10 weeks.

We'd march until you didn't think you could make it anymore. You used to have a full pack, but our drill sergeant would have nothing on his back. All he would have would be a walking stick that he would whack you with. And then he would run. He would say, "Double-time." And you would have to run.

160

You would start to hate him and say, "That son of a bitch, he's not carrying anything." And when you think about it, it was really a gruelling, torturous 10 weeks. And they used to degrade you. I used to scrub the toilets with tooth brushes.

This guy Haley-- I always told my kids about this-- he called the rifle his gun. And they said at the very beginning, in our orientation with weapons, that it is not a gun, it's a rifle.

So one day he made a statement about his "gun." And we were supposed to go on liberty for the weekend. And he was down in the barracks right where everyone walks in and out. And they made him stand there in his shirt, with the field scarf and his hat, shoes, socks, rifle, but no underwear. Completely bare. And he stood there and said, over and over, "This is my rifle. This is my gun. This is my rifle. This is my gun."

What was interesting was that you hated them, and then, after that 10 weeks and you graduated, they came out and said, "We're buying you beers." The drill sergeants and the G.I.s were saying that, and all of a sudden you forgot everything. They were hugging you, and you were hugging them. You realized they did it because they had a job to do.

Most of the guys made it, because most of them wanted it. They weren't drafted. They were all volunteers. Most of them were college graduates. Most of them were good athletes at college, so what they really had was the cream of the crop. I was so excited when I got in. We just hugged each other. It was so exciting to be picked, to actually be a Marine.

"The crew of a B-24 is like your own little family. We flew across the ocean to Dakar, Africa, and we were green as grass." *--Robert C. King*

I remember the day I went into the service. I got on a train to go to Nashville, Tennessee. The Aviation Cadets is what it was called at the time. That was November 11, Armistice Day, which was a great day to go into the Army. They had a classification

161

center where they give you all these tests to see whether you're qualified to be a pilot, or a navigator, a bombardier, or none of the above. And I qualified as a pilot, so they sent me home in the first year in '42. I was home for Christmas, with 10 days leave, and then it was on to Santa Ana, California, for Preflight.

In Preflight you don't see a plane. It's about 10 weeks of identification, physical, and all this kind of stuff. Then you go to Primary. That's another 10 weeks. And out of every 100 that get to Primary, probably 90 will wash out. So the 10 out of the 100 then go to Basic, which is also 10 weeks. And probably out of that 10 that have gone to Basic, maybe two more wash out. Then you go to Advanced and from there you're assigned.

When I graduated from Advanced they put me in Multi-Engine Advanced, so that meant I was going into bombers. So that's where I ended up. The training took almost a year.

In Primary, the reason most of them washed out was we only had 11 hours to solo, and if you didn't solo in 11 hours-- if your instructor said, "Well, he can't solo"-- then you're washed out. And I was the only guy left with my instructor. Each instructor had five students. You'd wash out because you couldn't solo, or you became airsick, or-- I guess that's the bulk of it, but I'm sure there are other reasons.

Then I graduated from Marfa, Texas, from Advanced, and then I went to Fairmount in Lincoln, Nebraska, to become acquainted with a B-24. And then to Salt Lake City to get the crew together.

When you're in a crew of a B-24 it's like your own little family. It's imperative that you get along. From there we went to Trinidad, Belem and Brazil. And then we flew across the ocean to Dakar, Africa, at low level at night. My navigator, Ray Baleerzak, had graduated from navigation school the same time I graduated from pilot school, so we were green as grass. And here we are low level over the ocean going across to Africa at night, and he's up there in the dome sighting the stars and I say, "Boy, Ray ..." because you don't have a heck of a lot of gas

162

left, that's a long flight. Well obviously he did very well. The sun came up, there was the coast. And from there I went up into Marrakech and then to Tunis. And then as the Allies started taking over part of Italy, we moved into Italy and I flew out of southern Italy near Foggia. That's where I was flying from when I got shot down.

"'Let me give you a tip,' he said. 'Volunteer for the butcher shop. You'll have a good voyage and you'll eat well.' "
--Livy Goodman

My friends and I moved up to Camp Kilmer. It must have been June or July of '44. It was after D-Day. We were getting re-outfitted and we knew we were going to ship out, but we didn't know when or where to. We kept hearing it was going to be this week, then this week, etc. We didn't mind Kilmer, because we went into New York whenever we wanted to.

Anyway, we went into New York about every night. At the bottom of Times Square was a place called the Crossroads Cafe, and that was our meeting place. The four of us would meet there and then walk down to Penn Station to get the train back to Kilmer.

So I was sitting at the Crossroads Cafe this evening, and there was a civilian sitting next to me, and he looked over and said, "Oh, 84th division eh?" And he said, "And 334th infantry, huh?" I said, "Yeah." He said, "Well, we're taking you guys over tomorrow." And I said, "What?" And he said, "Yeah, you're shipping out tomorrow, did you know it?" I said, "No, I didn't, but we'd been hearing."

He said, "Your regiment is on my ship, the *Thomas E. Barry*." And he said, "Let me give you a little tip." He said, "I'm a quartermaster. They'll come around tomorrow morning early, and ask for volunteers for different things." He said, "When they ask for volunteers in the butcher shop, you be sure to volunteer."

163

I said, "How many do you need?" He said, "Three or four." He said, "I'm not kidding you. If you want to have a good voyage, eat well, volunteer for the butcher shop." So when the other guys arrived I told them and introduced them. This guy looked straight, I mean he was a nice talking, friendly man.

And it turned out to be right. The butcher shop was where we cut up all the steaks, all the chickens, cleaned all the oysters and things, for the officers, mainly. Not for the troops. We ate at the table with the officers and the crew, we had three good meals a day, we could order anything we wanted, if we wanted three eggs for breakfast.

It was wonderful, it really was. And I didn't ever feel any seasickness or anything. We cleaned chickens, and the chow line went past the door to the butcher shop. And as they came by we would clean chickens, or open oysters, and one day, one fellow in the chow line just couldn't handle it, he was so seasick. He came through the butcher shop heading for the port hole, but the port hole was closed, and he fell right down in the sink.

"We ticked off the names on that list and came to the conclusion that only four of us were still alive out of those original 93."   *--Thomas A. Kindre*

We graduated in May of 1942, and all of us who were in Advanced ROTC got our commissions as second lieutenants at graduation. I didn't really know what that meant. I found out later. It entailed danger. Second lieutenant infantry was arguably the most dangerous rank in the military because you were a platoon leader. You were the guy who said, "Follow me," and I never thought of things like that at the time.

Just before graduation, I'd also got my private pilot's license as a result of completing the Civil Pilot Training program there at Rutgers. I got into that because I wanted desperately to be in the Air Corps, but I never could, and that's another story.

A month after graduation, a bunch of us-- members of my

164

Class of '42-- were shipped to Camp Croft, South Carolina. Camp Croft was an IRTC-- Infantry Replacement Training Center-- and we were there essentially waiting for them to figure out what to do with us.

The waiting wasn't hard. Camp Croft was known at that time as "the Country Club of the South." We went into town, we were invited to parties, we went horseback riding. There was a golf course, too. There wasn't too much else to do.

One day I happened to be standing in the day room, near the door to the adjutant's office. I was talking to some of the other guys, I guess, when the door opened and out popped the adjutant with some orders in his hand. He looked around and said, "I've got five for Fort Benning-- Motor Maintenance School. Let's see"-- and he started pointing-- "you, you, you, you and you." I was one of the ones he pointed to. On my Officer's Qualification Record I was identified as a "Student, journalism." That was my chief qualification for being an auto mechanic. But-- I didn't know it then, and later I even resisted the idea-- Motor Maintenance School turned out to be my ticket to survival.

A few days later we were shipped to Fort Benning, where we went through the three-month Motor Maintenance course. We disassembled auto engines, learned about the caster and camber of wheels, and road-tested jeeps and Army trucks. When the course was over, we were sent to Fort Jackson, South Carolina, to be part of the cadre of the then-forming 100th Division. We began to get our troops in-- most of them were raw recruits-- and we went through the winter months in training.

Then in the spring of '43 I guess they were beginning to use up a lot of people in the European Theater, and there was a big need for replacements. They pulled 600 enlisted men and 93 second lieutenants out of the 100th, and we joined thousands of others at Camp Shenango in Pennsylvania, went from there to Camp Kilmer in New Jersey-- just across the river from Rutgers-- and from there by truck convoy to Newport News,

Virginia, where we shipped out-- 15,000 of us-- on the British troop ship *Andes*. We were headed for Casablanca and then on to the African war front.

In a replacement depot somewhere in Algeria, I was called into headquarters, and a major had my personnel record in front of him, and he said, "It says here that you have a private pilot's license. We have an opening for a job as assistant headquarters commandant to a corps commander. Part of your job would be piloting a light plane to scout out new locations when Corps wanted to move."

It sounded like a very cushy job, and my answer to him-- I can still hear it reverberating in my head-- was, "Thank you, Sir, but I've come this far and I'd like to go on and see what's happening up at the front."

I was so dumb. I don't know what I was thinking. When I think of it now, it sounds like something Errol Flynn might have said in *Dawn Patrol*.

Then it was on to another replacement depot in Tunisia-- it was in a grove of cork trees on the edge of the Mediterranean-- and this time I was saved despite myself. The 34th Division was short an officer in its 734th Ordnance Company, which handled ammunition and vehicle maintenance for the Division. There were no ordnance officers available, but with my Motor Maintenance course, I was the next best thing. This time they didn't ask me, they just assigned me. And I went through the war with the 34th.

Toward the end of the war, I was in a bar in Rome, and I met two of those other lieutenants I'd come over with on the *Andes*. We went through the rosters and ticked off the names and came to the conclusion that only four of us were still alive out of that original 93.

THE FAR SIDE OF THE WORLD

Just as the funnel of history had thrown us together onto this narrow segment of continental seacoast, it later reversed itself, sucked us all up again and spewed us willy-nilly across the world stage-- from Europe to the Pacific, from the Arctic to the tropics, from China and India to Africa.

Most of us, born and bred in this small state, had never traveled much beyond its borders. Many had never been south of Philadelphia. Some, from south Jersey, had never been to New York City when they entered college.

Now, with the coming of war, geography suddenly exploded. Stints at specialized training camps took us to Miami, California, the deep South, the Midwest or Hawaii. With training completed, the troop ships, Navy vessels and Air Corps bombers moved out, and their destinations were Africa, Europe and the Pacific Islands. But special assignments took military personnel to almost every remote corner of the world.

The places we went, the people we met, the assignments we were given, were beyond anything our imaginations could have conjured. Aboard the cruiser Augusta, during the Atlantic Charter conference, David Robinson watched President Roosevelt fishing and shook hands with Winston Churchill. "Why me?" he mused. "How did a 22-year-old kid from Perth Am-

boy get to do this?" Charles Getty, flying across England with fellow Air Corps officer Lt. Col. Jimmy Stewart, had to bail the famed actor out when Stewart, who was navigating, said, "Charlie, I think we are lost." Irving Pape and Ed Kolodziej had personal encounters with General Patton, and John Berglund played poker with Admiral Nimitz-- and beat him.

Jack Ambos, on his Navy PC boat, went up a river in China as hundreds of people lined the banks, waving American flags. Joe DeMasi was elected honorary mayor of Airola, Italy. B-24 pilot Morton Sobin, in civilian clothes, flew black-painted "carpetbagger" planes into neutral Sweden with supplies for the Norwegian underground. In a restaurant in Stockholm, he taunted a Luftwaffe pilot.

Lew Bloom and Lloyd Kalugin helped liberate concentration camps, and years after the war Bloom met a former inmate who remembered the day he'd been there.

Some of the assignments were strange, unexpected, and not always welcome. Physicist George Reynolds wanted action in the Navy, but Vannevar Bush and James B. Conant, who were building the A-bomb, wanted him in Los Alamos, and they won. Reynolds was to "nurse" the Nagasaki bomb up to the moment it was dropped, but fate bumped him off that B-29 and onto another carrying Bomb No. 3, which was never used. But then fate seated him next to Admiral Richard Byrd, who drafted him as an aide during his time in Japan.

Carleton Dilatush, in the Quartermaster Corps, drew this assignment: Build a plant in India to manufacture 55-gallon steel drums used to carry aviation fuel over the "hump" into China. Dilatush had to pick a location, order a shipload of steel from the US, get hundreds of civilian laborers and a US Army unit to the site. The plant was open in three months.

John Dowling had no idea what to expect when he and his B-24 crew were assigned to the Counter Intelligence Corps. What they did was fly missions into France, Belgium, Holland and Norway, dropping saboteurs behind enemy lines.

168

" 'What have we here?' asked Churchill. I opened the box and showed him. 'This will make Mrs. Churchill very happy,' he said." --David Robinson

Before Pearl Harbor, the most memorable event in my Naval career had to be the Churchill-Roosevelt meeting, the Atlantic Charter conference. The cruiser *Augusta* was off Newfoundland, and I was her assistant navigation officer.

There's only one Roosevelt, there's only one Churchill, and how did a 22-year-old kid from Perth Amboy, New Jersey, get to stand behind Roosevelt while he's fishing, and shake hands with Churchill, and talk to him? There were 135 million people in this country. Why me?

Even aboard ship, very few guys had met Churchill as I did or got that close to the President. I was there because we were winding up our gear, our paravanes. Admiral King and the others were fishing. They're not catching anything. I just came down from the bridge. I had taken the President's chart down to Captain Beardall, his Naval aide. I thought, "I'm going to see FDR," but he took it and took it in to FDR.

But then I looked down the passageway, and a wheelchair is being wheeled, with Franklin Delano Roosevelt in it, portside. Oh, it's open and he's being wheeled right towards me. "Holy God," I thought. I'm the only officer there, my boys are there, "Attention on deck. Good morning, Mr. President." He just

169

kind of waved, no salute. (laughter)

Anyway, they switched him around, I'm standing there like that, and he picks up his fishing rod, and he casts his line. There was a cartoon in the newspaper at that time of Roosevelt in a rowboat. He says, "My friends," and all the fish come jumping into the boat.

He has a strike the moment it hits. Holy Jesus, he reels it in and it's a big, ugly dogfish, a small head, a big body. Roosevelt says, "It belongs in the Smithsonian Museum," and then he says, "It looks like Cotton Ed Smith." Who was Cotton Ed Smith? A senator, worse than Strom Thurmond down there. He did have a heavy beard, a dark complexion. He kissed Jean Harlow on the steps of the capitol. He hated Roosevelt and Roosevelt didn't like him. It did look like Cotton Ed Smith, but then the President says, "It reminds me of a number of senators I know, all mouth and no brains."

Roosevelt looked awful. His face was drawn. He was wearing this old sweatshirt and a soft hat, and I looked at his thighs, and they were flat on the chair. There were no legs there-- and his lower leg just dangled in the breeze. I was appalled. "I shouldn't see this. This is my President," I thought.

I turned to Mike Reilly, who was the head of the Secret Service, guarding the President, hell of a nice guy. He lived in the JO bunkroom with us. I said, "Mike, should we get the hell out of here?" He said, "Robby, finish up your work. The President doesn't want to disturb you."

That was my meeting with Roosevelt. I saw him several times after that, but how that man accomplished what he did in that physical condition, I'll tell you, just read this book that Doris Kearns Goodwin wrote. He was tremendous.

She writes that one moment he could look like hell, and two minutes later, in conversation, he looks great. And that's right. Six days later, when we're breaking up, he's sitting up there, and Churchill's just leaving on the *Prince of Wales*, FDR with his fedora and his brown, two-breasted suit, and a tie. "Happy days are here again." He looked like the champ. "My God," I said, "How could that man look so good?" But as she points out in her book, he had been with Churchill for four days. He had been at sea. He loved the Navy, and he was a different man.

This was a very important meeting. Churchill came for help. Hitler was threatening to invade, and then the jackass went up into Russia. That took the heat off, but Churchill lost all of his equipment at Dunkirk, and he was rearming and he came to Roosevelt to say, "Look, we appreciate the help you're giving us." He wanted to bring America into the war. He knew he couldn't do that, but "If we don't get help, we may go down."

I was in charge of a working party of 40 men, we put up 2,000 boxes, each box containing a half pound of cheese, a carton of cigarettes, and three apples. We put them up in the morning. Then Churchill came aboard. I came up to watch him come aboard. It was like out of the movies, the band, God Save the King, the piping, and, Oh, God Almighty.

"We put up these boxes," I said, "and we'd like to take them over to the *Prince of Wales*." "Sure, Robby, sure." So, after lunch, Churchill had had lunch on the *Augusta*, he went back. We're on the *Prince of Wales* with two motor launches, stuff piled high. We came alongside the port quarter, which is where their quarterdeck is, and I went up to the officer of the deck. I had two side boys. As an ensign, I rated two side boys. I tell him about the boxes. "Oh," he says, "fine. We'll get our own working party and we'll work together." This was the first cooperation between the British and Americans, I think. So we got them up the gangway there and put them on the deck.

Out of the crowd on the fantail comes Winston Spencer Churchill, with that hat, you know. He wasn't using his cane. Nobody was paying any attention to me. Churchill was walking straight towards me. I said, "My God. Yesterday, the President; now, Churchill; tomorrow, God."

I can't call, "Attention on deck." It's not my ship. "Good afternoon, Mr. Prime Minister." "Good afternoon," he sticks out his hand and we shake hands. "What have we got here? What have we got here?" I showed him. I opened up the box and showed him. There's a card there from the President of the United States. You know why Churchill's here. All of Europe is gone. He has his finger in the dike. What did he say? He said, "This will make Mrs. Churchill very happy." Well, that was a big love affair.

Meanwhile, Sumner Welles and the British undersecretary were working on the charter. They would go back to the battle-ship, the *Arkansas*, work on it, come over, and talk to Churchill. It did not go smoothly. Churchill didn't want the empires torn apart, Roosevelt did. Roosevelt didn't want a "United Nations" type of organization. So they compromised.

It was a great moment when Churchill left. As he went past the ship, he waved his hat and gave the "V" for victory. What a tremendous man. He went over to the *Prince of Wales*. We remained at anchor.

Roosevelt's sitting there, and, about 15 minutes later, the *Prince of Wales* draws past us, close to our port bow, and there's Churchill on the fantail, by himself, with the band in back of him, and our band is up in our forecastle, and he and Roosevelt are waving to each other. Then both bands broke into Auld Lang Syne. I didn't cry, but I was damn close to it. It was very moving. I have never seen a picture of that, and not many of us saw it, just those of us up in the forecastle. I get worked up about it, but it was even better than I say it was.

"The CIC wore civilian clothes, and I looked like a draft dodger, but then I'd open my jacket and they'd see my .38 in its holster." --Thomas La Costa

I had no choice in the service. When Pearl Harbor happened there was really no intelligence whatsoever in the services. They had what they called the "counter subversive system," which was a very simple thing, where one guy would squeal on somebody else. But there was no intelligence. And then all of a sudden they realized that we were very, very weak in that aspect of the work. So I think they got me for the languages-- my Spanish. Most of the guys who went in were lawyers, and some of them were people who had already been in the investigative fields, in border patrols.

I didn't have any preference, actually. I wanted to be a part of it, and I did hope that I could use my language. So I think that had a lot to do with my being called. Professor Turner taught French at Rutgers. They grabbed him also. He ended up in the European theater and I went to the Pacific. So they did take some people because of their language background.

I remember I went to Governors Island and everything was all secret, hush-hush stuff. And they started to investigate me. It was a very comprehensive investigation, you had a report a couple inches thick. So they were doing that while I was hanging around doing some substitute teaching and just waiting.

When they finished that and I got the clearance, they had "no reason to doubt my loyalty, integrity, and discretion," which is the way you end up all those reports. Then I got into it and they called me up. I went to 50 Broadway in New York, where they had a school, the Counter Intelligence Corps School.

Basically what we went to was the FBI school, and we shot on the pistol range. I never had any basic training. I never had a rifle or a carbine. I was issued a .38 snub-nosed police special and a .45, and that's all I ever had. I never had to salute. I went through the whole war without ever saluting anyone because we were operating as civilians.

I never wore a uniform while I was in New York. Later we wore khakis with a special civilian patch, and just the "U.S." on the collar. Everything we did there was as civilians. My travel orders never showed any rank or anything. So it was a very unusual set up. I never belonged to anything, any large unit.

The group I trained with was small-- maybe 20 or 30 people, mostly lawyers and people who had worked for the FBI.

It was interesting because I used to commute from Plainfield to New York in civilian clothes, riding the train, and all the people stared at me and wondered what that draft dodger was doing. But in the summer, it was awfully hot, so I would take my jacket off or open it, and they could see my .38 in its holster, so they were really wondering what was going on there.

We had some very interesting assignments in New York before we went overseas. For example, we used to go to Yorkville and they'd give us $15 or so, and we would buy drinks for the wharfies (dockhands) to find out if they were spilling any classified information about what they were loading on the ships.

That's when we started posting those signs, "Loose lips sink ships." We went around putting those signs all over the place.

In wartime you could do things that you can't do in peacetime. You could have a suspect under surveillance 24 hours a day, have his mail checked, incoming and outgoing, read it all, have his telephone tapped 24 hours a day.

I had another case in Princeton investigating one of the professors there. Somebody said he was a Nazi and that he used to have secret meetings at night in his home. So we had to conduct a big investigation. And it ended up they were playing poker. There was nothing wrong at all.

I went to the Elco Boat Works, in Bayonne, where they made PT boats, and checked on a couple of the workers there who were suspected of sabotage. We got rid of those guys fast.

Then they discovered that right across the street from our office building, someone was taking pictures of all the agents as they went in and out of the building. That did it! Everybody was sent away and spread out all over.

When we finally got to Manila, everybody was doing the same work. We had the one office there: the FBI, the ONI, and the CIC. We were all together.

I had some interesting times which, unfortunately, nobody knows about. There are not any records. I didn't get any Purple Heart or anything. I still got a piece of shrapnel in my finger, right here. Nobody knew I got that. I had malaria and dysentery. I never went to a hospital, no record of anything. I was in Borneo, which was very unusual for Americans. No mention of that in my service records. They don't even know I was there. That's the kind of war I was in.

I don't know who I reported to. My travel orders were just by order of General MacArthur. We didn't report to anybody else. We were out there alone. Half of the people didn't know what we were doing.

You could only operate in an area for a short period of time. As soon as you're "made," as they say, as soon as they know who you are, you have to do something else. So in the combat areas in the Pacific, they tried to alternate assignments. You had a difficult one, and then for a month or so an easy one.

I was on three or four beachheads. I was living in a hotel for a while. I even worked in a factory in Brisbane, Australia, undercover. And I got paid for that. I got paid for the military service. I had a liquor ration from the military service, I had a liquor ration from the Australians, and I lived in a hotel. So you went from one extreme to another.

There were never more than two or three people in a particular area. In a combat area, you were supposed to try to get prisoners and capture documents. So you're supposed to be the first among the people to go into an area and, in case of retreat--and we didn't have much of that--you were supposed to be the last to leave so you could destroy any documents that were around.

When we were on the easy assignments, we'd go to the movies in Australia and see the newsreels, and we would see long lines of Germans and Italians marching as prisoners, hundreds of them. We couldn't even get one or two of them out there. And even if we did, we weren't really sure that they were Japanese. They might be Japanese, Koreans, Filipinos, or what.

It was only at the very end of the war that we were able to distinguish what they were from looking at their toes, because each of those people wore different types of sandals, and the thong

175

went in between different toes. But we just couldn't get any prisoners. It was tough out there. Those Japanese were pretty vicious soldiers. They would not surrender.

I was in on four assault landings. I was with the first wave of Australians in Borneo, the last amphibious landing in World War II. And Leyte Gulf, I was on that invasion. As soon as we hit the beach, we put up a CIC sign, and people knew that meant they were supposed to take prisoners. But that didn't work: no prisoners, very few Japanese materials.

The Japanese wouldn't let themselves be taken as prisoners, they were fanatics-- just like those kamikazes and those one-man subs in Borneo. They knew they were gonna die, and they did it for the Emperor.

One interesting thing, though. We didn't have time to even try to learn Japanese. So we had Nisei boys as interpreters. Some of them, their parents were in those concentration camps in California, and those guys are out there being shot at. I thought that was unfair.

In one of those places, I think it was the Admiralties, we captured a whole bunch of documents and papers. They were different colors: red, blue, yellow. We thought we had really found something important. And then the Nisei interpreted what they were, and the little red one said "short time," so many yen; the blue one said "long time," so many yen, and the yellow one, "all night," so many yen. They had their prostitutes there with them, right in combat.

"I'm in Shanghai. I knock on the door, and this little man comes out. 'Are you Parag Tibor?' 'Yes.' I said, 'I'm Leonora's husband.'"   *--Mark Addison*

I knew pretty well where my unit was going. I knew I was going to India, and probably that I'd be flying across "the hump" to China, and that's how it worked out. I was in India from, let's see, we left in March, it was 63 days to Calcutta. Arrived Calcutta in May of '44. And left India just before Christmas to fly across the Himalayas to China. We stayed in China until the end of '45, and we steamed home out of Shanghai.

While I was in Shanghai, I had a very unusual experience involving one of my wife's relatives. My wife is of Hungarian background. Her father had three brothers. One of them was in the Hungarian army and he was captured by the Russians in World War I. They sent him to Siberia. But he managed to escape. Apparently he got to China and opened an ink factory in Harbin. Visited his folks in Hungary once, and then nobody ever heard of him again.

So when I was in China, my wife wrote, "If you get an opportunity, see if you can find my uncle." Sure. That's like somebody in Russia saying, "Oh, you're from America, you must know my cousin in Chicago." But I said, "Sure, I can find your uncle."

I asked someone for advice and was told that if he's Hungarian, he's an enemy national, and I should talk to the Swiss consul. So I went down to the Swiss consul and gave him the story. He said, "Every nationality in the area has an organization, and they'd know where all their nationals are if they are in China. I'll get in touch with him this evening. Come back tomorrow and I'll tell you what I've been able to learn."

I go back the next day. "Yes, he's in Shanghai. And he's living at 17 St. Catherine's Way," which is out past the race course. I went out there. Now I'm in uniform, wearing a sidearm. I knock on the door. This lady comes to the door, sees me, turns all different colors. "Something the matter?" I said, "I'm looking for. . ." and I gave her the name. And she said, "He's working at the American port on the river. He'll be home such and such a time." I said, "I'll be back."

I come back, it's about 5 o'clock in the afternoon. Knock on the door. This little man comes out. I said, "Are you Parag Tibor?" "Yes." I said "I'm Leonora's husband." He said, "I don't want to go in the house, come on outside. These people

177

were Nazis." What the hell, he'd been living with them. He was a Hungarian national. So anyway, we talked, and a couple of times I took him to dinner, because he looked as though he could use 10 good meals. He was a chemist who was working as a plumber's helper just to have a job, so he could put food in front of him. That was a very unusual experience.

"There was a hole cut in the bottom of the B-24, and we would drop these 'Joes' behind enemy lines at night to conduct sabotage."   *--John Dowling Jr.*

We were doing anti-submarine flights off the southern coast of England daily with our B-24s until the Navy got enough airplanes into southern England to take over all of the anti-submarine patrols for that part of the Atlantic. When that happened, they moved us up to the Midlands and assigned our outfit to the OSS, Office of Strategic Services, which had to do with sabotage work behind enemy lines, and there were two bases in England that did that. One was our base at Alconbury and another base that the British just called "Base X."

That's where the work was done, and I feel that's the important thing we did during the war. We were involved for about a year and a half in working with the French Underground, supplying people behind enemy lines for sabotage ventures.

When a man was behind enemy lines, he had to be supplied with equipment, bombs, ammunition, guns, everything, so we would drop supplies to him on predetermined, pre-designated signals. It was very interesting work.

The people that did this work were called "Joes." The man going behind enemy lines, he didn't want anybody to know who he was, and so everybody was Joe. There was a hole cut in the bottom of this great big B-24 airplane, and it was covered with a plain piece of plywood, and we called that the "Joe Hole."

We would get to where the person was to do his sabotage, blow up a building, blow up a bridge, blow up an ammunition

178

dump, or something like that, and we would take that plywood off, and he would fall out the Joe Hole and parachute to the ground. Now mind you that this is done from the big B-24 bomber flying at high speed, flying at low altitude, and flying in the dead of night. One airplane to a target, no protection, no guns, no armor plate, just an airplane flying as fast as it goes. It was hazardous to drop people out that way, but we did it.

We would drop the Joe and his equipment, but we could never drop enough, because the airplane was flying so fast that we covered too much territory, and you wouldn't dare make a second run, because then people would know what you were doing, so you had to come back another time to surprise them. We would come back again later and drop whatever he would need. We flew all over France, Belgium, Holland, even up into Norway. It was a different kind of operation.

The men who did this, surprisingly enough, many of them were prisoners out of jails in the United States, and they traded the dangers of serving their country in this fashion for their freedom. So a lot of the Joes who volunteered for this work were people who had been in jail for very serious crimes. They got their training in a place in northern England. We visited it a couple of years ago.

Most of them were from the United States, although many were from the country where we dropped. You'd take a guy from France who escaped the country, and he would volunteer, or we'd get word to him, and he would come back to do a certain job, but most of them were Americans, at least those that we worked with. They didn't have to know the language because even if you're fluent they can tell by the accent that you're faking. So it didn't necessarily mean they had to be fluent. All they had to do was keep their mouths shut.

One thing that always intrigued me was the fact that, at night time, just before they were to take off on a mission, most of the Joes would go to the edge of the taxiway and pick up some mud or grit and put it in their mouth, and rub it all around their teeth, and they said they did that in order to make their face, their mouth, look dirty and soiled, because if they got picked up immediately, if anyone saw that they had clean, bright, shiny teeth, they would know that they were just not a native walking down the street. Most people didn't have toothpaste to clean their teeth, so they did that for their protection.

Now these people would do their job and they'd come back. You'd go to the mess hall at six o'clock in the morning and you'd see a guy sitting in the mess hall that you'd dropped out a couple of weeks ago. He would have to be picked up by a man in a different kind of airplane. We had people with real small, fast airplanes that could land on a very small field, and they would locate such a field, and he would land but wouldn't even stop the airplane, and the man would run out of the woods and jump in the airplane and come home. In the morning, he'd be sitting there eating his corn flakes and eggs and you'd wonder how he got back.

These Joes carried a military rank-- most of them had a little higher rank-- but, they didn't display it. They wore no uniform. They were dressed like the country they were dropping into so they could blend in with the crowd.

We had one fellow who was about six foot six, a great big husky fellow, and he did what he was supposed to do, and his instructions were, "If you lose track of where you are and you lose track of your contact," which was always some kind of French Underground people, "walk towards the coast."

He walked towards the coast, all the way to the ocean, and nobody stopped him. He just kept walking, paid no attention to anybody, and he was finally picked up, put on a boat and brought home. There he was eating his corn flakes and eggs one morning.

By the way, some of those Joes were females. They always kept the females in a truck until they were about ready to get on the airplane, and then they would run them into the airplane and we could tell they were females.

When they came back, the Joes were kept separate until they were debriefed, then they could do anything they wanted to, but they never said a word about where they were, or what they did, or anything at all, not a word. It was just like they were part of the party and we all had enough sense not to talk to them about it. That's the way it went.

We would deliver everything-- guns, ammunition, all kinds of food. I remember one night we were getting this airplane ready to load, and I broke a package, and out rolled an egg. Here we had a two-million-dollar airplane delivering eggs, but it was an important commodity.

There were other people on the base, but they couldn't go near our airplanes. We had guards on every one of our airplanes. Even the permanent parties, even the base commander, was not permitted to see what was in any of our airplanes. People thought we were going out and doing regular Air Corps missions.

The radio equipment we used was very high frequency, very complicated, very sensitive. They had different sets, and a name for everything. We had a set called the "Mickey," and you just had to learn it. You just put it up on the test bench and just fool around with it till you knew how to work it.

We never had a day off. The only time you had a day off was once a month, you got a 48-hour pass, and if things were rough and you had a lot of missions, you didn't get the pass. We worked all the time.

"We went up this river, liberating China, and hundreds of people along the banks waved American flags to welcome us."   *--John F. Ambos*

Our vessel was PC-807, and it was commissioned in February 1944. We had six officers and about 80 enlisted men, and we did convoy duty to all those little islands-- Eniwetok and places like that. We were down in the islands, and then we

181

would escort up to the Philippines. And I remember we had an escort job with one or two small merchant ships, and we came to the inland waters. It was pretty because it was right amongst all the islands. Then they put us in Subic Bay, and we fared worse. We sat there for six weeks.

I hate to tell you what our life was. First week we worked like hell, painting everything, cleaning up everything, getting everything squared away. Then the second week we had a drill.

After that, we took it easy. We set up an awning on the upper deck, and after we swept down the deck we'd play bridge. We'd knock off for lunch, and we'd play bridge till 3:30, when a boat would come alongside to take us to the officers' club, which opened at four. We'd be there till about six, and we'd come back and watch the evening movie, and that was the day.

Finally they gave us orders to take the marines to Okinawa, and later we took them to Korea. The war was over by then. I remember once we were on convoy duty near the Philippines, and a Jap submarine hit one of our ships right in the forward magazine, and in 10 seconds the ship was gone. 250 guys dead.

That was one of the few actions we were involved in. Well, we were also on a picket line at Okinawa. The planes would come over, but they were looking for big ships. But we would fire with everything we had. We welded machine guns on the stanchions along the side, so the crew would have something to do when the planes were going over.

We were hardly regular sailors. The uniform of the day was jock straps and earrings or something like that. We were very informal. Not having a lot of laundry may have contributed to that. When we got involved with other Navy ships we'd have to tighten up a little bit-- at least wear dungarees.

We were in China for three or four months, I'd say. We went up this river, liberating China, and there were hundreds of people along the banks of the river waving American flags to welcome us. We stopped at a little town where we established our base, and we tied up there. We ran the traffic up and down

182

to Tientsen from there. It was a lot of small craft. LSTs and LSMs would carry their stuff up there.

While we were there, some of us got on the train with the marines and went into Peking. Local warlords still had control of the area. You could tell whose army it was by the arm bands. They had different arm bands. I remember the marines had machine guns on the roof of the train in case somebody wanted to get in trouble. When we came into Peking, they put us up in a very nice, big hotel, with hundreds of rickshaw drivers out in front to take you anywhere around town.

While we were up there, the river started to freeze over. It always froze over by early January. But we wanted very much to get out of there, because if it froze over we'd be there for the winter. So just before Christmas they gave us orders to go back to the States. We went down river and stopped at Tsingtao. It was miserable, cold weather, just around Christmas time.

They loaded us up with everybody that needed transportation back to the States, and we drew a whole bunch of senior petty officers who were beach commanders. They had been trained to go on the beach and handle the traffic as you came in. Most of them had never been to sea on anything smaller than a big transport, so they were miserably seasick all the way back, and it took us six weeks, because we sort of made a great circle. We took the longest way possible because of our need to stop for water and fuel. We went down to Eniwetok and all the little islands and then Hawaii and then home.

"I showed up with half a truck of C-rations, and they said, 'By God, these Americans are great,' and they made me honorary mayor." --Joseph DeMasi

So here we were, the 82nd Airborne, we're in Naples. Italy is full of dialects, and I was a Neapolitan, so I was right at home. It was very interesting. When we went into Naples, the Germans were retreating but we still had a little firing going on up through Sorrento and Naples. And it so happens that General Gavin says, "I think we are going to take the post office for our CP, our Command Post."

The general was starting to get the people to go into the post office and all of a sudden, some Italians came up to me (they knew I was Italian because I was talking their language), and they said, "Don't go in there, it's mined." I said, "What do you mean?" They said, "Mined." I told that to General Gavin, and other Italians came and said the same thing. So General Gavin said, "Well, the police are right across the street there and we'll put our CP there." So we moved into the questura, the police station.

But the General was still thinking about the post office. Six days go by, seven days go by, and nothing happens. Now the General turns to me, "Reddy,"-- he used to call me Reddy-- "what kind of information are you getting? Are you sure they are telling you right?" I said, "General, I don't know, but you never know, maybe they put duds in there, maybe it is not geared to go off, or maybe you've got to touch something before it goes off." I said, "There are all kinds of mines." He said, "Yeah, I know that." Then all of a sudden, on the ninth day it blew up.

That's the closest I got to General Gavin because I was his interpreter then. I was the reconnaissance man, because of my talking with the Italians. It's always nice to know about the enemy. How do you get to know about the enemy-- who they are, where they are, where'd they go? The Italians, those that deserted and those that had been around, were the ones that were able to talk to us.

When we started to get ready for Anzio, we moved to Caserta, about 15 miles north of Naples, and that's the time I told the general, "I want to go visit my relatives. I know where they're at. They are in the town of Airola." He said, "Okay." So I went there to visit my mother's family.

You know, I had red hair and most Italians are dark, or sup-

184

posed to be anyway, so I didn't know if they'd recognize me. The first thing I see, a girl comes out to me and grabs me, "Guiseppe, Guiseppe, we were waiting for you!" In Italian she says that. I said, "Well, how did you know who I am?" I said, "There are eleven million GIs," and I said, "You think that it would be routine that I would be here?"

Well, it appeared that when the Germans retreated, all the boards were torn off their kitchen floor because the Italians had a habit of hiding things, taking a few boards out and hiding wheat. And the Germans, when they went, they took all the pigs, the chickens, the cows, everything. They searched everywhere, and they cleaned house. They lived off the land, see, the Germans did. Everything was cleaned out. There were no chickens, no farm produce, no nothing. The Germans just took everything. Clean sweep.

So the people were in bad shape. So I said, "Look, tomorrow, I will see if the general will give me some food and I will bring you some food." I showed up the next day with half a truck load of C rations and all that. I passed them out amongst the people there and they said, "By God, these Americans are great." And they made me honorary mayor of the little town of Airola.

They showed me where my mother had been married and all the places of interest. I've been back several times, and I think this summer I'll go back for a couple of months. My relatives on my mother's side are farmers, well-off farmers. On my father's side is the fellow that owns one of the biggest restaurants in the area. It would feed 2,000 people. Over there, you've got the women in the kitchen, like 15, 20 women, cooking in the kitchen, and you got 15, 20 waiters serving.

I've been back to Normandy, too. When they had the big 50th Anniversary celebration in Normandy, I get a letter and it says, "You are welcomed to join us, join President Clinton at breakfast aboard the USS *George Washington*. Please call to tell us whether you will bring your spouse." So I called up the

185

War Department and I said, "Yeah, you bet I'll have breakfast with the President." "Are you bringing anyone?" I said, "No, I'm not bringing anyone, I'll be alone."

Now over there, I meet a friend, Jake Schneiderman, my military police friend, the guy I used to play golf with. He's married and we're in Ste. Mere-Eglise, and his wife says, "Joe, can't I be your wife and go with you?" I said, "I told them it's just me, but I'll stick my neck out and see what happens."

So, it's five in the morning and there is the helicopter to take me on board the USS *George Washington*, out in the bay there, and I said, "Major, I have my sister here, she'd like to go. It's a late entry here." "Well," he said, "let me talk to the Colonel." So finally he says, "Well, okay, you can take your sister." And I find out that there was one other man from the 82nd invited, the President of the Disabled Veterans of America.

So we get on the ship, and there is Senator John Glenn, there's Hillary, and everybody's talking and having fun and eating all kinds of stuff. Then we sat down to have breakfast. After breakfast, everybody got up and clapped and the President gave a talk. He said, "I want to thank the 1st Division, 9th Division, the 45th Division," and all the Navy people that were there.

Afterward, we got up to shake hands and I said, "Mr. President, you gave a beautiful speech, but you forgot to mention the 82nd Airborne." "Oh, yeah," he said, "I know they were there, and they were the greatest." He gave three other speeches that day, on Omaha Beach and right on down to the American Cemetery, and in every one he mentioned the 82nd Airborne.

" 'What am I signing for?' I asked. They said, 'Chinese currency for General Chennault's 14th Air Force in Kunming.' " *--Carleton C. Dilatush*

About a year after I was out of college-- I was now a first lieutenant in the Quartermaster Corps-- the Colonel called me into his office. He said, "Dilatush, I'm going to send you to

186

Command and General Staff School in Fort Leavenworth. You're a guinea pig. It was always captain and higher rank, but they're going to take 10 first lieutenants to see if they can handle the courses and graduate."

So I said to him, "I'll do my best, sir." He said, "You realize that if you don't succeed, I'll have to explain my endorsement, why I chose you." I said, "I understand, sir."

Well, I was there for 10 weeks. It was 10 months training condensed into 10 weeks. Classes started at 8:00 in the morning. We had classes on Saturday as well. They'd lecture to us in this great big study hall. You had a number assigned and were identified only by number, no rank. So a colonel couldn't be given preference over a first lieutenant. My number was 192.

I graduated, and all 10 of us graduated. Six were promoted to captain. I didn't get my promotion until after I came back. But I'll tell you, it was a wonderful experience. It was tougher than college. The Colonel said to me when I came back, "Well, I had an officer out there, keeping an eye on you. I want to congratulate you on being in the top ten of your class."

Next I went to Miami, Florida, and I was there for two weeks, then I was ordered to be a courier officer. They were loading all these cartons. I said, "What do you have here? What am I going to be signing for?" They said, "Oh, this is currency. This is American money printed up in Chinese currency, for General Chennault, for the 14th Air Force in Kunming."

The only time I got into a bed on that trip was on Ascencion Island. We took off from Miami, went to the British Gold Coast, to Belem, Natal, Aden and Karachi. I had five different crews going over to Karachi, India. Then I was ordered off the plane to proceed immediately to New Delhi.

I reported in and the Colonel said, "Dilatush, I want you to study this operation here for six weeks. After six weeks I want you to return with an organizational and a functional chart. So I studied all the operations. After six weeks I gave him my report, and he said, "You're going to be Chief of the Field Inspection

Division, that's your job. You report directly to me."

So for six months, I traveled all around the theater, first the base section, Karachi and Calcutta. The code names were Bent and Daub. I would visit the depots and see what was in short supply. Then I would go to all the Quartermaster units in the base section and inspect them. I would take corrective action where I could, then go to the intermediate section, and then visit the advance section in Assam where General Pick was building a road over to China.

That was some experience. I saw the Taj Mahal, because it was in Agra, right at the air base. I remember one time we were landing and there were two Indians. They had this goat and they were stroking its neck and, all of a sudden, I saw one take a big bolo and sever its head. They were, I guess, preparing it for the dinner that evening.

I went on down to Karachi, which was then part of India, and got a jeep, and started out from there, and felt my way through all of the CBI Theater. It got to the point I knew all the units in the field, and they would call me with their problems in connection with salvage or laundry or storage and distribution, or you name it.

So the next thing I knew, the colonel called us all together, and he said, "Now you know the executive officer is due for rotation. He's been here so long as lieutenant colonel" (In the meantime, I had been promoted to major). He said, "Major Dilatush is going to be the executive officer, and I expect you to take orders from him the same as if they're coming from me."

Now we had a bird colonel in our section, two other lieutenant colonels and me as a major. It was a big section, Services of Supply section of the Quartermaster, and it was a wonderful experience.

After I was made executive officer, the colonel came back from G-4. They were trying to get me assigned to G-4 section. He said, "I think you have the right to make your decision." I said, "I'll stay here. As much as I'm flattered that there would be this opportunity, there are many things to be done here."

A couple of weeks later he said, "We have a project assigned by G-4. It's a drum plant which must be constructed, we have to find a location for it. A drum plant to manufacture 55-gallon, 18-gauge reinforced chine band drums."

The colonel sent me to investigate the problem. I went to Calcutta and investigated the whole system. They had been using 55-gallon drums of lighter weight metal, loading these drums full of aviation fuel on the planes and going over the Himalayas. But with the pressure at that altitude, they had drums springing leaks, and they had to jettison them or lose the whole plane and the crew. So there was a very definite need for this new plant.

He gave the project to me and I looked at all the blueprints, about three inches thick, and I realized that we had to immediately order the steel, because it would take a complete Liberty ship just for the steel. So we placed the requisition.

The unit to run the plant was in California being staged, but the troop strength in the Theater would not permit the entire company to be brought into the China-Burma-India Theater. So I had to figure out which ones to bring to India. But by cutting back on the number of men from that unit, I had to then offset them with employees for labor. So I went to General Headquarters in India, and I said, "We need three companies." We had chosen a location 110 miles northeast of Calcutta, Tezcon Kermatola, off the Ganges River. So we got the three companies and moved them to the location. The building material was shipped from Cairo to India. It came into Calcutta and was moved to Tezcon Kermatola, and the building was erected.

To make a long story short, we had to plan the operation, and build the plant, and in three months we exceeded rated capacity of production of 55-gallon drums. We put a canning plant right next to it, and we filled the drums with aviation fuel and loaded them on the planes, and they took off from the airport right over the hump to support the 14th Air Force in the China theater.

189

"She screamed, 'It's Geislingen!' She'd been a slave laborer there. 'Oh, my God,' she said, 'you're the lieutenant who came that day!'"   --Lewis M. Bloom

We took the town of Geislingen, which is not too far away from Stuttgart. In its center is a factory called Wurtemberger Metalwaren Fabrik. They used to make very fine cutlery, and they had a process of binding metal to porcelain. And during the war they made vanes for jet planes. I had surveyed the plant for that reason. They also made parts of submachine guns and aircraft empennages--the tail sections for aircraft.

So we took the town, but they were still firing all around us. We got into the center of town, and we set up our divisional headquarters in a series of stores. Actually the G-2 section was in a little Rathaus, and somebody came running in and said, "We have a big slave labor camp nearby."

The camp apparently had been taken over by the prisoners. These prisoners represented many nationalities-- Russian, Polish, Czech, Hungarian. Our battalion commander was concerned because many of the prisoners were armed and had imprisoned German guards. There were so many language problems that we couldn't secure the camp.

I was talking to the Colonel (G-2), and the General said, "Well, we better get somebody down there right away." He turned to my Colonel, and said, "Why don't you send Bloom over? He speaks the language, and also this sergeant who speaks about five languages."

So we took two jeeps loaded with infantrymen, armed to the teeth, and we got up there real fast. The camp was surrounded by all sorts of wire about 15 feet high. I came into this circular section, and there's mobs of people, and they had already attacked some of the German guards.

I spoke to the prisoners through the sergeant, who used a bullhorn to convey, in the various languages, our request to meet with the leaders from each of the national groups. I calmed them down and told them they had to release the guards to our custody. And I asked them what they needed. And of course they all needed food and medicines. And I said, "We will get them to you." I turned around and went back and made my report and within 15 or 20 minutes we were already piling trucks in there. I never went back there because I moved on with the division.

Many years later-- during the early 70s-- my wife and I had a little reception for some people from our Temple. One of them was a woman by the name of Rose Ringel. Rose still has the tattoos on her arm, and she had suffered very badly. In fact, she was in bad shape. And she was browsing through some of our photo albums, and she picked up this album, and she suddenly screamed out, "This is Geislingen!" She was almost in tears.

She said to me, "This is Geislingen, isn't it?" And I said, "Yes, it is." She said, "How did you get there?" And I told her. She had been one of the slave laborers. And I explained to her that the picture had indeed been taken in Geislingen, and she very clearly remembered the day the US army jeeps arrived and a lieutenant-in-charge advised the sergeant about the instructions to be announced through the bullhorn.

And she said, "Oh, my God." She said, "You're the lieutenant who came in!"

"On our way back, Lt. Col. Jimmy Stewart said 'Charlie, we don't have to tell them about this back at the mess, do we?' " --CharlesGetty

After I finished my missions on B-24s--this was in England-- I was assigned to Second Bomb Wing Headquarters. The wing was composed of about seven flying officers, who would take the message from the division headquarters and put together a mission for the three groups that were in our wing-- the 389th, the 453rd, and the 445th. I was assigned to wing headquarters as an operations officer.

About a month or so after I got there, Lieutenant Colonel

James Stewart was assigned to the headquarters as the chief operations officer of the wing. Yes, that's Jimmy Stewart, the actor. So we got to know him because there were so few of us, particularly flying officers. He had been a squadron commander at the 453rd Bomb Group, and at that point had probably made 14 or 15 missions. So we got to know him quite well.

The most interesting story about him was when he was assigned as an investigating officer in a court martial case. It involved a major who was court-martialed for taking a Red Cross girl on his lap across England and back in a P-47, which is a single seat airplane. When he landed at the air base in Bournemouth, the base commander was in the tower, and he saw the girl get off the guy's lap and get out, and he made sure that he told the major, "Okay, but don't you dare take her back on your lap." Well, the major did, and he was court-martialed.

Stewart was named the investigating officer, so he had to fly over from Hethel, which was our base, over to Bournemouth, on the other side of England.

We had assigned to us in the wing headquarters a Canadian Norseman cabin plane with about a 250-horsepower engine in it. So that was the plane that Stewart was going to take, and he asked me if I would go with him. I said, "Sure."

Going across, Stewart flew and I navigated, and we got over to Bournemouth, and he did his business, and we took off from there to go back to Hethel. And this time I was flying and he was navigating. So we got about an hour out, maybe an hour-and-a-half out, and Stewart said to me, in that whiney voice of his, "Charlie, I think we are lost."

We were not far from an RAF field, so we landed at the RAF field, and I ran up to the tower and asked where we were and what was the heading back to Hethel, which we got, and then we took off again, and we got back to Hethel and landed.

We're driving back to our wing headquarters and were on our way to the officers' mess. We had a small mess of our own. So on the drive back, Stewart said to me, "Charlie, I don't think we have to mention this at the mess." Well, of course, I couldn't resist and I did tell the story. (laughter) So everybody got a kick out of Stewart's poor navigation, but he didn't mind. He was a good man and easy to know, no put-on airs or what have you. He was a real nice guy.

"The dog became a veterinary legend. When the marines tossed their butts, she'd knock off the ash and eat the cigarettes." --Paul W. Rork

I think our ship was manned by about 95 percent reserves and five percent regular Coast Guard. So we were really neophytes on the LST. The LST experience started in Pittsburgh. We went to Pittsburgh by train, and we did some more training there, but we really went to pick up our ship. We picked up the ship there, with the pilot, and we spent 10 days going down the river. It was quite an experience, going through 52 locks on the Ohio River alone. Now I think they have two.

Each lock was more beautiful than the next. The lock keepers took such pride in their little gardens and their houses and their locks. We went through 52 of those with the pilot and then, at Cairo, we met the Mississippi and continued to New Orleans.

We had seven officers and a crew of 130 on the LST. For me, after a sub chaser, this was a big ship. I was a first lieutenant, deck officer.

The officers ate meals together in the ward room, but we had the right protocol, you know. The captain was at the head of the table, the executive officer to his right, and the deck officer to his left. I was third in command. Then it went down depending on what your rank was. The ship was a big happy family almost from the beginning. We had a few trouble-makers but we got rid of them along the way.

From New Orleans, we went to Panama City for our shakedown cruise. We had some professional pilots aboard who were used to LSTs, teaching the skipper all the nuances of operating an LST, and practicing dropping a stern anchor. When you were making a beaching, you had to drop a stern anchor as you ran up on the beach to keep the ship straight.

From there we went through the Panama Canal, up the coast of Mexico to San Pedro, California. We were there a couple of days. That's where I picked up my cocker spaniel and took her with me.

Captain Kane had a cocker spaniel at home. I said, "Captain, you have a cocker at home, and I have a cocker at home. I see an ad in the paper. There's a kennel here. How about my calling them?" And he said, "Okay, go get it." So we brought her aboard. She was six weeks old.

That dog became a case history in the veterinary legends. When we had marines aboard, they would smoke and throw their butts over the side, but they didn't know the lee side from the windward side, and the butts would fly back on the deck. Inky would come over to a butt and sniff it. It would burn her nose. She would knock off the ash and eat the cigarette, literally eat it. And she did this for over two-and-a-half years.

When she had her puppies, the veterinarian called me and said, "You have to tell me the history of this dog." I said, "What's wrong?" He said, "There's not a worm in any puppy. Tell me what she did."

I said, "Well, she was famous for eating cigarettes." "Ahhh," he said, "you know what a worm capsule is made of? What kills the worms? Nicotine!" (laughter) He said, "I have to write this up for the *Cornell Veterinary Journal*." He sent me a copy of it.

Everything was comfortable on the LST except the ride. If there were a sea running, you could stand at the superstructure, and it would bounce you all the way to the bow. Never bothered my dog, though. She would just walk. She had her sea legs. I trained her to go on the cargo hatch, and I let the crew know I was going to clean up after her, but that only lasted a couple of days. They just wanted to see if I meant it.

194

And then the chief came and said, "No more, Mr. Rork. We'll take care of it. When we hose down the ship in the morning, we'll take care of everything."

From California, we headed out to Pearl Harbor, where we picked up some Army troops and took them down to the Guadalcanal area.

We didn't pick up marines until we were going in toward the end of the Philippine invasion. And then the main one was Okinawa. We staged at Ulithi with thousands of other ships and then went in to Okinawa on Easter Sunday, April 1, 1944.

My most vivid memory of those days was leaving Okinawa to go to Saipan. We were shuttling for several months to pick up ammunition for five-inch guns for the destroyers that were on picket duty at Okinawa, where the kamikaze planes would come in and try to sink the ships. The destroyers were out there trying to keep them away, but they would run out of ammo, and we had to carry 20,000 tons of ammo on our ship.

We'd just unloaded on a destroyer and we were on our way to join a convoy. It was in the evening, still light. I was standing with the forward 40 millimeter gun crew on the bow, and one of the men says, "Mr. Rork, look to the starboard, please." And I looked and here comes a torpedo. And I called the captain on the intercom and said, "Torpedo, 500 yards, starboard bow." And he tried hard to maneuver, but an LST you can't maneuver that quickly.

Fortunately, the Japanese intelligence wasn't too good. If they had shot a torpedo at us when we were loaded, we would have been way down in the water. Now we had only six feet under us. And the torpedo, I swear, it went right under my legs and just kept going. It just kept going. It wasn't set right. It was set too low. That's a vivid memory. (laughter)

We had a near miss with a kamikaze at Okinawa, too. It was diving on the ships, and they were firing like mad. This guy couldn't get to them, and it looked like he was almost out of control. We were off the beach about a half mile, and all alone, and he was coming right at us. And, suddenly, the deck was full of hail. Actually, it was the ships shooting at this kamikaze, and all the rounds of ammunition were falling on our ship. Everybody dove into the gun tubs, or in the boats or anything. This fellow crashed about 100 yards astern of us. We had our only wounded during that experience. Six people were hit by shrapnel. But nothing serious.

Another memorable experience, more on the light side. We were on Guadalcanal, and we saw a bunch of drunken marines standing around by their jeep, and so we pulled up, and we said, "You guys are out of beer?" And they said, "Yeah, we're out of beer." So we said, "You want to make a deal?" They said, "What kind of deal do you have in mind?" "We'll get you eight cases of beer for your jeep. You can just tell your C.O. that somebody stole your jeep." They said, "That sounds good." So we went back and got eight cases of beer and traded it for the jeep. We were the only LST in the Pacific, and maybe one of the few ships, that had their own private transportation.

On our way back to Pearl, we stopped at Guam, and we were in the officers' club, and I said to a couple of guys at the bar, "Are you guys interested in buying some equipment?" They said, "What kind?" I said, "We've got a jeep aboard." And the one guy says, "Jesus, you've got a jeep aboard? You got a receipt? A custody receipt from the government, official, stamped, numbered?"

"What do you mean a custody receipt? We got eight cases of beer." "Oh," he said, "do you know what they'll do when you hit Pearl? These officers come aboard and they make an inspection. And anything you don't have a receipt for, you're in big trouble. You could be court-martialed."

I said, "Well, what do we do?" He said, "Follow me." So we went out to the ship, and he said, "Where's the jeep?" I said, "Down in the tank deck." So I opened the bow doors, lowered the ramp, got in the jeep, and I drove it out into Guam Bay. The jeep sank and I just floated and swam back to the ship.

I swear I could have heard it hit a thousand other jeeps at the bottom of the bay! (laughter)

We finally made it to San Francisco-- that was at the beginning of 1946. I went to the transportation office of the Coast Guard, and there's a classmate of mine there. We were yakking about old times, and I told him I had a dog, and our executive officer and I were both heading east. So he said, "Call me in the morning."

So I called him, and he said, "You're all set. I traded five lowers, three uppers, and two roomettes for a compartment, a full compartment." So we had enough room for the two of us with the dog. And the two of us and the dog went first class all the way across the country.

When I brought her home, remember she had never seen grass, so she would only go on the sidewalk. It was the closest thing to a cargo head. And she swayed a bit when she walked. It was really funny. She was a real heroine. Everybody loved her.

"And into the room walked Admiral Nimitz and Admiral Lockwood, and you never saw two lieutenants sober up so fast in your life." --John Berglund

I went back to Guadalcanal and we were supposed to invade Kavieng, New Ireland. And I remember the briefing. They showed us all these pictures, aerial photos and stuff. And they said, "The first battalion of 9th Marines will land at Government Wharf and then sweep up to the airfield." And I thought, "Who's doing this sweeping?" because there were six-inch guns on each side of Government Wharf.

As a matter of fact, there was a real neat gimmick that was going on. We were to land on an island in the harbor, on D-Day minus 1, and support the landing. But then I was shaving and the S-2 went by me and he said, "We're not going." I said, "Bullshit, Major." "No, we're not going, Berglund." And it had been called off.

Now, what it was, apparently, was the MacArthur vs. Nimitz thing, who had had the most casualities and got the most headlines. That's all. I mean it had been planned that we would have this bloody operation and land. There were signs there, saying, "Welcome, 9th Marines," that the Japanese had painted on the beach.

So then I was selected to go back to the States to Fort Sill because I had this experience in sound ranging. I was in an artillery training regiment in California, waiting. And this was in Camp Pendleton. I met Ida Lupino when I was there, and went around-- I won't say I was going with Ida-- but I was in a crowd that included Ida for several weeks.

Now I was this overseas marine who comes home, so I was probably a pain in the neck. In fact, we were nasty. The Army wanted us to wear dungarees and leggings, but we told them that wasn't considered uniform in the Marine Corps. And we had a colonel in charge of our class. We called him "Neon," because he had a false grin. We used to sing barber shop at lunch, and he thought there must surely be something in the Articles of War that forbids officers singing barber shop in the field.

I broke my arm at Fort Sill-- the only time I got hurt in the war, really. I jumped gracefully out of a truck, but I tripped getting out and broke my arm. I splinted it with an artillery slide rule, a graphical filing table, and duct tape, and I rode 30 miles to the hospital like that. And it hurt every time we went over a rut.

Now I'm back in the Pacific, and in the middle of the battle of Iwo Jima, in the fire direction center of corps artillery, 5th Amphibious Corps, the phone rings and I answer the phone. And I said, "Captain Berglund."

It was a guy named Dave Swanson, a major in one of the gun battalions. He said, "Hey, Berg, how's the second verse of Little Orphan Annie go again?" because we used to sing commercials in the mess in Hawaii. "Always wears a sunny smile. Now wouldn't it be worth your while, if you could be like Little Orphan Annie." That's a true story. He called me up and I sang it there in the fire direction center.

Another time, the phone rang and it was a guy named Pesko. I don't know where he went to college. I don't think he went to Rutgers. He was a Jewish guy from Atlantic City, from my high school. And I answered the phone and I said, "Captain Berglund." He says, "Berglund. Bill Berglund from Atlantic City?" And I went over to him and he showed me, they were living in a Japanese pillbox, using that for their fire direction center. And there'd been a Jap in the walls, in a chamber for, like a week, with hand grenades, and he finally committed suicide. They didn't know he was there.

And then there was the time I played poker with Admiral Nimitz. There was a Marine named Rick Ohrstrom. He was from Connecticut, his father was a very wealthy man. Because of Rick, I lived in the Bohemian Club in San Francisco, on my way to Hawaii, for four days. This is a very plush place where Rudyard Kipling visited in the 19th century, and Jack London was a member and all guys like that.

When we went to Pearl Harbor, Rick and I were traveling together, and he called up this family named Walker in the Nuuana Valley. He had been at St. Paul's School with their son, and at Easter time, rather than go all the way to Hawaii, the Walkers' son would go to visit Rick in Connecticut. So he said, "I'm here, in Pearl." And Mrs. Walker said, "Come on out." He said, "I have somebody with me." "Bring him along."

Well, we had a few drinks at the club at Pearl Harbor, at the BOQ. Then we went to the Walkers' and we had another drink or two. And it was a beautiful home. They were reduced to five servants because of the war. They were suffering. And they said they were expecting more guests. Well, okay, that's fine. There was an Army major there and the two lieutenants, two Marine lieutenants. And I can remember to this day the sound of a car on the gravel, and I said, "Well, I guess that's the guests." I was feeling mellow and so was Rick. And into the room walks Admiral Nimitz and Admiral Lockwood, the submarine commander. And you never saw two lieutenants sober up so fast in your life.

So we had dinner and then after dinner, they played ten cent limit poker. And I wasn't in the game to begin with, but I got in later on when somebody dropped out. I won the last hand. It was a short hand, but I won a hand against Admiral Nimitz, and I never saw him again. On Guam, I went to his headquarters to buy shorts, because the Marine Corps didn't have any. But he wasn't around when I went to the ship's steward there.

"I was to ride on the B-29 with the Nagasaki bomb, but some VIP wanted the glory, so I got bomb No. 3, which we never used." --George Reynolds

I came to Princeton University for graduate work in 1940, and we started working on the mass spectrometer, probably one of three in the country that was turning out first class research results. By the spring of 1940, it was clear to the faculty here in the Physics Department that the US was going to be involved in the war. We were involved with a program sponsored by the National Research Council to do bomb damage analysis, and what is called "exterior ballistics studies," that is, "What happens when a projectile hits a wall or ground?"

It was called the CPPAB, Committee for Passive Protection Against Bombing. Our object was to design air raid shelters for Great Britain, which was under terrific siege at the time. This went on until about 1942, when we were doing field tests, full-scale field tests, on the effects of bombing on structures above ground. I still took courses, and did a thesis, and got a PhD in 1943-- one of my thesis advisors was John Van Neumann-- but the main activity was to be involved with the war.

In 1942, we had a program at the Aberdeen Proving Grounds, studying the effects of bombs on German structures. In 1943 the emphasis had changed from defense to attack. We had a program in Camp Gruber, Oklahoma, to study the effects of bombs or detonations on the pillboxes on the beaches of Normandy, because there was planning for the invasion by that time.

At that time, I felt that anything I could do from then on was not likely to affect the war. There was too much of a lag time between the research and its application to the war front. So I determined that I wanted to be in the US Navy. I applied and got a commission. I was on my way to assignment in an amphibious warfare training program, and was looking forward to it. I liked small boats, I was young, I wanted action, I wanted involvement, I wanted immediate results.

In the meantime, I had been "asked" by Vannevar Bush, head of the OSRD (Office of Scientific Research and Development), and James B. Conant of Harvard University, who was head of the National Defense Research Council, to go west and work on a project that several of my acquaintances here had already gone to work on. Everybody knew what that was. However, I didn't want any part of it. I wanted the action that the amphibious warfare training promised.

I was summoned to Washington and interviewed by Conant, and he said, "You're the only one that we've been trying to get that has refused to go there. And I don't think you're very patriotic." And that's where I made my slip. I said, "It's not that I'm not patriotic. I've got a commission in the US Navy."

I had, in the meantime, married Virginia, and we were living with my parents in Trenton. I got my orders for the amphibious warfare training, and everything was set up. The date was June 15. So we went to the Jersey Shore for a last weekend together, and when we got back there was a telegram that said, "Old orders cancelled. Proceed in four days to Santa Fe, New Mexico." So that got me to Los Alamos.

I wasn't happy. I was assigned to the group that I knew were after me: a Harvard chemist, George Kistiakowski, a very colorful fellow, who is well known in the history of the atomic bomb. He recognized immediately that he had an unhappy camper. He said, "Hello, I'm glad to see you." And I said, "I'm not glad to be here." He said, in his Russian accent, "Oh, God! What's wrong?" And I told him I'd gotten married, and my wife, Virginia, was down in Santa Fe on a street corner with our luggage, and I'd been taken by MPs and brought up to the hill. There I found that military officers couldn't have wives on the site.

So Kisti got on the phone and called General Groves. He said, "Reynolds is here." And then he said, "No, that's not good. His wife is in Santa Fe." And then Kisti put his hand over the phone and said to me, "Any children?" And I said, "No." Then he said to Groves, "No. No children." And then he said, "Just a minute, I'll ask him." He turned to me and said, "Expecting any?" I said, "No." And he said, "No."

The next day the Military Police brought Virginia to the hill. She was the only Navy wife there. All the Army officers were a little unhappy too because they couldn't have their wives.

Anyway, we got involved with the workings of what's called the "Fat Man," which was the Nagasaki bomb, and our assignment was the detonation system. We went down to Alamogordo, New Mexico, to decide on the site for the test, and they decided to have it there.

If the test had been a failure we would have gone back to work. The test was a success, so I went that same night to Tinian, where our field assembly station was, and did some dummy runs in a B-29 with the pilot who ultimately delivered the Nagasaki bomb, a fellow named Sweeney.

After the field tests of the firing and all, the bomb was delivered. I was to fly with it, and my responsibility was to check out the detonation circuits, right up to the last minute. Another junior officer, an Army lieutenant, had worked on the proximity fuse, and he was to go along and do the proximity fuse test. But at the last minute some VIP wanted to ride for the glory, or the whatever, and we had to bump one of us off the flight. So we each learned the other fellow's job, and we drew lots. I lost. He went, and I didn't. I was then due to go on number three, which never went, of course. When the war was over, I was held on

202

Tinian until the surrender, and then, the day after surrender, was flown into Japan.

On a bus ride from the airport to some seaside hotel at Nagasaki, I happened to sit alongside Rear Admiral Richard E. Byrd, who was along for the ride. Everybody got in on it: archbishops, gentlemen, everybody showed up in Tokyo to get his name in the paper. I was sitting next to Byrd, and he said, in a polite way, "What do you do?" I said, "Well, I'm really a physicist." And he said, "Oh, I've always been interested in physicists. Talk to me about this." Well, that night he went to General Farrell, whose group I was in, and had me transferred to be his aide for his stay in Japan, which had its perks.

A hospital ship came in, the Admiral got himself quarters on the air-conditioned ship, and of course his aides went with him. So I spent my time there on an air-conditioned hospital ship. I had to moonlight on damage analysis for whatever I could do. But it was fun being associated with a fellow like that. He was not arrogant. He was very humble. He said, "You know, people think I'm a scientist. I'm not. I just collect the data and hand it over to them." He just wanted to talk about physics, so we did.

Anyway, in due course, I came back to Los Alamos, and then began planning the future. I had several offers. I liked the one from Princeton. So I came back here to teach physics, and I've been here ever since 1946.

"I knew German, so local people would talk to me. What everyone wanted to know was 'How was New York after the bombing?'" --Kurt Leuser

When I was in Germany, as a personnel sergeant major, I had no trouble communicating because I had grown up speaking German. So local people would talk with me. And one of the big questions that I was asked over and over again was, "How is New York after the bombing?"

In 1944, or '45, Adolf Hitler decided he wanted to bomb New

York in the same way that Jimmy Doolittle had bombed Tokyo. They set up a plan, a complete plan, where aircraft would fly from Germany, they would be refueled at sea, bomb New York, and then ditch in the sea off New York, where they would be picked up by submarines.

Then, somebody, I have no idea who, came up with the idea that they could save a good many lives and a good deal of equipment if they just did this all on paper. Consequently, these fastidious Germans took that original plan and they worked it out to the last dotted "i" and crossed "t," the names of the squadrons that were flying over, names of the fliers, the submarines, the names of the submarines. They decided who the survivors were going to be. Every detail was worked out.

They manufactured photographs, which were published in the newspapers, and I saw those papers. Everybody in Germany had a relative in the US, and New York was symbolic of the US, so this was important, and consequently many people cut these articles out and saved them.

I was one of the people who could communicate and was authorized to communicate with the Germans in that period, in that time of non-fraternization, so I had access to this whole story. What they had done, they had photographs from the air, very good, realistic photographs, showing the destruction from the bombing.

Some of them were supposedly taken from the bombers, others from reconnaissance aircraft afterwards, some of them were claimed to have been smuggled out by Nazi sympathizers in New York, showing all kinds of damage, very convincing.

I saw photographs of fliers being helped off submarines, that had been picked up and brought back in. It was a complete story. There was no truth to it at all, and of course the question everyone had was "How is New York after the bombing?" "What bombing?" "Well, New York was bombed." "It was not." "Oh, your propaganda is hiding it," you know, that sort of thing. I'd say, "Listen, I was in New York two months ago.

It was never hit. I was never far away from New York. It was never hit. There is no damage." Some of them believed and others didn't believe, but that is what propaganda can do.

The people we knew were generally not Nazi sympathizers, and Germany was not, and I still believe that to this day, Germany was not, primarily, a Nazi nation. The Nazis were a group of men who took advantage of the country, but this was not a Nazi country. Most of them wanted to disassociate themselves from Nazism.

When the truth came out about the concentration camps and death camps, I think the average German was shocked. The average German was in disbelief that these things could happen. Yes, there were concentration camps, they knew that, and, yes, not everybody who died of pneumonia actually died of pneumonia. I mean, this was taken for granted, but these death camps were unbelievable, even to them.

"Bud O'Toole and I are standing there, and in come Lord and Lady Mountbatten, Cordell Hull, Jimmy Byrnes and Jim Farley." --Richard J. Mercer

I thought the Navy was wonderful. It really is a good life. They ran us every morning, the entire company. And you know, there's something uplifting about it. It makes you realize why wars can be popular. I loved every minute of the Navy. I just loved it. And even though there were things about it that were confining and rigid, I think I found satisfaction in being able to do those things.

I was very good at shining my shoes, and you had to do all your own laundry, your hat and everything, and I stole from Gamba, the boatswain's mate first class who was our company commander in Newport. He was from Newark, New Jersey. He was about 40 years old, and God, was he Navy! He used to soak his white hat in salt water so that after it dried it would sparkle. It would be absolutely virgin white but it would sparkle, because there were little particles of salt all over it.

So here we were, at Pier 92 at 52nd Street, waiting to get on the Queen Mary and ship out to Europe. They lined us up one morning-- we all had to work while we were there waiting-- and we were in our dress blues all the time, and the reason for that was very interesting. If the spies saw you in your dress blues, which was the way you had to travel in the Navy, they would never know when you were going to leave. But if they saw you running around in navy dungarees and chambray shirts all the time, and then one day you are suddenly in dress blues, they go (snap), the ship is leaving.

So we were in our dress blues, and I had soaked my hat in salt water, just like Gamba. And there was a new officer there. And he walked down the line and said, "You, one step forward. You, one step forward. You, one step forward." Well it turned out that we were to go to the Waldorf-Astoria that night, they had Lord and Lady Mountbatten there, and Jim Farley, the Post-master General. And, oh, the biggies that were there. And we had been selected because we were so smartly dressed. (laughs) I always looked like a million bucks. And apparently three other guys did too, because they chose the four of us. And we had a fantastic dinner in the Waldorf. What a night we had.

One of my pals, Bud O'Toole, and I were posted on each side of the entrance, and everyone had entered, the banquet had begun. Lord and Lady Mountbatten had come by, and Cordell Hull, and Oh Jesus, the people, Jimmy Byrnes who was the Governor of South Carolina, and a pal of Roosevelt's. And we saw all these famous people.

And he and I are standing there at attention. All of a sudden there was electricity in the room. I swear to God, the air crackled. And all by himself the Honorable James A. Farley had stepped into the foyer. And he came down that hallway, and he turned to me and he said, "At ease, sailor. My name is Far-ley, what's yours?" He stuck out his hand. And I said, "Dick Mercer, sir." "Where are you from?" "Elizabeth, New Jersey." "That's a good Democratic town." (laughs) Then he turned around to my friend Bud, and he said, "You're Irish." He said, "That's right sir, my name is O'Toole." He said, "Well, mine's Farley, ever heard of me?" And Bud said, "Yes, I have, sir." Bud O'Toole went on to be the youngest judge in the history of the State of Florida. We're still very close.

Mountbatten, too, he exuded charisma. I learned that there are such things as electric personalities. I learned it in the presence of Jimmy Durante when I did a recording session with him. I tell you there are people who are bigger than life, people who have personalities that make the air crackle. I swear I've seen this. I've witnessed it. It's an amazing thing.

"Our lead tank broke through the gate, and we saw bodies burning on wooden railroad ties, and dead bodies were all over the place." --Lloyd Kalugin

After we captured Wiesbaden, we were mounted on tanks and chasing the fleeing Germans. At some point, one of our objectives was to capture the V-2 underground rocket factories that were producing the rockets that were bombing England. I guess we knew pretty well where they were, and it was just a question of finding them. I was on a patrol with the Fourth Armored Division. It was their tanks and we supplied the infantry support, and we mounted the tanks that morning, and we were going off to where we felt the factories were.

We reached the top of the hill and started to smell something burning. We didn't know what it was, and as we went farther up the hill, we were able to look down. We saw smoke, and the odor was overwhelming. We saw a camp and we felt we had to look at this camp. So the tankers took off, with us on them, and, as we approached the camp, we started to see fires.

The lead tank-- I was on the second tank-- broke through the gate and we all dismounted and went in. We saw bodies burning on wooden railroad ties, and dead bodies were all over the place.

One of the barracks was burning, and the lead tank sheared off the front of the building so we could help the people out.

We went into the building and there must have been 75 or 100 people left still alive. Most of them were in very bad physical shape. We were able to put the fire out and we tried to help many of the people as much as we could. I asked one person, who was Jewish, I asked him in Yiddish, "What happened?" He said, "As soon as the Germans heard that the Americans were coming, they killed as many prisoners as they could."

I found out later that this was orders from Hitler, so that there would be no evidence. But they couldn't do it fast enough, so they locked the rest of the people in the barracks and set the barracks on fire.

We got there in time at least to save those people. And it's interesting that this was not our objective. We didn't know it was there. But it turned out that Ohrdruf was a labor camp that supplied workers for the V-2 rocket factories. That's why we knew that the V-2 rocket factories were in that proximity.

Once the support troops started coming up, with the ambulances, the people that could help the inmates, we continued on our mission. We found the V-2 factories, and they were all abandoned. There were no German soldiers or anybody around. Everything was abandoned.

So that's how we captured our first concentration camp. And, you know, it's interesting that Ohrdruf was the first concentration camp liberated by American troops. There were only two Jewish kids in my outfit, so I might have been the first American-Jewish soldier to be involved in the liberation of a concentration camp.

When we saw it, we were all in a state of shock. This big sergeant that I was friendly with started to cry. He said, "How could people be so cruel?" We were all wandering around, saying, "How could this happen?" I was in a state of shock for 50 years. I repressed it.

Then last October, my wife and I went to the Holocaust Museum in Washington and, as soon as we got off on the fourth floor, which is where you start your tour, it was as if I was walking back into Ohrdruf, because there was the picture of Ohrdruf taken the day after I was there, with Generals Eisenhower, Patton and Bradley, and I took that same picture the day before.

That kind of shocked me into reliving these memories, and I felt that I had to start talking about it, because there are people today, some politicians, who are saying that this never happened. Well, I'm here to tell you it did happen and I was there.

"'Eleanor Roosevelt is letting niggers into the Marine Corps,' she wrote. 'Those kikes in Washington give her the power.'" --Herbert Gross

I heard only one anti-Semitic remark the whole time I was in the Marine Corps. And they all knew I was Jewish. There was a major who went to Virginia Military Institute, a real typical southern military guy, and when we landed in Kwajalein after everything was over, we stayed there until they were going to pull us out. He came and lived with the officers of my company.

I had three second lieutenants, and a first lieutenant, and myself. So there was five of us. I was a captain then, and this new man was a major. All of a sudden he comes in and throws his gear down. And he had someone bring him a cot, and he said, "I'm moving in with you guys." And that was fine.

He was living there a week when, one night we were all lying in our bunks, reading, and mail-call came. He got up. He opened his letter, and he read, and he burst out laughing. He said, "Listen to this," he said, "this is from my wife." He read, "It's just horrible what that Eleanor Roosevelt has done to the Marine Corps. Now she's letting in niggers."

Now he's reading us this, and he knew I was Jewish, and he went on: "The only reason she's able to do that is because those kikes in Washington give her the power." And he laughed. He said, "What do you think of that?"

209

Now he was a major, and the Marine Corps was different, I guess, from the Army. No captain in the Marine Corps ever said anything untoward to a major. These other guys all looked up. They were all my friends. They were officers with me for years. They all looked up. And he said, "What do you think of that?"

I said, "I would expect that from a fucking whore." He looked up and he said to me, "What did you say?" I said, "I said your wife is a fucking, dumb, bigoted whore." And he said to me, "If we weren't in the service, I'd kick the shit out of you." And I said to him, "Why don't we just forget it? We won't report each other. Let's go outside." And he said, "We're going outside, but we're going to the colonel."

Now we had a colonel with an Italian name, Negri, and we went to him. And the major said, "I want to report this man for showing disrespect and calling my wife, whom he doesn't even know, a 'fucking whore.'" The colonel said, "Why did you do that?" And I told him the story. And he said, "Major, step outside." And the major turned around and stepped outside.

And the colonel said to me, "You shouldn't have done that in front of your officers, but I know just where you are coming from." He said, "I've been called a 'fucking wop.' I know just where you are coming from." He said, "What would you like to do?" I said, "I like my outfit. Could you transfer him?"

And he said, "I couldn't do that. Would you like a transfer?" I said, "Yes." And I got transferred. But that was the only experience I ever had with that kind of thing.

"We were monitoring American guerrillas. Once in a while one of them would be captured, and then he'd go off the air." --Richard Kleiner

I went into specialized training in the Signal Corps, and it turned out to be interesting. That was my Army career. I turned out to have an aptitude for the Morse code, which I never knew I had. They give you a whole series of tests. There was a series of dots and dashes, and you had to figure out if they were the same or different or something like that. And I had this aptitude for it.

So they took me and about four or five other guys who were good at this thing, and they put us in special training in Warrenton, Virginia. They trained us in Japanese Morse code, which is entirely different from international Morse code. International Morse code has only the 26 characters for letters of the alphabet and Japanese Morse code has 30 characters: the 26 plus a few others.

It's very difficult, because they have a character called dit-dit which is "i" in international Morse code, but in Japanese it's called a "nigori." That changes the sound of the previous character. So in other words if you've got a "ka" with the "i" after it, and dit-dit after it, it becomes "ga, ka." Dit-dit becomes "ga." So it's really quite difficult to copy Japanese Morse code. Toward the end, I think there were only about 10 or 12 of us in that specialty.

We learned just enough Japanese to understand a few words of procedure. When they would come on and say something to indicate that they were going to change frequencies to such and such a frequency, or if they were going to go off the air until such and such a time, you know, procedural stuff, that's all. That's the only Japanese we learned.

The outfit that I was assigned to was called the Second Signal Service Battalion, which was in charge of radio intercept, Japanese radio intercept. It had stations all over the world. They had stations in Alaska. They had stations in the Philippines, mostly in the Pacific. But I think they had a station in Europe too, somewhere. But I was originally sent to central California and then eventually to Hawaii.

I was in Petaluma which is just a little north of San Francisco. It's a lovely town. Now it's quite a big city, but it was a very small town then. At first I lived on base. Then I got married to a girl from NJC. We were married in 1944. I got permission to live off the base in a nice little house, on a nice little street. She had a job, and I had work. We had good friends who were in the same situation as us.

It wasn't nine to five. We switched. Every week we had a different shift. We had eight in the morning to four in the afternoon one week. The next week four in the afternoon until midnight. And the next week midnight until four AM.

Later, we went to Hawaii, but we could hear the Japanese stations better in California than we could in Hawaii, because of the way radio waves bounce. They sort of skipped over Hawaii, but they hit right in California.

We had a number of very definite schedules that we would monitor-- certain stations we would listen to. At one point for about six or seven months, I was monitoring American guerrillas in the Philippines, which was quite interesting because they would be very hard to find, and they'd be switching around all the time, because they would be chased by the Japanese. Every once in a while one of them would get captured, and then he'd go off the air.

But mostly it was Japanese stations. Some of us would monitor the commercial stations and some the small army stations. We'd take turns. And then we'd sit at the typewriter and copy the messages. Then we'd send them off to our headquarters in Warrenton, Virginia. That's the headquarters of the Second Signal Service Battalion, where they would decode them.

I really got to know those guerrillas. I don't know if you know this, but everybody has what's called a "fist." It's like handwriting. Everybody who has a signal has his own little quirks, so that you can recognize them. Joe's dashes are a little longer than normal. So you get to know these people. Sometimes they'd send personal messages and sometimes they'd make jokes.

They were American guerrillas who had been planted there, or had been trapped there and escaped from Bataan or wherever and gone out to where the natives were pro-American and helped them. But they had to keep moving all the time or they could be traced.

The Japanese messages were always in codes, groups of letters or groups of numbers. We had no idea what they actually meant. But we did get a commendation because one of us intercepted a message that led to the victory at Wake Island, so we got a special commendation for that that permitted us to wear a wreath on our uniform.

"We walked into the Georges Cinq Hotel. Shooting is going on a block away, and here's everybody sipping cocktails. It was weird." --Irving E. Pape

So I drove the whole way into Paris. We got into Paris at six o'clock in the morning. We went across the Alexander Bridge and we took a turn and there was some small arms fire, but it wasn't in our immediate area. We were assigned to live in a beautiful mansion in the Sixteenth Arrondissement, which was the swankiest spot in Paris. The house was owned by Henry Hodges, who was J.P. Morgan's partner in France.

We got in there, and the high-ranking German Gestapo officers had used this for their headquarters, and the place was immaculate. They had gold dishes. And all we had to eat was K-rations. There was no hot water. There were no utilities, but the electricity finally came on.

One of the fellows in our outfit was a German refugee who spoke French as well as German and English. And he was a student up at Syracuse. He held a Maxwell Fellowship in political science so we had a lot to talk about. He said, "Let's go. We'll go see what's going on."

So we went out and we walked into the Georges Cinq Hotel, sat down, took off our helmets and put our weapons on the table. There were civilians in there drinking. Shooting was taking place a block away and here's everybody sipping cocktails, two o'clock in the afternoon, and enjoying themselves. It was weird.

The bartender came over. They couldn't tell us from the

213

French soldiers because they wore brown uniforms just like us. They thought we were French. I remember ordering in English a Manhattan and he said, "I'll make it for you," because he spoke English also.

At a table near us was a young man with four very pretty girls, and I was smoking a Camel cigarette. And he came over to me and said, "You know, I haven't smelled a cigarette that good since 1939." We didn't realize at that time that a pack of American cigarettes on the black market was worth the equivalent of $400. So I gave him a cigarette and cigarettes for the four ladies. It turned out that this guy was a movie producer who was friendly with a relative of DeGaulle's or something, so we were traveling in fast company now and we got invited to dinner.

We puffed on the cigarettes and had a drink and then Fred says, "Let's go, we'll see what's going on." So we walked over to the Rue de Rivoli, where the shooting was taking place. And the German commandant of Paris was in the Hotel Maurice and we're standing behind a big tree because there's all kinds of small arms fire, machine guns and stuff going off, every now and then a bang of a grenade.

And here comes a Frenchman down the middle of the street walking with a little dog on a leash. And he sees the two of us standing behind a tree and he's hollering out, "Tirez! . . .tirez!" in other words, shoot. Well, we couldn't see anyone, who are we gonna shoot? We didn't see a German the whole time. The firing was coming from inside the buildings and we weren't gonna shoot because we probably would've killed civilians.

We were there for two weeks, and I want to tell you it was a single man's paradise. We had a welcome from the French people that was the most incredible thing. The minute they heard you were an American they wanted to hug you and kiss you. They couldn't do enough for you; it was great.

From there we got shipped to Longwy, France, which was a mining town. We had our headquarters in a building that was the headquarters of the mining industry in France, a beautiful

214

marbled building with huge columns in the front. We were there for like five or six months and it was very quiet until the German breakthrough.

When the Germans broke through, the first news we got was from the French. They needed passes to get out of our area because now we were in a combat zone. We were close to the forward lines, but until then it had not been considered the combat zone.

One day I was the charge of quarters, and you had to walk up our entrance, then down a long corridor. At the end of the corridor I had a desk, and two of us had been filling out passes for the officers to sign so people could leave the area. They were panicking. The Germans are coming. It's just like 1939 again.

On this day nobody came in. So my folks had sent me some comic books, and I was reading them. (laughs) I'm sitting at the desk with my feet up, my helmet and my rifle are on the desk, and it was quiet.

I hear footsteps coming down the hall and I look up and Oh, my God, it's Patton. Here he comes, all by himself, General Patton. I leaped to my feet, stuffed the comic book in the desk. (laughs) And he says, "We're gonna need a place where we have absolute privacy for a meeting. What have you got?" I said, "I'll take care of it sir. Wait here a minute."

We had an anteroom to a glassed-in office, which was perfect for him. Our enlisted men and the French officer were in the anteroom. So I walked in and I said, "All right guys, grab your gear and clear out because I need this for a meeting with General Patton." So everybody starts laughing.

All of a sudden, the grins turn to horror because Patton is standing right behind me glaring at these guys. And in a matter of five seconds the whole place emptied out. So he went in there and I realized this was the Third Army coming up to blunt the Bulge.

I went back to the desk, and it didn't take maybe five or six minutes, Eisenhower comes in with General Bradley. So I opened up the door for them and they went in with Patton. And, subsequently, a whole load of brigadier and major generals came in, division commanders. And they were there for about 15 minutes and then they left.

Patton said to me, "How do we get to Arlon?" And I told him, "Just go right back up the hill like you came from, but take a left and that'll take you right into Arlon. It's 16 kilometers from here." I said, "If you'd like, I'll escort you up the hill with the jeep." "No," he said. "it won't be necessary."

I looked out the window then, and there was this whole army bumper to bumper. If the Germans had any kind of air force up that day they could have had a score because it broke every rule in the book about concentrating everything. It was like one huge pile loaded with tanks. (laughs) And there were no civilians around. The civilians were petrified, so most of 'em had left.

So he went up there and he did the job.

"We're in a restaurant, and there's a Luftwaffe pilot. 'What's the matter?' I asked. 'Don't you have an airport to go home to?'" --Morton Sobin

I trained in Romulus, Michigan, which was a Ferrying Command base. The Ferrying Command was a section of the Air Transport Command that got the orders to move certain planes from here to there, and it depended on where the initial plane to be picked up was, who got the assignment, whether it was Baltimore, or Detroit, or Great Falls.

From Romulus, Michigan, let's see, I got there in February, '43, and I think I was there, on and off, probably about a year. Then I was transferred to Great Falls, Montana, where we brought planes up to our friends, the Russians, up in Fairbanks, Alaska. From there they flew them to Siberia and put them on the Trans-Siberian Railroad, which they ran for about 5,000 miles. They cut the trees all along the right-of-way so they wouldn't have to remove the wings. They got four or five different kinds of aircraft from us.

And then I was transferred to Florida, to Homestead. We knew pretty much what we were being prepared for was something in Europe, or Africa. It was terrific training, four-engine. You took off in that darn plane from Homestead in daylight, with a curtain around you, so you got to take off by instruments and come in for a landing, until the last few seconds, with the curtain around you.

We were told in advance, "It's B-24 advanced instrument schooling down there, you're gonna get it, and you're gonna be a co-pilot because you don't have enough time yet to be a first pilot." You needed 1,200 hours and I didn't have that much time. So, it was as simple as that, and while we were down there, we went to ground school, went to some classes and did a lot of flying and it was nice, it was interesting.

Then we were ferrying bombers, '17s, and '24s, to Scotland. I took planes to California, to Canada, to South America, flew across to Africa, went into Egypt once. I did quite a bit of traveling. I was lucky, compliments of Uncle Sam, except there were a couple of bum spots. I remember having to land in the Hebrides, the islands off northwest of Scotland. It's still wild, they have sheep grazing, and we landed there once and we were given bunk beds in a Nissan hut, and it was raining on me and my bed was all wet. I wasn't very happy there. I asked, "Where is the men's room?" They said, "You see that field out there?" We had a few spots like that.

The most fun place to ferry a plane to was Newark, New Jersey. I did ferry quite a few-- small planes that were going aboard a ship. I'd fly over the house, land in Newark, go out on a date that night, or see the folks, then head back.

From Homestead, several of us were shipped to the Ferrying Command base near Baltimore, and we were assigned two crews of five people each to a plane to take over to Scotland. We went there and then we were assigned to a place in Cornwall, and our job from there was in uniform and in marked planes. We flew quite a few times down to Casablanca, around France and Spain, through the Bay of Biscay, and then some of us, not everybody, were called into London to a briefing room.

A major stood up and said, "You have a new job as of now," and he explained. He's gonna give us civilian clothes and passports and we're gonna go into Norway, into Sweden, even as far as Poland, and he went through the whole business. We're "carpetbaggers," and we fly black planes. "Any questions?"

I raised my hand. The major said, "Yeah, Lieutenant?" "What happens if we go down?" Meaning in civilian clothes and everything, "Any back up?" He says, "Go down, why the fuck do you want to go down?" and walks out.

So then, very shortly after that, we were standing in Selfridges Department Store in London, right out in the open, the guy is measuring me for civilian clothes. I said, "Don't you think we ought to go in another room?" "Oh, nobody here would give you away."

So on one of the very first trips we took to Sweden, we usually took off about 5, 5:15 in the afternoon, but that was double British war time, like daylight savings time doubled, and as soon as we got up, we'd turn the radio on to a station from Germany, because Lord Haw Haw would come on with Glenn Miller's music, trying to make us homesick, and he mentioned the names of all of us who were on that flight. He said, "We know what you're doing." They had pictures of us in the gestapo headquarters in Norway. One of our guys had been in Oslo and he said, "They had pictures of all you guys."

Now, after that, it was a long haul to Stockholm. We go out of East Anglia, up through the North Sea to the top of Norway, across Norway, and then down into Stockholm. It was 10 hours plus, sometimes as much as 12, and the same thing going back, so one mission could be 24 hours plus.

As soon as we landed, we went to end of the runway, the Swedes would look the other way, and a bunch of young Norwegians with a big truck would empty us out and then drive away. If we had dropped the supplies over Norway, the Germans might get more than the Norwegians.

Inside our C-87s, which were converted B-24s, there were racks and racks of bags, let's say four to five feet high and about two feet square and in them were guns, ammunition, grenades, in other words, all war supplies for the Norwegian underground. It was in white sacks and the Swedes called it Norwegian diplomatic mail so they would not get in too much trouble with the Germans, because they were neutral.

We'd land there two, three o'clock in the morning. By the time we cleared customs and got a ride to our hotel, wherever we were staying, and got to bed, maybe it's five o'clock in the morning. And we'd make the return trip in one day, or up to five days, depending on what had to go back with those planes. For example, we were trying to outbuy the Germans for ball bearings, which were very important.

Staying in this hotel would be Swedes, Germans, just about everybody. We went pretty regularly for lunch to a place called the Rainbow Restaurant. It was big and clean and bright, had good food, and in the beginning of December, I think it was in 1944, when our fleet out in the Pacific had really racked up the Japanese fleet for about the last time, there were headlines in the papers. So we took the newspapers, wrapped them around a trench knife and had the waitress bring it over to a Japanese group who were sitting there. Crazy kids, I was 23 at that time, something like that. The Japanese stood up and walked out.

We got to speak to some of the German Luftwaffe pilots who were hanging out there. One time at a party, we were having a drink and one of the German pilots was there, and I said, "I noticed you're not here very often anymore." I said, "What happened, you don't have an airport to go back to?"

He just shrugged his shoulders. He took it good-heartedly, you know, we were so-called professionals at what we were doing and we all knew what was going on. Hitler was talking about Festung Norway, Fortress Norway. He was beginning to send his fighter pilots and planes up there. He figured they'd make a last stand up there, and make some sort of peace.

We took our own route across Norway, up a fjord because the mountains were about 13,000 feet, and we were near a German air command in Norway with the planes and night fighters and everything else, and again, as I said, we were 23 years old and brash. We felt we should do something about their brazenness that they kept their lights on at night.

So we took some empty whiskey bottles and in the floor of our flight deck was a hole through which you could drop flares, or what they call navigational bombs that, when they hit the water, they'd smoke. So we dropped our whisky bottle bombs, and all of a sudden the lights went out, and we laughed and laughed. That gave us great pleasure.

We got shot up once over the North Sea. Remember, we had no guns on us or on the plane, we were flying into neutral countries. The Germans had Intruder planes, night fighters, and they'd follow you, and we got shot up pretty good. There were five of us in the crew-- three were dead, one was dying and me. I told you, I'm a lucky guy. I had one gear that would come down, one that wouldn't, and one of my engines was out, so I landed on the one gear and kept it that way as long as possible, until we had no speed left at all and then we fell down, and I was fine. *(The interviewer noted at this point that "Mr. Sobin is shaking." He obviously could speak no more.)*

"We went by, did 'Eyes left,' and there's De Gaulle. I couldn't believe this. One minute I'm in a war, now I'm in a parade in Paris." --Vincent J. Gorman

We had nothing at all to do with the liberation of Paris, I gotta make that clear. But we did march. We were on our way toward Rouen, and we got this order to move. We were loaded onto two-and-a-half ton trucks, and we rode toward Paris. And then, we were let off in the Bois De Boulogne, a beautiful park.

220

It was after midnight, and they said, "No digging in." You aren't allowed to do any digging. We had to find our equipment truck, which had our barracks bags, and you'd have a uniform in there. We had to put on an OD uniform, and it was hot.

And then we had to shave, too. We were given so much water in your steel helmet, and you poured it from the five-gallon water can. And you had to find yourself a razor, and you had to shave in the dark. (laughter) So about two o'clock in the morning, you are trying to clean up as well as you could.

And, during the night, I can remember, it started to rain. Everybody started to get under trucks, to stay dry, which we did well enough. And that's the first time we knew we were going through Paris.

They wanted us to dress for this. And then the guns were hooked up, the infantry guys were in formation, and we came out of that park, we weren't trained for a thing like that, but you'd swear we had been. That thing was precision. Amazing. I was on a weapons carrier, and we were in formation, four across, and the guns were lined up.

We went in a sort of semi-circle. To the left was the Arc de Triomphe, and there was this big platform. And, General Cota was up there, and De Gaulle, and the other French officers, a lot of high officers. And then, we had to do an "eyes left." Beautiful parade. Then we went down the Champs-Elysees.

Oh, this was great. This is Paris. I'm in a parade. I couldn't believe this. Jesus! I have been to war one minute, and now I am in a parade, for God's sake, in Paris, which I never saw before in my life. But that parade was something. The French people were going wild. There were thousands on all sides.

The parade would move and it would stop. It would move, like parades do, and stop. And, people were throwing apples. I don't know whether they are throwing at us, or throwing to us. (laughter) At any rate, they had champagne. They had cider and all kinds of wine. And guys were drinking, and women were hugging the guys, and then you had to get back on your vehicle,

221

and get going. And, some of the drivers got drunk. They couldn't even drive. I understand that some guys went AWOL. I don't know this personally, but I heard they went AWOL there. They didn't catch up with their outfits 'til maybe a week or so later. But nothing was done to them. And that was a wild party, a wild parade.

"I was ordered to proceed to Tsingtao, alone and unarmed, and take over the Japanese naval base with its 20,000 men." --Vincent Kramer

My mission was to train Chinese irregulars to harass the Japanese troops. I had a supply officer, a pharmacist's mate and a couple of gunner's mates, maybe 10 of us altogether. That was our whole unit. The enemy was in the Yellow River bend area. I knew where that was, and my job was to train the Chinese and then take them out there to fight the enemy.

So what I did, I went out to where the fighting was and encouraged them to hit the enemy. In guerrilla warfare you entice the enemy, you hit them, and then you withdraw. It's that type of warfare. I thought what we did was quite successful.

I was on this mission for about nine months, in 1944 and '45. When V-J Day came, I was up there with the guerrillas, and I received a one-time message. A one-time message is something only two people can read-- the man that sent it and the man that receives it. It's a coded book you carry in your pocket and you use it to encrypt and decrypt messages.

I was informed that the Japanese were about to surrender. I received this message about the 10th of August. I guess the old man must have been informed about the atom bombs or maybe they'd already gone off and I didn't know it.

I spoke pretty good Chinese by now, and the old man knew it. I was ordered to leave the troops and proceed to Tsingtao in Shantung Peninsula, alone, unarmed, and take over the Japanese naval base with its 20,000 men until the Navy came in from the

Pacific Fleet. Now I was 27, a Marine major, I'm in a Chinese uniform, with a Marine hat-- I always wore that-- and I looked at this message. I knew where Tsingtao was, but I thought, "How in the hell am I going to get there?"

I didn't dare tell the Chinese general where I was going. I just asked him, "How would you get to Tsingtao, from here?" "Urr." You always get that "Urr." Oh, it's so annoying. I said, "How many miles, maybe, or kilometers?" I think he said, from where we were, about 600. So I thought that's 350-some miles. Wondering, how I'm going to get there, you know, it's a long walk. And I had to go through Communist territory.

But I remembered there was an airfield in the town of Xi'an, which is the capital of Shaanxi, and if I could get the boys to drop me there, at that airfield, there'd be a train.

So I went back to the city of Xi'an, which was easy for me to do because that was all through friendly territory, and I went to the airfield and the war had just ended. I asked the Air Corps there if they would just put wheels down and drop me at this Japanese airfield in Xi'an. The commanding officer said, "We'll drop you there, but my men won't stop. My plane will go in wheels down, they'll swing around and they will take right off, and you jump out of the airplane." I said, "Fair enough."

So they dropped me on this Japanese airfield, and I was picked up by the Chinese immediately. The Chinese saw the American emblem, and the peasants around there came over, and then I was chit-chatting and joking with them, and I was the first American they had seen.

Then I went into the city of Xi'an and there was a Japanese lieutenant in the railroad station. By this time, I had 500,000 Chinese with me. They're cheering me on, and you've seen the pictures of those crowds, how they followed you everywhere. And I asked the lieutenant if he would get a train for me to go to Tsingtao, and he feigned he didn't understand me. And I kind of figured he might understand some of it. I saw his sword there, the Samurai sword, so I pick that damn thing up, and indi-

223

cate that I was going to break it, you know, and desecrate it.

Then he said, "I speak a little English." I said, "Good." So I told him all I wanted was a train, with one engine and one car, and that they had to let this train go through and not to dick with it, that I was going to be on it, and I don't want to die now. So, by God, they got a train, and I got on the train and I arrived in Tsingtao and after that it was a piece of cake.

I was the only American there, and I had to take the surrender of this whole naval base. When I got off the train, this ill-informed Japanese soldier had a bayonet on his rifle, and I told you I was ordered to go in unarmed, and I was unarmed. When he saw the Marine emblem, because I had the Marine hat on, he put his bayonet down, and I thought, "Well, here it is!"

I hit him on the side of the head with my cameras, and he went sprawling. And the Chinese were cheering. You know, wherever you go in China there's a million of them. So I took his rifle and removed the bolt, took his ammunition out, gave him his rifle back, shook my finger at him, and he had lost so much face he didn't know what to do.

I could see a big hotel, the Edgewater Hotel, and I had a rickshaw take me there. I went in and it was fully occupied by the Japanese. When I walked in, they had a man who had been Consul in the United States, spoke fluent English. I told him I was taking over the hotel, and that I wanted to see the Chief of Staff of the Japanese Navy immediately, and that he should go get him. And within five minutes the guy was there. And then everything went as smooth as silk after that.

I am now fully in charge of all these Japs, and I put them on alert that they had to keep the Communists out of town. I had ordered all roads to be blocked, coming into Tsingtao and beyond the airfield, too. The Communists were trying to take over but they weren't prepared yet to quite move in.

I was a pilot, you know, and I began taxiing one of their twin-engine Betty bombers around to get the feel of it. I wanted to get out of there and get to Shanghai, because that's where the old man would be by now. Of course, no Japanese planes were supposed to be in the air, and I might get shot down. But I began taxiing this thing around, and Okabi, the Japanese Chief of Staff, was getting more and more nervous because they had been forced to remove all compasses and radios from their aircraft under the terms of surrender.

So I said, "Hell, you don't always need all that equipment. As long as you know which way the wind is blowing, you can head where you are going." And so, finally I told him that I would like to take that airplane up and around, but I wanted a pilot with me. So we did, we flew it around a couple of times.

I realized that I would have difficulty, not so much taking the aircraft off, but landing it, because, boy, it went down very, very abruptly. I told him I wanted to go to Shanghai.

Okabi insisted on going with me, so we took off one morning and we've got this Japanese pilot, and I sat in the copilot's seat. There was pretty full cloud cover, and American planes were flying over all the time now, but we would fly under the cloud cover where they wouldn't see us.

We took off without a compass or a radio and stayed pretty close to the water, and went almost into Nanking. And then turned to the east and took this Japanese Betty into one of the airfields in Shanghai, which had already been taken over by the US Air Corps.

And, Oh, my God, the red lights began going on all over the place, and they had no communication with us, and I said, "Put her down the runway. What the hell, we've got to go in." So the Jap landed it, and I told him, "Pull off that runway and get behind the hangar over there."

By that time the MPs, the air police, grabbed me. I started out of the nose of the bomber and, boy, they grabbed my feet and pulled me down, and they were surprised to see an American. "Where the hell did you come from?" "Well," I said, "I had orders to get here." And I said, "Don't bother my crew." "All right." So they took me back and got me all the way to Shanghai. I saw the old man. I thought he'd die laughing when I told him I landed a Japanese Betty there.

And then he said, "You're the only American up there. The Navy will come in eventually." But I said, "I had no way to communicate with you." He said, "I know, I know." He said, "I need you back there, you've got to get back immediately." I said, "How?" He said, "You got here, you get back." I said, "All right," because he had no way of getting me there.

So we managed to refuel that Japanese plane and take off and go back and landed there, and then I waited there. And eventually the task force came in with their cruisers.

You must be very careful in a situation like I was in, where I was alone and couldn't get any help. I had to determine ahead of time how I was going to do it. I got this consul who spoke fluent English. And I said that I wanted him present at all times when I was dealing with the Japanese Navy, and I asked to see the Chief of Staff of the Navy because I didn't want the Admiral, the commander, to lose too much face.

Okabi, the Chief of Staff, had had several tours of duty in the United States, and he was very fluent in English, so I worked all my orders through him. You don't take command of foreign troops yourself; you tell him that he must see that certain things are done. I told him, "I want a chart of all the mines in the area, and I want a chart of the latest channels."

When our Navy first came in, they laid off shore, and I signaled to them as best I could. They didn't want to come in sweeping if they didn't have to, so they sent a boat in. And I went out with all the charts to this Navy captain and showed them to him, and then they came in within a day or so and pulled right into the harbor.

And then I was ordered back to Shanghai. It must have been about the 10th or 15th of September, and the old man sent a big PBM to pick me up, one of those big black cats, and it landed in the harbor and picked me up, and I bid farewell to Tsingtao and headed for Shanghai.

THE CHAOS OF COMBAT

Killing was not taught in our schools, and no one really wanted to do it, but killing is what war is all about. "The Army trained us to kill," some have observed, but that didn't always make it easier to accept. Ed Kolodziej, after gunning down 30 German soldiers during his first night in combat, visited his chaplain for assurance that he wasn't a murderer; and George Boggs, who fired his pistol first when he and a Japanese soldier jumped into a shell hole at the same time on New Guinea, was eager to wipe off the bloodstains.

The sheer noise and confusion of battle was often overwhelming, and unseen dangers lurked everywhere, in the form of artillery shell bursts, snipers, machine gun fire, torpedoes, mines and booby traps. The skills learned through training might be ruthlessly overruled by bad luck-- simply being in the wrong place at the wrong time.

Lives were snuffed out quickly. In France, Maurice Meyers recalls the sadness of not knowing a man before he was gone. "It was tough," he says, "to see people get killed that quickly. You wouldn't even get to know them by name and they'd be dead. Someone would say, 'Remember that kid who came in last night from Kentucky or somewhere? Well, he was killed.' "

Those who survived can recount many times when life hung

227

in the balance. Over the North Sea, tail gunner Forrest Clark, his plane "full of spent shells and blood," is ordered to bail out. He looks down at the frigid white-capped waters and hesitates. On Okinawa, Roland Winter's lieutenant orders him to set up a machine gun in a position that is exposed to direct Japanese fire. Should he disobey the order? Bomber pilot Bob King is parachuting from his burning B-24 over Austria when he sees an ME 109 heading directly for him. Franklyn Johnson, shot in the chest by a sniper on D-Day, tells his second-in-command, "Take the men back, Gardner. I'm dying." Andrew White is swimming away from his sinking ship in the English Channel in the dark when he sees his last chance for rescue-- a tugboat-- barreling past him. Morton Sobin, on a secret mission to neutral Sweden, is attacked by German night fighters, and with three of his five-man crew dead and one dying, tries to nurse his crippled plane back to base. All of these men lived to come home and tell their stories.

Bill MacKenzie, on Okinawa, found that action was sometimes bred by hopelessness. "You did what you had to do," he notes. "You might as well go forward as go back because you're not going to make it out of there anyway." Frank Kneller, in surrounded Bastogne, almost didn't make it. He was one of two men left alive out of a 65-man platoon when Patton's tanks rolled in to rescue them.

In France, Nathan Shoehalter captured the effects of combat succinctly: "The men we were relieving trooped wordlessly past, haggard, slumped, with glazed expressions. Our silence was the silence of fear."

Even so, the boys not only survived, they conquered. "It amazes me," says Maurice Meyers, "that our Army was made up of people like me, who were far from being military types, but we were actually better soldiers than the highly-trained soldiers we fought. It was American traits-- independence and ingenuity. We'd attack at night, and the Germans actually said to us, "Don't you people ever sleep?"

" 'How many did you kill,' asked General Patton. 'About 30.' 'That's that many of the bastards that'll never reproduce,' he said."   --Edwin Kolodziej

On my first night in combat, I was a combat scout. I had volunteered for the 379th Regimental Combat Scouts. They were a unit that did behind-the-lines patrol work, acting as an armed force for the intelligence and reconnaissance platoon.

The I&R had said that the Germans were across the Moselle. We were overlooking the river, on this bluff. On the other bluff, across the river, were the Germans. The distance is maybe a half mile. It was like, if you're driving along Old Bridge Turnpike in South River, you're looking down and you see Sayreville. There was a little settlement there in a place called Vezon.

The Germans had an outpost there, and our assignment was to go through our lines to that outpost, capture a German, and bring him back. So we put our black-face on. I think there were about 15 of us. We had about three guys in the point. Captain Lewis had me with the machine gun so we had high-power fire available. And when we went into no-man's-land, we had a getaway man. There was always someone who had to get back with information on what happened. Then, we would sort of leapfrog. The point would go out, then I'd move up and establish a position. Then they'd move again, and I'd move.

In the course of this, we got into town. This village square was triangular. We were set up in the right-hand corner of the triangle, and our point men were down at the point of the triangle when all of a sudden two German machine guns opened fire on them. Then a big green flare went off so everything was illuminated. When that happened, we froze. If you didn't move and were quiet they might not be able to see you in that light.

That was the first hint that something was wrong. Somebody knew we were there. They must have heard us. So that flare goes off, and Grondahl and I have our machine gun on a tripod, and then music starts playing over a loudspeaker, American music. An American woman's voice says, "Men of the 95th, we know you are here. Why don't you come over and join us? We have nice warm beds, and there are very beautiful women here, and if you come with us that will solve all your problems."

You know, everything was a secret in the Army. I didn't know who the hell knew where we were. We go through our lines, we're in no man's land, in the German position, and all of a sudden, this voice is going off, telling us they know we're here. You think we ought to be scared? Try it.

At this point, the music and the talking stop, and I'm laying here, and Grondahl's laying here, and I see a flashlight go on and off, right over there. When I looked, I saw that there were a squad of Germans and the guy in the front, with the flashlight, was looking at his watch. He didn't know we were here. So I unswiveled the machine gun, shot up the whole group and wiped them all out. One of them got as far as here (*indicating a half dozen feet or so*) and was laying there, crying for his mother.

While I was doing that, our getaway men left to go back. On their way back, they found a bunch of Germans under a tree getting orders and they threw hand grenades into them. In the meantime, I'm in a fire fight with the two German machine guns.

The Germans used green tracers; we used red tracers. When I took over this job, one of the things I did, the standard belt of ammunition comes with a tracer every five, I made mine every

20, because I felt that when you fired the weapon at night, with the tracers, if you had them every five, it makes a straight line to your gun, where the bullet's going. Our guns had a lower cyclic rate of fire than the German guns did. Theirs fired much faster. These guys were shooting at me, but because of the higher speed, there was a straight green line over to where they were. When I fired back at them, there was no straight red line, just red dots that showed up once in a while. So I was engaged in a firefight with these two.

Meanwhile, the three point men were trapped in front of those guns. One of them was killed, and the other two laid there, making believe they were dead. What I did, since I'm not sure what's going on, or where those guns were-- there were buildings along either side of this square--I grabbed the machine gun and just ran to every doorway and window all the way down the line and shot them all up. You don't need a sharpshooter's medal to do this, because you just blast them all. Later I was told by one of the point men that I knocked out both of those machine guns in doing that.

So I took care of one German squad, the getaway men took care of the other one under the tree, and I took care of the two machine guns. Then we were given orders to disengage, so we went back. We were living in a barn, and I went up in the loft and went to sleep.

I was there sleeping when somebody picked me straight up into the air. It was a very big guy called Jumbo Curran, who played football for Cornell. He was one of those two point men out there making believe they were dead, and after we left, when they felt it was safe, they crawled out of there. He comes in, and he's a big guy, and he picks me up and hugs me and kisses me, and says I saved his life.

I went back to sleep, and the next thing you know I got awakened again and there are two huge MPs standing there. They looked like they were about 15 feet tall. One of them lifted me up, and they said, "Get up, soldier. They want you downstairs."

231

So I went down the ladder to the other part of the barn. There's the general, and the brigadier general from Division, newspaper reporters from the Chicago paper and the INS and other reporters. They wanted to interview me about what had happened. That was a press conference, my first press conference, or whatever the hell it was, okay? And that was my first night in combat.

The next morning, the Germans put up a white flag, and our people told us they took out 30 dead bodies from there. And that's how I got the Bronze Star, my first night in combat. I didn't know anything about medals; I didn't even know we had medals. I was an 18-year-old kid picked out of a town called Sayreville and put down somewhere else.

After that, I went to see the chaplain. I said to the chaplain I was deeply concerned because I knew I had killed a group of men and it never dawned on me that I would do that. And since I'm Catholic, that I was unhappy with the fact that I had killed these men, and I wanted to know whether I'd committed a sin in the eyes of my Church or not. And he said, "No." In effect, what he said to me was I should continue to do what I do because I had God's blessing for what I was doing. Now, as a mature adult of 76, I might question that a little bit, but I accepted it at the time.

The next day I walked over to my old outfit, B Company, who were in a static position. They told me they'd watched the fire fight the night before. You know, when you get into an outfit like the Scouts, you sort of throw the book away. I was wearing a polkadot bandanna, and I'd let my hair grow long in what was Tarzan style in those days, and I was wearing a rabbit-skin vest that I'd found somewhere, and I was walking along a ridge on my way back when all of a sudden I see a guy walking toward me. He gets closer. I think, "Jesus, he's got a silver-handled pistol."

I get a little closer, and the voice says, "Don't salute, soldier." It was General Patton, out there on the battlefield. So I said, "Excuse me, sir, but you shouldn't be here." He says,

"Where'd you get that outfit?" I said, "Well, you know." He said, "What's your name, soldier?" I said "Kolodziej." He says, "Oh, you're one of the guys I'm here to decorate today." He says, "Why are you dressed like that?" I answer, "Because of the job I do, I got a right." He says, "You're right." So he said, "We both should get out of here, shouldn't we?" I said, "Yeah, you don't belong here. You're the general of all the armies."

So then later, we all line up, he drives up in the jeep, and he goes down the line, handing out the medals and shaking hands with everyone, and he comes to me and he says, "Oh, here you are. Where's your vest?" I said, "Oh, over there." He says, "Tell me, how many of them did you kill?" I said, "They tell me maybe 30." He says, "That's that many of the bastards that'll never reproduce," shakes hands with me and off he goes.

I got my silver star at Metz. Where we were located, a major stumbling block to the advance of the US Army was Fortress Metz. The fortress wasn't what you might expect, the childhood dream of a fort with walls around it. This was a series of in-ground concrete vaults. They had heavy cannon that were in units that sunk into the ground and then came out of the ground, and fired at you, and disappeared again.

General Patton's theory of attacking was called "walking fire." He would line up a company, battalion, a regiment, a division, in line and everybody would start walking at once and everybody would start firing at once-- firing at random. The enemy had too many targets-- you sort of overwhelmed them. And that type of attack was used in a frontal assault on the city of Metz. In doing that, they ran into this fort where they were completely stopped.

This strong point, I learned later, was a concrete bunker buried in the ground. It must have been at least 75 feet long and four feet thick. The Germans in the fort wouldn't give up, even though they were being fired on and they were decimated from the artillery fire that was coming in, six shells every 30 minutes.

So the whole assault was stopped right at that point.

Because our people were in such difficult shape, we were given the assignment of carrying our own weapons plus additional ammunition, food, and medical supplies up to them since they were stopped there.

We went out at night as usual. The fort is built into the ground and they had built a big trench all the way around it. They also had a small bunker, to the side of it, to use as an outpost. Most of the troops in that bunker were shell-shocked by now and crying and stuff like that. When we got there, it was raining.

Grondahl and I were told to set up at one end of the trench. We took the machine gun and set it on what we thought was a hump of ground, and we leaned against something that we thought was a pile of dirt. It turned out when it got to be daylight these were bodies of people that had been killed, that were covered by raincoats, that we were laying on. In the trench was all the water from the rain, the blood from the guys that had been shot up, and we were there.

Meanwhile, every 30 minutes, six more shells came pounding in and they were caving in the sides of the trench on you while you're laying there. We were there through the whole next day, and when the next morning came, Grondahl and I thought it over and we said we'd had enough of this shit, we're not going to have anymore. And Grondahl said, "You know what, when they're in there in that concrete thing they don't get much air, so they must open their little portholes at night to get air." And I said, "If the sun is in back of us when the sun comes up, if we could take this machine gun and move it up another 20 feet and if we could catch them with their portholes open, we could fire through those portholes."

And that's exactly what we did. We did it because, you know, if you didn't you're going to die. So we got out there and I carried the gun and I tripped over a body. When I did, Grondahl ended up behind the gun and I ended up feeding the belt into the gun and we started firing and, fortunately, we caught them with their portholes open. The portholes are only about four inches by two inches, or something like that. But when the bullets went in those portholes, when they got inside this concrete building, they ricocheted all the way around.

All of a sudden a white flag went up and a voice shouted out that they surrender. The lieutenant said to me, "You go down there and check it out." And I said, "Well, you're the officer, why don't you go down there?" He said, "No, no, I'm telling you to go down there." So I took out my .45 and cocked it and I took a hand grenade and pulled the pin out and put it in my hand and walked down there.

And there I met a young German officer and I asked him if he was going to surrender, and he said, "Yes." I said, "Well, come over here," and I put my hand on his stomach with the hand grenade in it and I said, "Now don't fool around with me because if this is some sort of a trick, I'm going to let this hand grenade go and we'll both be dead."

He happened to speak very good English. He was an SS officer and they were trained in English. He said, "You have no need to worry, sir," and out came 30-some soldiers from inside.

At this point, our division started the walking fire again, so our part of this enterprise ended. So the lieutenant says, "You captured them, you take them back." Well, to take them back to regiment was like a two-mile walk through these muddy fields, so I said to the German officer, "Pick up that machine gun." He said, "The Articles of War say that I can't be made to do that." I said, "This hand grenade says you can be made to do that. How would you like to do it?"

He picked it up and put it on his shoulder, and I give the man credit, slogging through that mud was a real job; walking back took several hours. He had his head up high and he carried that gun straight up and never bent once, to prove to me that he was a superior German officer. And, of course, we looked just the opposite. I mean, we were all muddy and dirty. So we got them

235

back, we turned them over to the Intelligence and Reconnaissance people, and then I went back to another barn to rest because we worked at night. So that assignment was done, and the attack was still going on.

"My lieutenant was trying, over and over, to get me killed. He was fearful that I'd reveal his moment of weakness, and it terrified him."   *--Roland Winter*

We were all green. We had our first contact with the enemy on Guam. Although marines were already on the beach, it was still under fire. We spent the first night in front of Marine long toms. The long tom was the biggest gun in the Pacific, and every time it was fired, we got bounced out of our holes. I'm half deaf today because of that. On the second morning, we were committed to marching behind the marines toward another beachhead that was in trouble, to hit the Japs from behind.

I've got my pack on, and I'm carrying my 88 pounds of ammo, and every time I hit the dirt with all that stuff on my back, it knocked the wind out of me.

Now the head of the whole operation was a one-star general whose nickname was Howling Mad Smith. He was a tough guy, he was wearing a baseball cap with a silver star on it. And he sees this midget trudging along with four ammo boxes, two canteens, all the gear I told you about. He says to me, "Stop!"

I immediately knew who it was, I'd read about him. You don't salute in combat, and I looked at him and he said to me, "How the fuck you gonna fight with all that shit on your back?" I said, "Ask my sergeant." So he says, "Who's your sergeant?" I said, "Him." "Come here. Are all these assholes decked out this way? This is jungle." He says, "Take that backpack off your back. Put a box of ammo in each hand and leave that pack behind. Now go fight."

It was on Guam where I got word my father died. We were in the only battle zone in the world that didn't entitle a soldier to some home leave. We were actually involved in a fight. We were being counterattacked and we were in shallow holes, and small arms were firing all over the place, and through the noise of battle, I heard someone say, "Winter's hole is over there!"

I had an intuition that it was a chaplain trying to reach me to tell me one of my parents died. And I looked up and I see a young, fresh-faced kid with a helmet and a little metal cross on it. I said, "Over here, Father. And who is it? My mother or my father?" "It's your father."

I said, "Let me ask you something, doesn't the 77th Division have a Jewish chaplain?" He said, "Yes." "How come they risked your ass to get up here and not my chaplain?" He said, "Soldier, don't be bitter." He said, "Your chaplain is busy doing the same thing. The assignment came up and I'm here to commiserate with you." I said, "Fair enough."

And he had a letter from the uncle that I finally practiced law with, that was written to the chaplain so it didn't come directly to me. He wanted it read to me. Given that it was my father's death and the circumstances and everything else, I said, "Gimme the letter." He said, "It's not addressed to you. My instructions are to read it." I said, "You're gonna get your head blown off. Here, give me the letter and get the hell out of here." "No," he said, "this is my job." And he read it.

Well by that time the other guys in the outfit knew. They say there were no Jews in the infantry. There were a lot of Jews. And from that day forward, every day for 10 days, nine guys would come around my foxhole-- in combat-- and help me say the Kaddish. You need 10 to say it. They would stay there above the ground, and expose themselves to fire, so I could say the Kaddish for my father.

It was after that first night on Guam that my platoon leader-- the lieutenant-- began trying to get me killed. He was from the midwest, he was 32 years old, he had two kids and a wife, he had been a school teacher. And I know why he disliked me.

Every time those long toms went off, there was a big flash,

and it created shadows from the scrub brush and the little trees and the bushes, and it looked like somebody was moving, and everybody was trigger happy. They were shooting at shadows. The lieutenant had directed everybody where to dig in, and by the time it got dark, he didn't have a hole. He said, "Winter, I'm gonna share your hole with you tonight."

He started crying. And all through the night, in the flashes of the long toms, he had his wallet out, he was showing me pictures of his wife and children and saying "I'll never see them again," and he was crying. And I was commiserating with him, you know. I wanted to see my family again too, but I didn't have any children and I felt for the guy.

That's what he had against me. He thought I was going to relate that and embarrass him in front of the men. I never did, and I told him I wouldn't, but he wanted me dead. He was fearful that I would reveal his moment of weakness, and it terrified him. I even told him, "I know why you're doing this to me," but it didn't make any difference.

It got worse and worse. When we were in thick jungle, you lose contact with the squad on your right and the squad on your left. He would say, "I want you to be the scout. Tell me how far they are on the right." That made me a straggler. I didn't know if I was going to find my own troops or the Japs. I was always the guide. There was no doubt in my mind he was trying to get me killed. Nobody else had to do that, only me.

On Ie Shima, we had the deadliest and worst combat I ever saw. Ie Shima was like an inverted ice-cream cone. From the top of the mountain there, you could hit any exposed person with a rifle. If you weren't behind a building, they'd pick you off one by one.

Just before nightfall, he wanted me to put a machine gun out in front of the line of riflemen, in a field. We saw bullets hitting there every time somebody stuck a nose out. I couldn't live long enough to put the gun where he wanted it.

There was a marine tank and a crew sitting there with the engine off. They could hear what he was telling me. They said to me, "Soldier, we'll get you out there, don't fight with him." "How you gonna get me out there?" "Roll the tank out there. We'll wait till you dig your hole. Then we'll roll back." And that's what they did.

Nobody asked, no officer told them to do it. They knew that this guy wanted to get me killed. They listened and they knew.

Finally, on Okinawa, we relieved an outfit on top of a ridge. We didn't own that ridge. We shared it with the Japanese. And the machine gun squad that we replaced had built an emplacement. You couldn't dig up there; it was all rock. And they had taken rocks and made a pile to put their machine gun in it. And toward the front of the ridge was an enormous boulder. When we relieved the guys, they said, "Don't get in front of that boulder. The Japs got a machine gun right on the other side of that boulder. You stick your nose out, they'll blow it off."

So my lieutenant came up. He looked around my position. After the other guys are gone, he said, "Move your gun up to the front of the ridge." I wasn't going to tell him what the other guys told me. He wouldn't have believed it. He'd have made me go there. He'd done worse than that to me. Much worse. I don't know how I survived some of the spots he put me in. I said to him, "I don't know where you mean." "God damn it! Are you blind? I mean over here!" And he walked out from behind the boulder. They cut him in half, and he fell off the ridge.

It would've been me.

"I let go with the twin .50s and filled the whole sky back there, but they kept coming. I could see the pilots' faces, they were so close." --Forrest S. Clark

My most harrowing mission was the 18 November, 1943, mission to Kjeller Air Base, the Luftwaffe base in Lillestrom, Norway. It's a miracle we didn't go down on that one. We've got a memorial over there to the Second Air Division, Eighth Air

Force. We dedicated it in '93 on the anniversary date of the mission, and the Royal Norwegian Air Force is the custodian of it, because it's on their base.

We'd gone to Rjukan, the heavy water plant, Norsk Hydro, a couple of days before and didn't experience any opposition. So on the 18th, we went to Kjeller, because it was one of the leading bases in Scandinavia being used by the Luftwaffe, and they were refitting planes to ship to the Russian front, so it was a major maintenance base.

It was a long mission, and a cold one, very cold. It was November in the North Sea, about 35 degrees below zero, something like that, and we had to go about 700 miles up, make a big turn, and come back again, through the Skagerrak. The Germans had Luftwaffe squadrons in Northern Denmark and as we were going in we saw these German fighters off there, flying parallel with us. They were apparently radioing down positions.

As it happened, the German High Command was having a maneuver that day at the base, and they had given all the civilian employees a day off. So there was a whole cadre of German troops there and they were having a defense maneuver. They were practicing antiaircraft defense, running around, having a ground deployment of troops, and General Von Falkenhorst, the Luftwaffe commander in Scandinavia, was there reviewing the troops. I learned all that later, of course.

I don't know how, but we caught the Germans totally by surprise. The story is-- I learned this when we went back over there about 10 years ago-- that General Von Falkenhorst was up on this hill, looking down at the base, and he saw these planes (we had about 110 bombers in our force) and he said, "Was ist?" (laughter) and his aide said, "Oh, I can assure you, Commandant, those are ours." Then, when the bombs started to fall, they had to run for their lives, hide in a bunker. So we almost got the German general.

We dropped 836 500-pounders in about 12 minutes over that base. It wiped out 85 percent of it. The RAF came back a couple

240

of months later and wiped out the rest. Some of us made two turns over that target, and the funny thing was that nothing got off the ground. They had all these aircraft, and not one got off. They were taken totally by surprise, I don't know why, because some of their reconnaissance planes had seen our formations coming in over the North Sea. We were at about 15,000 feet, and I could see the flak batteries on the ships down there in the fjord, but they weren't firing.

Years later, I met a man who was a 16-year-old schoolboy back then, and he remembered it. When we came over, he said, all the Norwegians were cheering, because they hadn't seen any Allied planes. The Norwegians had gone five years or so under German occupation, and they'd never seen many mass bombings by the Eighth Air Force. So this was a big event, and we wiped out that base. The casualties must have been very high among the Germans. They must have been in the hundreds. They were exposed, and the aircraft didn't get off the ground.

Well, we dropped our bomb load, and coming back out of the Oslo Fjord there were a couple of flak bursts, but it wasn't until we got out over the open water that the word had gotten out to the Luftwaffe squadrons, and they had beefed up their squadrons around that time in the area of the Skagerrak. I would say it looked like they had 100 or more fighters up there-- ME 109s, I even remember seeing some Junkers, JU 88s, FW 190s.

We had lost some turbo-charger power, so we were lagging behind. And I was the tail gunner, so I could see everything. But I couldn't see the rest of our formation. Where were they? They were gone, headed out of there as fast as they could. I didn't see anybody else, and I said, "That's not too good."

Then I saw the fighters-- they started lining up at our tail. They were coming in right at level (laughter) with everything going. We were told to fire, watch our tracers, and then adjust for the lead, but I just let go with both the twin .50s and was filling the whole sky back there. But they were coming in and coming in, and I could see the pilots' heads, and helmets, and even their faces, they came in so close. I thought they were gonna ram us. I said, "They're gonna ram us. They're gonna ram us." The pilot said, "Shut up and shoot."

They'd come in level, then they'd dive down at the last minute and go under us. You couldn't miss them. I learned later that they were firing rockets, which I had never seen before. In those B-24 turrets, they had a big piece of thick plexiglas there, but not too much protection. The ball-turret gunner, Bill Kuban, came up out of the ball-turret, bringing ammunition back to me, in the tail, because I was running short. I was leaning over, and a shell went right over my shoulder and hit him, and he went down.

Then the bail-out bell rang. I heard it in all that noise, and I said, "What the hell is that bell?" At first I thought it was a dream, but then I realized it was the bail-out bell. I rolled back out of the turret and there were all these hot shells, spent shells, covering the whole bottom of the aircraft, and blood. Kuban was bleeding, and I looked at him and said, "He looks like he's gone." He had his eyes rolled up.

Then Gibboney came back and said, "Get the hell out of here. We've got to bail out. Don't you hear that bell?" I said, "Wait a minute." They were still attacking, so I said, "Well, I've got to go back into the turret and finish up shooting." He said, "No, forget that, start throwing stuff out."

So we threw flak suits, everything we could, oxygen bottles, to lighten up the back, and I opened the rear hatch and looked down-- the camera hatch we called it-- and looked down and saw the North Sea and the white caps, and I said, "Wait." He said, "Go, go, go." I said, "Wait a minute," and then, I don't know what made me stop, but something did. Gibboney said, "What are you doing?" and I said, "Well, I'm praying."

I got down, and I really prayed, and just about that time a layer of clouds formed over the North Sea and we went into it. We were heading straight down for the water by this time, and the German pilots probably had written us off. Maybe they lost us or they were out of range. We were pretty far out by then.

So they broke off their attacks, and from that point on, we just limped back over the water. It just looked like 100 feet in some places. We'd sink down, then roar up again, then sink down and roar up again, and I looked out there and I could see a hole in the wing. It looked like it was big enough to drive a jeep through. One engine was completely shot up. We had no hydraulic fluid, no landing gear, that was shot away, and later we found there were about 150 holes in the plane.

So for about three hours-- it seemed a lot longer--we just limped along, and we'd see other planes going down. We saw Lieutenant Houle go down. You couldn't ditch those B-24s. They were not ditchable, really. They'd break up with that Davis wing they had. It wasn't like the B-17 wing.

At one point, we devised a plan. The pilot was gonna ditch, then-- no, first, we were gonna bail out, use our Mae Wests in the water-- and that water is about 40 degrees-- and then he's gonna ditch the plane, inflate the big raft, and go around and pick us up, which was about a million to one shot that we got everybody out of there.

Anyway, we limped on and on. Then I saw a coast coming up. I wasn't sure what coast it was. I thought it might be the Dutch coast or the French coast. I was completely disoriented. Then the order came back, "We can't get the gear down. The wheels are shot away. What are we gonna do?" and the pilot's command came back, "Jump, parachute, everybody out," except him and the wounded gunner.

So we bailed out and I remembered that you've got to free fall so you don't get tangled in those big vertical stabilizers on the B-24. We had cases of guys who pulled their cord too soon, and the chute got tangled, and that was it. So I counted to 10, and then, I said, "Gee." I looked up and the airplane was still there, so I counted again to 10.

When I finally pulled the cord, I came down over this farm field. Luckily, it was a very muddy field, and I hit, "Bang," like that, and rolled over about 10 times in the mud, and my chute was pulling me across the field, and I saw a farmer with a pitchfork come running. He stuck it out at me. I put my hands up. (laughter) I thought, "Jesus, we've made a mistake. That damned navigator screwed up again and we're back in Germany." But luckily, it was England, about 20 miles from the base. I said, "Where are we?" and he said, "Why, you damned Yankees." He said, "Don't you know your geography?"

Then I remember I dug my hands into the dirt and wiped them on my flight suit and I said, "That's enough for me. I quit." They took me to the hospital, and I did have a bad foot, I still have it, from that landing, 'cause, when I landed, instead of rolling, I put my feet down and hit, and you're supposed to roll. See, we never had any parachute training. I don't know why that was. Actually, we did have a couple of crews who practiced jumping, and we thought that was stupid, but now that I look back at it, I think maybe it wasn't so stupid.

The day we were finally shot down was April 13th, that's an unlucky day, April 13th, 1944. We were on a mission to Lechfeld, Germany. I believe it was an ME 262 base. The ME 262 came in late in the war as a German Luftwaffe fighter and was a very effective jet fighter. I used to see it go through our formations like a blink, you know. You'd see a little dot, and then, "Swish," it's gone, and I remember them very well in the later missions.

On this mission, that was a rather deep penetration, to Lechfeld. It was way over near Dachau, not far south of Augsburg in southern Germany, quite a way across enemy territory. Anyway, we got over the target, and got hit by flak, and lost a lot of fuel and the fuel was streaming out in big streams, I remember. It was a very dangerous situation. The pilot, with the help of the engineer, calculated how much fuel we had left. We couldn't possibly make it back over 700 or 800 miles of German-occupied territory to a base in England.

From 20,000 feet, we could see the Alps, over to the south. I was the radio operator that time, because we'd lost our radio operator. Sofferman had gone down. We got rid of our bomb load over the target. I remember seeing the bombs go right into the runway, hitting those 262s and blowing them to bits there, and it was a pretty good bomb pattern.

We didn't have any bombs left, but somehow or other we kept the bomb bay doors open. I don't know exactly why. Part of a radio operator's job on a B-24 was, if the bomb bay doors crept-- sometimes they'd slowly close-- there was a manual crank. You had to go and manually crank them open.

So I was back there, trying to manually crank open the bomb bay doors, (laughter) and you try that at, say, 15,000 feet or so, and the pilot said, "Okay, we're going. We're gonna try to make Swiss territory." It looked like it was right over there. So I said, "What are we gonna do now?"

He said, "We'll send a message in code, that we're trying to divert to Swiss territory and we're very low on fuel," So I coded this message and sent it, in bomber code. I don't think they ever got it. Just as we got near the border, there were four bursts of flak, "Bang, bang, bang, bang," and the waist gunner, Sergeant Harmon, got his finger shot off. He was holding one of the waist guns, because there were still fighters around, and he got hit by a piece of flak.

Then, the pilot, "swish," dove down to the right. We looked up, and, "Bang, bang, bang, bang," there were four more flak bursts just where we had been. If we had been just a second or two later diving, we'd have gotten blown to bits. They'd got our range, and the pilot was smart enough to know to go into a quick dive to the right.

We were very lucky. We went into Dubendorf with practically no fuel at all-- that's near Zurich-- and crashed, cut the trees off as we went down. We cut the trees right off with our wings, rolled into a big ball on a grass field.

It was a Swiss Air Force base, and they were flying ME 109s so it looked just like German planes. When I got down out of the bomb bay, I let myself out, and I flicked the switch on the IFF to blow the plane up. We were told to do that if we came down in enemy territory. As soon as I got down out of the bomb bay, I saw what looked exactly like German soldiers with automatic rifles all around the plane, surrounding the plane, and so I said, "What the hell is going on here? Did we make a mistake? We must have landed at Munich."

I started walking away from the plane real fast, because I thought it was gonna blow up anyway, even though it didn't have much fuel in it. You could smell the fuel. It was leaking. So I walked away, and I walked about 50 yards and all of a sudden I felt this gun at my back. I looked around and there was this little German soldier with a gun, looked like about 17 years old. They took us in to interrogation and asked us about the bombing of Schaffhausen, which was the big controversy at that time.

We had bombed some Swiss cities, the Eighth Air Force had. We'd bombed Zurich, Basel and Schaffhausen, that was the famous one, just a few days before this happened, so they were very uptight about that, the Swiss were, and they interrogated us for about eight hours, held us in this operations center, and then, they put us in a van, took us to the schoolyard, where we slept on the ground for three nights, and then they put us in a train, took us up to Adelboden.

That's a whole chapter of World War II history that not many people know about. We had 1,500, mostly Eighth Air Force and some Fifteenth Air Force men, in internment camps at Adelboden, at Wengen, and at Davos.

I came out in December of '44. A group of us, British and Americans, there in the internment camp, had gone to Zurich and were under guard there, and we're coming back to our camp up in the Alps. We knew we'd never get out of that place, because you had to be an expert skier, so we got in the train going to Bern, which was the capital, and I knew that if we could get to the American embassy in Bern, they would help us get out, over into France.

We had about five armed guards, Swiss guards. They would march us off. We said, "We want to have a rest stop at Bern. We have to go to the john." So a group of us-- I'd say there were about 15 of us-- got off the train at the Bern station and mixed with the crowds there. We had Swiss clothes on. We sat at a café, an outdoor café, and one of our guys, Carl, spoke German very well, so he hailed a cab and said to the driver, "Take us to the American embassy."

We got in the cab, went to the American embassy and ran right past the Swiss guards. We found there were about 15 Americans in there waiting to get out. We were there for four or five days, and then we walked along the streets to this big villa.

Behind the house there was a moving van, and the whole van was filled with GIs trying to escape. They sealed the van up, and drove us about five or six hours to some place up in the mountains, outside of Geneva. There we met a couple of Maquis, French Resistance guides, who took us walking.

We walked by night and hid in these different farmhouses by day for three days, 'til we got to the border. This was December, you know, and it was cold. At the border, there was barbed wire, and an ice-cold stream. We had to wade through that stream, go under that barbed wire, and run up a snow-filled, icy field to a farmhouse and knock on the door three times.

The French guides told us that would be France, and someone would pick us up there. The next morning, instead of waiting to be picked up, Carl and I got anxious, so we started walking in what we thought was the direction of the nearest town. Along came this patrol, coming down the road on a jeep, and it was an American colonel with the Seventh Army, I guess, and he had an assistant with him.

We hadn't shaved in about a week, and we were dressed in civilian clothes, and he said, "Those are our men. I can tell they're Yanks." (laughter) He said, "Jump in." So we jumped in and went to Annecy, where we were given new uniforms and showers and taken to Lyons, France, where we were given our

247

first meal. We hadn't eaten in about seven days. The meal was served by German prisoners of war, I remember that. The Captain said, "Now, I don't want any of you guys to say anything to these men or cause any incidents." He said, "I just want you to mind your own business and eat."

When I saw these prisoners of war, and this was in December of '44, I said, "Boy, Hitler is in real trouble," because these guys looked like they were on their last legs. They looked terrible. They were all about 16 or 17 years old. They looked like they had malnutrition, they looked very bad.

From there, they flew us back to London, and eventually back to the base. I was only at the base about two weeks and I got orders to return to the US.

We lost about 62 men in Switzerland who either crashed, or were killed coming in, or died of wounds, and they were buried over there, and very few people know that. There was a lot of anti-American feeling, especially in the German-speaking part of Switzerland. There were stories about how taxi drivers would abduct American and British airmen and turn them over to the Germans at the border for a bounty, and those stories were pretty well proven to be true.

We have a Swiss Internees Association, which was formed about 10 years ago, and they have gone back to Switzerland to visit some of those places.

"His blood was all over me. I shot him because he was the enemy; but when he was lying there dying, he was a human being." *--George Boggs III*

When we were in New Guinea, we were in one of the upper perimeters, and I still don't know where it was, but we had gun fights every night, and they lasted all night, but we were dug in, and we had fairly secure positions there with sand bags on top of logs and things like that. But then I went out with a few scouting parties, and we went around to the rear of the Japanese lines and we were told to scout the capabilities of the Japanese and learn where their concentrations were, and where their munitions dumps were, and things like that-- and to take prisoners.

But it was a hairy thing, taking prisoners when you're behind the enemy's line because, when you'd bring them back through their own lines, you would have a chance of being killed because they'd warn some others. So this was bad. At times you forgot the Articles of War and after you would question somebody, you'd find a convenient bayonet and eliminate any possibility of him telling about you being there.

I had some close encounters, but the closest of all was really eye to eye, eyeball to eyeball. We were out once on one of these raids when they started firing. I jumped into a shell crater for protection-- and a Japanese jumped in at the same time. And that was a bit hairy. What saved me was that my family had been nice to me and gave me a shoulder holster, so I didn't have to reach way down to get my Colt pistol.

I had looked on the Japanese soldiers as some sort of wild animals. It was hard to think of them as human, but when they died in your hands, they were human. In other words, you could shoot one of them, and you shot him because he was the enemy, but when he was lying there dying, he was a human being.

I was only in that crater for a matter of minutes. His blood had splattered all over me and I was anxious to get out and wipe his blood off me.

"The US Submarine Grayling comes limping into port, and those sailors are mad because they'd been bombed by a flight of B-17s."   --Frederick Wesche III

From Hamilton Field in California to Hickam Field in Honolulu took 13 hours and 55 minutes in the air. That was normally beyond the range of a B-17. But in our bomb bay, we had extra tanks that carried 400 gallons of fuel each, and you could pipe that into the regular fuel tanks on the airplane. Back then, you have to remember that Pacific air routes were hardly developed. But Pan American had been flying that route fairly regularly before the war, and we were relieved half way across to pass a Pan Am plane. We figured, "Well, if they're on course, so are we."

We landed at Hickam Field and we were assigned to the Second Provisional Bomb Group. This was in May of '42. So we did some patrols and other duties around Hickam Field. Then one night, again in the middle of the night, the charge of quarters came through the barracks and said, "Everybody over to the base theater for briefing." Then we learned of the breaking Battle of Midway.

So the next morning, early, we were out on the line waiting, supposedly to be bombed up, and my bombardier was ready to supervise the loading of bombs. Meanwhile we got some briefing on navigation. Eventually, here comes a bomb carrier truck and starts unloading "bombs." My bombardier says, "What the heck is that? They're coast artillery shells." Some of them had been stored up in the hills of Hawaii since World War I. He said, "What do we do with coast artillery shells? These aren't bombs." The answer: "So, well, the sheet metal shop is going to cut out some tail fins and attach them. We'll give you a few hours to go out and drop a couple for the ballistics."

Normally, when you bomb, you have ballistics tables all made up for specific bomb loads. So we put them in and went out and dropped a few. I think we dropped five, of which three were duds. So we came back and said, "This is impossible." So they said, "Well, unload it."

In the meantime, they had a munitions ship on its way out to Midway, so we went on out to Midway. It's a long trip to Midway from Hawaii, and we're cruising along and suddenly the navigator said, "Hey, there's somebody in a rubber boat down there." We looked and there was some poor Marine pilot floating around in a rubber life raft, so we went down and took a look at him and took his position and radioed it. I couldn't help him. I can't land the airplane on the water. I understood later they did pick him up.

When we got to Midway, the place was in a shambles. They'd had a major Japanese attack the day before. They'd hit the distillery, so there was no fresh water. On the other hand, they'd also hit the PX, so you could walk around the island and pick up cigars, cigarettes, candy.

So we parked the airplane there and waited for instructions. It was hotter than blazes. We put a cot under one of the wings in the shade and played poker and all of a sudden the air raid siren went off. The rule is you get in the airplane and go. They don't want airplanes caught on the ground.

So we all jumped in the airplane, a couple of the guys right out of the lagoon, with nothing but a pair of shoes on. The airplane had been sitting in that hot sun, and to touch the metal was murder. But we got the engine started and took off. It turned out to be a false alarm.

But it was funny. I couldn't sit on the seat because it was too hot, so you sat halfway hunched up over the wheel, trying to fly the airplane. I looked back, I could see back through the bomb bay into the waist, and all I could see were naked bodies.

On one of our combat missions out of Midway, we were chasing a Japanese ship-- I think it was the *Mogami*-- that had been crippled by submarine action and was limping away. Now B-17s were never meant for bombing naval targets. By the time you drop the bomb, the ship can see it and turn right out of its path. And the B-17 is not a dive-bomber, but at least we would have the range to do it.

But we never did find it. The Pacific is a pretty big place, and it turned out later that we had an improper position report. So on our way back, our group leader said, "We'll bomb targets of opportunity." "All right, fine." Not long after that, he said, "Here's our target. I don't have this on my disposition list." My navigator said, "That's a submarine down there."

So we all bombed it. When we got back to Hawaii after a few days, here comes the US submarine *Grayling* limping into port, and the sailors onboard were ready to go over to Hickam Field and clean up on the Air Corps because they'd been bombed by a flight of B-17s. It shows you how mixed up and chaotic things were in the beginning.

"They wanted volunteers to bring the bodies back. I volunteered because they were my men. We brought them back and accounted for them." --Robert F. Moss

In one of our patrols in the early period on Morotai, two of my men were killed. We had to bury them in the middle of the island. Well, a month later, they wanted a volunteer patrol to go and bring the bodies back. I volunteered because they were my men. So I was the lieutenant in charge of the whole expedition.

I knew there was some risk; you could run into a pocket of Japs that would try to ambush you. We had a patrol of about 50. We left and I moved those soldiers fast. It wasn't like in training, where you walked for 50 minutes and stopped for 10. I didn't let them stop, and they felt pushed too hard. They even complained after we got back, but I didn't have one casualty. I kept them moving fast enough so any Japs could not really organize anything in front of us.

We had to camp overnight and we had our watches. Guards were at every point around the camp. We did find the graves and we wrapped the bodies in canvas and we had those little yellow life rafts for pilots. The bodies fit right in. Then we took a different route out. We found a stream and floated the bodies downstream and got them back to the graves registration unit, and so we accounted for all our men.

I never could understand why all this attention is given to the MIA problem. The military in World War II tried really hard to find its dead, and mostly they found them. There were no MIAs. If they were missing, they were dead, or they were prisoners. If a family can't accept the death of a person who is missing in action for a year or a couple of years, I feel sorry for them.

"They took those 60 guys who'd tried to escape and lined them up against a wall in front of us, and they shot every other one."   *-- Robert C. King*

I belonged to the 485th Bomb Group. By the time I was shot down, there were only two of the original crews left. That's how bad the attrition was over there. You were supposed to get a rest after 25 missions in Italy. You go to the Isle of Capri. So two of us were up for this, and this guy and I flipped a coin. He won the toss, so he and his crew went to the Isle of Capri. I stayed and we flew two more missions and then we were shot down. But we all survived that. He came back and flew more missions but he and his crew didn't make it. They were all wiped out.

You didn't have a choice on where you were going. I can remember the pilots would all sit around in the briefing, and they would unravel this red ribbon and put it across the map to Breslau. We all knew we couldn't go that far. And when they came to Ploesti-- I was on that run three times-- man, you died. You just died, but there's nothing you could do. So you go. You just do it! That's all, you had no choice.

I didn't know the other pilots and crews very well. It sounds strange, doesn' it, but we really didn't know them. You're a little knit group, you and your crew. And they were dying and disappearing and new ones were coming all the time. You didn't really get a chance to know anybody. The only ones we knew were the 10 of us in the crew and maybe the couple of guys on the ground that serviced our plane. But other than that, no.

We were very, very dependent on that ground crew. Our relationship with them was almost like love. And I'm not trying to be smart. It was a lot of affection and a lot of respect. Us for them and them for us. We were very dependent on those guys and they appreciated what we were going through. So you know, it worked both ways.

We had this B-24 with big round tails, and every group had its own marking on the tail. And it was an unwritten rule between the Luftwaffe and the U.S. Air Corps that if a plane was in trouble, even though it's over Germany or Romania or Hungary or wherever, and it can not get back to its base, if it will reduce its speed and lower its wheels, the German fighters will no longer attack it, but they will escort it and make sure it doesn't get out. And they'd escort it down to a field. Which I thought was a gentleman's way to do it.

Well, in a group near us in Italy was this guy who thought he's a hot shot. He thought, "Well, we'll lower the wheels and when German fighters come in, we'll shoot them down." Which he did. And he got back. But I'll tell you, from that mission on, they had to disband that group. Because from that mission on the Luftwaffe targeted that group and annihilated it. And I think they had every right to do it. They even changed the markings a couple of times, but that didn't work because the word got out. But isn't that stupid?

I was shot down in Austria, right outside of Vienna. The flak caught one engine and I had to feather it. With one engine out you have trouble staying, so I fell back. And then the fighters got the second engine. With two engines out and now the wing's on fire, and that's what scared me. Because I had seen on occasion where a plane off in the distance would be on fire and all of a sudden there would be an explosion and it would almost vaporize.

So I figured this was the time. Let's take this big step. So I put it on automatic pilot and gave orders to the crew to start getting the ball turret gunner out. "Hey, pass to Ken, we've got a problem." And we got everybody in and so they all jumped out and then I jumped out.

As I'm floating down, I could see these people coming out from town following the flight of my chute. I tried to get the chute off and jump to one side or another, because I saw this ME-109 coming at me directly and then he came to me and went straight up in the air and I thought he was going to shoot me, but he was obviously just marking me for the people who were coming out from town.

So I ran through the wheat field to try to get away, and my electric flying shoes came off and I'm running through this wheat field with my bare feet, scared to death. So I did what Little Orphan Annie did. I back-tracked four or five steps and then jumped off my path and decided to curl up in a little ball and I was there-- Oh, a long time-- maybe five minutes. (laughs) And they got me and that is when it all started.

So there I was, no shoes, I had plenty of nothing, and I'm trying to remember some of the German I learned at Rutgers. I remembered Professor Bierschmitt. I said, "Ich weiss nicht was sol es bedeuten das ich so traurig bin." I tried to say, "I'm your friend," and "Help me," but it was an exercise in futility.

The civilians were tough on me, but I don't really blame them. The Burgermeister puts a gun in my back and says, "March." And we go down this country road to the little town. And the people are lined on each side of this road, and they're calling me names and throwing rocks and spitting at me, and I'm thinking to myself, you know, I might have killed their brother or father or who knows what. I can understand that.

First they put me in this latrine, this concrete structure with just tiny slits. And they threw me on the back of an open truck with a wood burning stove and a bunch of other people. They were all Americans, fish like me, and we headed for Sagan in East Germany.

But before I got there, they put me in isolation for about eight, nine days. And they knew who I was, they told me who my father and mother were and all that stuff. It was scary."They'd say it like this. "Well look, we know that your mother's name is Anna, your father's name is John, your copilot is Bob Peterson and you graduated from Rutgers in 1942 and you're parked on Hardstand number 46, at Spinazola, Italy. All we want to know is some information about the Norden bombsight."

This guy would be talking just like we're talking, with all the idioms and everything else. I mean he spoke English as well as we do, which made it kind of scary. They had a tremendous espionage system. But they were hung up on the Norden bombsight, which was just getting started. Well I didn't know anything anyway. They threatened me, but they never did any violence to me.

My first prison camp was probably the size of a football field, with the barbed wire and the sentry boxes. None of my crew members were there. I never saw them again until after the war.

We got a Red Cross parcel a week. It had Canadian biscuits. It had Spam, D-bars, chocolate bars. And I think it had oatmeal or some sort of cereal. It was supposed to sustain a person for a week. And then the Germans would give us kohlrabi once in a while and a little soup. I found a mouse in my soup. I found a horse's tooth in my soup. But I'll tell you, you'd eat anything. We had congealed blood in a casing they gave us. We ate that, because we were starving to death. And then the parcels got cut because of the transportation. The rail lines were all shot up and the Red Cross couldn't get them in. It wasn't their fault.

Once they distributed a letter to every American flying officer. It said they wanted us to join the Luftwaffe, to fight our common enemy from the East in exchange for amnesty. But nobody did.

These things are coming back to me now. I remember toward the end of the war, Hitler had ordered the Wehrmacht to get rid of all prisoners of war, because it was a tremendous drag of manpower just to watch us. But the Wehrmacht was not as crazy as he was. This is like March, I guess, of '45. And so the Wehrmacht wouldn't do it. Thank God!

And then we had what was called a "death march" from one prison camp to another. They would shoot you if you straggled on that "death march." And we slept in the ice and the snow in the fields, and we had hardly any clothes, so we were freezing. It was in February. Guys were starving and freezing. And we were strafed once by our own planes, which was not their fault that they saw a formation in Germany. It was a bad scene.

We walked for about a week and then they put us in boxcars and took us down to Moosburg. So that was like two or three days, I guess. I don't know how far we walked or where we walked to, but it was at least a week. And then we got on these boxcars and wound up at Moosburg. That was a big camp with an area that you walked around in, and we were digging a tunnel and we had a radio.

But the Germans had tunnels too, under all the barracks, and they would crawl under the barracks and listen. So we had spies out all over. One guy brought out his little homemade crystal set to listen to the BBC news. If they would have caught this, there would have been all kinds of repercussions.

I remember one attempted escape. Captain Atkinson was with me in my little quadrangle of eight bunks. And the bugs would eat you alive. Well, he tried to escape in a honey wagon. A honey wagon is the wagon that comes by and sucks all this excreta from the outhouse into the tank and then hauls it away. He tried to ride out in this tank with the stuff up to his neck.

But they caught him. They got him going out the gate. They opened the lid and there he was, trying to keep his head above the excretion. That's the last we saw of him. I don't think they killed him. But I don't know. I never heard.

In the camp next to us there were 60 British who escaped. I think the movie was The Great Escape, and they caught them, and they brought them all back. And they brought us out. And they brought Heinrich Himmler down from Berlin. I'll never forget this. By now we were pretty weak. We had just about enough strength to stand up and be counted twice a day. And they'd come by with their guns and dogs, and they'd count us.

But this day they took the 60 guys that had tried to escape and lined them all up against a wall in front of us, and there was Himmler in his black leather coat. And they shot every other one. They shot 30 of the guys right in front of us. As an obvious deterrent for further attempts to escape. And I'll tell you, it was very effective.

257

We had a light at the end of the barracks. A red bulb. Theoretically if someone was sick, you'd turn that red bulb on and medical care would come. But it never did. The guy died of emphysema or lung disease, whatever it was right there in the barracks. Nobody ever came. You had maybe two spigots of water for a couple of hundred guys. And outhouses. Well, nobody had to move their bowels much because you weren't eating. If you went once a week, that was something.

It was like someone cut your legs out from under you. You had all that time just sitting around, and everything had stopped. We're all hungry and we're scared. And so what are we going to do. We walked just like they do in prisons. Walked like the lions do in the cage. And you talk. And so that's about all there was. There were no books. There were no cards.

And what we talked about-- that's interesting. You know, Freud tells you that sex is the prime mover. It's not true. And we commented on this. We'd lay there in the barracks at night and talk, talk, talk. After the first week or so, you didn't hear talk about girls or anything. All we talked about is food. I made a list and I have it somewhere, and it has like 100 things-- peanut butter, milkshake, Tasty Cakes. And where we were going to eat when we got out of there, if we ever got out. Sex-- and this surprised me-- was a low second.

Moosburg was in the center of a woods, and all around us in the woods were the Gestapo, and they were fanatical right to the very end. When the tanks came in to liberate us, there were two guys that were killed, two American prisoners of war. They were killed as we were liberated, because of crossfire between the Gestapo and the tanks. We had been warned to stay in the barracks.

I can still see that tank coming through the gate, like King Kong coming through the wall. And guys were running out of barracks, jumping on the tank to ride it. It's tragic that they go through all this and be killed on the day that we were liberated. Yeah, but it happened.

"The British tanker kept trying to pull himself out of that burning tank, but he kept falling back, and he probably was burned alive." --*Frank Gimpel*

Two of our regiments were assigned initially to the British to take a salient they called the Geilenkirchen Salient. We were there to take that salient. One regiment was loaned to the 30th Infantry Division, and our battalion was supported by a British tank regiment called the Sherwood Rangers.

Your first combat experience is miserable, and you are scared. A person who says they're not scared, they're lying. Everyone was scared, even colonels. I remember one of the first towns we went into, there were two captured German pillboxes, and this colonel was there exhorting the troops, and suddenly a bunch of shells started coming in, and he hot-footed it for one of the captured pillboxes, and that's the last we saw of him.

You would always hope it wasn't going to be you, because if you thought you were going to be hit, you probably never would've been able to survive. You had to live on faith and on hope and, if your feeling was that you're going to get killed, I think your whole morale and your whole being would have collapsed on you.

On the very first day, when we were on the attack, we were moving forward, and we started getting shells on us, and I dove onto the ground, into the mud, and a piece of paper came flying by. I put my hand out and turned it over and it was the Twenty-Third Psalm. Your morale is really boosted a lot when you read it, "The Lord is my shepherd. I shall not want. He leadeth me into the Valley of Death." I figured, "Okay, I'll have to put my fate in the hands of God."

If you survived the first week, you did well in combat after that. The first week, that was the great leveler. Our battalion had about 800 people when we went in, the first week in combat, and, at the end of the first week, if they had 100 or 150 that were combat ready, that was a lot.

Trenchfoot was one of the big problems. Your feet got frozen, and they would evacuate you back. One of the things they eventually had was the discipline for keeping the feet dry and warm. After a while, they would send up, along with food, fresh pairs of socks, and you were supposed to take your shoes off and rub your feet, and dry them, and then put on fresh socks, and put your shoes back on, and send the other pair of socks back to get washed and replaced.

When I got wounded the first time, besides being hit in the arm, my feet were partially frozen. We were outside this town of Prummern. We were trying to take some pillboxes, and we were pinned down there for a day-and-a-half. Three British tanks came up to try to knock the pillboxes out with flame-throwers. They put the flame-throwers on the pillboxes, and the first thing we heard was, "Bang, bang, bang," the German .88s. The first two British tanks were hit directly and burst into fire, and the third one tried to back off, and three more shells came over and hit it.

One of the most vivid things I remember was one of the British tankers trying to get out of the burning tank, and he kept trying to pull himself out, and he couldn't. One of the fellows from our company jumped up on the tank and tried to help him out, and the Germans fired at him, so he had to jump down. He couldn't help. The last thing we saw was the fellow sinking back into the tank, and he probably burned alive.

This one fellow that went over with us on the ship-- Sy, a big, burly fellow-- crawled out of his foxhole and picked up one of the British tank drivers. This tank driver had his whole rear end shot off, and he was laying there, and Sy put the fellow on his back and crawled on his hands and knees to get off of the ridge and then, once he got out of the line of fire, ran down to the aid station, and took the British officer with him.

The next day, since we weren't able to take out that pillbox with the British tanks, they decided to send the infantry up there. We had engineers who would put satchel charges on these pill-

260

boxes, but first you had to get past their protective trenches.

The Germans had these automatic pistols, and they fired on us. Three of us were in the same foxhole. The sergeant got hit in the stomach, and another fellow was hit in the back of the head, and I was hit in the arm. They took us down to the aid station in the little town we had captured, and the doctor told me the sergeant had died on the way back.

Before we went to take the pillboxes, the sergeant, the platoon lieutenant and I were in the same foxhole together. The lieutenant said we had to take the pillboxes, and the sergeant said, "Do I really have to go, lieutenant? I want to stay." He said to the lieutenant, "You know, if I could just go home, I'll work on the railroads and dig ditches for the rest of my life. I just want to go home and see my wife and son." He never made it.

"The explosion was tremendous. I looked around, and the top turret gunner was lying crumpled at the foot of the turret." --Frederick Wesche III

One night, right after the Battle of the Bismarck Sea, we were out on what's called "armed reconnaissance." The Japanese had failed to bring a convoy in to reinforce their troops on New Guinea, so instead of using transports, they'd load a bunch of stuff on a destroyer, which can go up to 40 knots or better, and they'd run it through at night, drop the stuff overboard on rafts, hope it floats into the shore and then get out of there.

But our intelligence got wind of this somehow, and we were out alone looking for them. It was a half moon, and my bombardier said, "Hey, there's a ship down there." We looked again, sure enough, there's a destroyer. You could see it by the reflected path of the moonlight. So we made a circle and dropped a flare. There wasn't just one. There were four, and here we are all alone. We made two passes on one of the destroyers, dropped on it, and the first one, we had a near miss, but the second one, we hit it on the stern, and all hell broke loose.

261

By now, 40 mm antiaircraft shells were flying all around us. Only one hit us, but it came in right next to the cockpit. The sound from that explosion was tremendous. My ears were ringing; I could hardly hear anything. Right behind me was the top turret gunner. I looked around and here he was laying crumpled at the foot of the turret. I had to wait till we got clear of the enemy. Then I rushed back, and a couple of us got him out of there, and he was peppered with shrapnel.

That hit knocked our radio out; in fact, our whole electrical system was gone. We didn't even know what the condition of the airplane was, and I had to land it. I headed for one of our forward bases.We had to crank the landing gear down by hand. We had no flaps. We couldn't reverse the propellers to stop. We couldn't even use the brakes. We got down by the skin of our teeth.

The top turret gunner didn't have mortal wounds. He was hospitalized and eventually sent home. Next morning, recon found a lot of debris where the ship had been, so we were credited with having sunk it, and we all received the Silver Medal.

We were fortunate. If that round had come in a few inches farther to the front, it might have taken out the main wing spar, in which case the wing would have come off. It was probably the worst combat mission I had.

"We started with 65 in our platoon, and I was one of the last two when Patton's tanks came up. It was me and Kelly, Kelly and I." *--Franklin J. Kneller*

After our jump training, we went to little huts in the forest-- Quonset huts-- and on December 18th we were shaken out of bed, "Get ready to leave," and we did, but we didn't have complete equipment. We didn't know what was going on, just that the Germans were coming through. They drove trucks down the street, throwing out equipment. (laughter) So you got whatever equipment you could find.

It was the fastest any division had ever activated, I read later. In just a couple of hours, we went from rest time, without equipment, to being what they called combat-ready. We had rifles and some ammunition, we got on trucks-- 100 men to a truck, I heard. I remember that the trucks were cold, and then, during the night, I'll always remember passing the trenches from World War I. Over the years they had filled in. You could see the outlines. I didn't want to get in trenches. The last thing I wanted was trenches.

We arrived at Bastogne and were told the 82nd was pulling out, and we started in. It was daylight, we'd been up all night. We moved, dug in, moved, dug in, and then at last they found a place where they wanted us to dig in and stay.

Then the Germans came in. I was frightened when we were hit. The Germans came and I kidded around, tossed a coin, said, "That one's mine," and things like that. I was acting. (laughter) Once the big shells came in, and they came up with their tanks, I was extremely frightened. Then the joke was, "Where am I gonna run?" We were surrounded.

When you don't have any food and only limited ammunition, (laughter) you figure it's kind of bad. Artillery said, "We've got 12 more rounds, where do you want them?" That was the end. It was bad, but what can you do about it?

For the first 10 days, I worried. Gee, I was frightened. I spent days being so concerned, and then, it turned around and I thought nothing could hurt me. From complete vulnerability to thinking, "Nothing's gonna happen to me."

They say it's usually the opposite way; people think they're indestructible the first time. I knew I was destructible, and then, I became indestructible. (laughter) It got so my companions thought I was trying to win the war all by myself.

There was a little knoll out in front of us, and I thought we could have a lookout there, an outpost. I took the wire, and I said, "I need something to defend myself." They gave me a submachine gun, the only weapon I had not qualified on or even handled. I did not know how to use it. They said, "Well, it goes to your right when you shoot it." So, I took the wire out and I thought I was really doing something. But the Germans and my people knew more than I did. They just let me alone, and I put up this telephone, and soon after the Germans knew I was almost finished (I later found out they had a man in a tree who was watching), they bombarded me

Sometimes I'd get up in the morning and sing, "Oh, what a beautiful morning. Oh, what a beautiful day. I gotta feeling everything's *coming* my way." (laughter)

And then, during the '30s, was it *Balalaika,* with Nelson Eddie? Nelson Eddie was a Cossack, and he sang *Silent Night,* in English, to the Germans, and the Germans sang back to him, *Silent Night* in German. So, you know, those things stick with you, and here I am in battle on Christmas.

So on Christmas Eve I stood up and sang *Silent Night.* It was a little quiet. (laughter) A guy's standing beside me, we're talking, and I finished singing it, and we heard, "Zing," and I said, "That came in my left ear." He said, "That came in my right ear." It came between us.

I got really mad, so I called up for some fire, 'cause our artillery was zeroed in on the Germans. I picked the phone up and requested shells. They probably were phosphorus, because they got a couple of Germans and they were running around, screaming, their backs on fire, and I got the worst sense of guilt. I always remember that. Jeez, I felt extreme guilt, that I had ordered that.

When McAuliffe sent his "Nuts" message, I heard it. I was listening to the messages and broadcasts. I'd told my mother, "Don't worry, I'll stay safe," and I'm away a couple of months and here's Franklin Roosevelt saying, "Let's pray in all the churches in the US for those surrounded at Bastogne."

We had a road that went into Foy. Our company was along one side of the road, and, gee, we were wishing for Christmas packages. "Packages are coming, packages are coming," we kept saying, "and we'll get some." Finally they dropped them in, and at night I heard the truck come up. I was listening in my foxhole, and I knew nothing else was moving on the road that night, and we said "Here come our packages." But the truck didn't stop; it kept going. (laughter) It went right through our lines and "Bang," it hit a mine, and that was the end of our Christmas packages. I wanted them, but I sure didn't volunteer to go out and get them.

Food was pretty horrible. We had some farmers in our group. We killed a pig. I guess we didn't know anything about hanging it up. We used to kill chickens and try to eat them, and then, one day, we had chickens in a pail, cooking, and a bombardment came, and the chickens were filled with shrapnel.

An Army Air Corps liaison officer parachuted into surrounded Bastogne to relay directions to the fighter pilots, I was told. I was on an outpost in a house, on the ground floor, at the top of the stairs to the cellar, looking out at a house where the Germans had an outpost a hundred or so yards away. It was annoying because the Germans appeared to be living comfortably, as shown by the smoke coming from the chimney.

I called for some artillery rounds on the house. I was switched to the liaison officer and he relayed my request to a pilot overhead. Two or three bombs were dropped. I wanted to bring the pilot in closer. The liaison officer patched me through to the pilot. I asked the pilot to drop between our outpost house and the Germans' house. The pilot confidently stated he would put the next bomb down the smoking chimney.

The next bomb landed closer to me, and the explosion lifted me up and threw me down the cellar steps with the telephone in my hand, snapping the wire. Obviously, it was not possible to inform the pilot that he had not done me in. The pilot sounded as if, in a year or so, he would be celebrating his twenty-first birthday, as I would also.

At one point when it was felt that we would be overrun and some would be captured, word was passed that everyone should take off their dog tags, so the Germans would not be able to identify men of the Jewish faith. After a bit of depression and worrying, I concluded it best to put a dog tag in each boot, so that "graves" could identify me.

We heard stories like how the Germans had come in at night and killed 16 of our men while they were asleep, so then you didn't want to go to sleep at night.

The Germans were shouting "Death! Tomorrow, you die!" When you know they're going to send the tanks in, you want to dig a foxhole near a tree, because you don't want the tank to get on top of you. Then, at night, sometimes, we'd move fast to where they were attacking, and it was so cold at times-- 10 degrees below zero-- and they didn't have body bags, so they stacked up the bodies, three across, three one way, three the other way, and that affected me. I didn't like running into a battle area passing those stiff bodies. That was a negative.

In one place, where we ran to one night, it was pretty horrible. I don't know what happened there, but we stopped and I'm digging a foxhole, and my backside's up, and a tree is suddenly cut off about two inches above me right across my backside. Boy, did I dig faster then. I didn't sleep that night, 'cause bullets were coming in and I was hugging the ground.

You didn't care what was happening a half mile away. You were only worried about yourself and the people beside you, waking them up if something happened or so they didn't sleep too much. At the start, I was awake for almost three days. I was so tired, and I remember going to sleep. They were yelling for me to go on patrol but the sergeant says, "Hey, Frank's done enough. Let him sleep." I heard that. That patrol never was found, as far as I know. You know, it was something I was glad I had missed.

We started with about 65 in the platoon, and I was one of the last two before Patton's tanks came up. Oh, there were only two of us. We were running our own war then. Me and Kelly, Kelly and I. My feet were frozen black when they got to us, and we just put our rifles against a tree and went back.

The first doctor I got to cut one pair of socks off my feet and they were frozen solid. He couldn't bend them back and forth. (laughter) Then he cut another pair, and by the last pair, he could bend them; they were moist. I said, "I've been walking on those feet," and he said, "No, you've been walking on your heart."

Originally, back in Mourmelon, I never got the shoes I should have had. I'm size 13. They were cooperative. They kept saying, "We ordered them," and then the lieutenant came in when we were getting ready to go to Bastogne and said, "You don't have to go. You don't have the proper shoes to go." I didn't want to be left there, so I said, "No, I'm going."

So it took no time for my feet to be frozen. Then they dropped galoshes, size 17 galoshes, and some socks. I put on four pairs of socks and the galoshes so I could move.

Being frozen is unusual; first your feet hurt, and then they stop hurting. It's when they stop hurting that you have a problem. Later, in Paris, they wanted to cut my toes off. Several toes on each foot were black. I had one of the biggest arguments I ever had. The doctor was saying, "Those toes are gone." He was going to operate the next day, but I had him give me another week.

So, they were going to fly me back, but it was bad weather. They put me on a litter, and I lived on that litter in the tent, waiting to get on a plane, for maybe seven days, and then they sent me back to another place, and I guess it was an apartment house. I woke up and I was in a hospital, in a VD ward. They didn't have room anywhere else. (laughter)

They were nice to me. They even carried me to the john. I was very ill, and the guys couldn't do enough for me. I was taking 18 sulfa pills per hour or so, trying to cure whatever I had-- pneumonia, I guess. I was thin. You could count all the ribs and perhaps see my backbone. They made sure we had C rations every night, warmed up. In a week or so, we got on the train and went to Paris, to the American hospital. Then I went back to Cherbourg, then back to England, and then, in mid-May, 1945, back to the States.

"We had Rutgers professors, ministers, people of all kinds, working on this project. They wanted to be part of the war effort." *--Elliot Bartner*

We graduated in '43, but prior to that a lot of us went to enlist. And I applied for the Navy. I wanted to go into the Navy. And I waited, and waited, then I got a letter, and they said that all the openings were filled. After I graduated I had a number of calls from various industries for jobs. One of them, I remember, was RCA and this was the beginning of television. They were starting to make television tubes. But my interest was in the biological end, and I became a biochemist. And I went to work for the Bureau of Biological Research that had been started up here at Rutgers, working with the Squibb pharmaceutical company.

A lot of the work that we did was for the war. We had contracts with the Office of Scientific Research and Development. So I worked there and I taught at the chemistry school. The project had to do with human blood. The country was divided into three parts, and Squibb had the contract for the East Coast.

What we did was, the Red Cross got the bleedings all up and down the East Coast. And we got approximately 10,000 bleedings a day. They would ship them to us, they would arrive about seven in the morning and we'd start working on them right away. They came in special cases-- huge cases, about three to four times the size of a desk-- and while they weren't refrigerated, they were insulated to keep them at room temperature.

We were working on a method that was called the Cohen method, developed by a Dr. Cohen at Harvard Medical School. We fractionated the blood. We took the human blood and divided it into the different parts, the different proteins that it consisted of. We were after one protein, called serum albumen. And the reason for that was, this was a Navy contract. Everything we made went to the Navy. In a confined space, on a ship, you only have so much space allocated to different things. You couldn't take thousands of pints of blood, you didn't have the room for it. So essentially what we did is we took serum albumen out of the blood, made it into solutions and put it in small bottles.

Each bottle held the equivalent of five pints of blood. We condensed it that much. And it was in bottles that could be given immediately, intravenously. It was used in the case of shock.

Shock was a great killer in battle. The blood would leave the veins and go into the body cavity, and that could result in death. But this serum albumen kept it within the veins and arteries.

We turned out millions of pints of blood that way. This was a new method that was far different than the method ordinarily used for the purpose, and it required working in cold temperatures. We worked at five degrees below zero and the storage rooms were 60 below. We fractionated by alcohol. As we went along, we made improvements and modifications, to the point where we recovered practically everything of value.

We had all these other fractions, the globulins and the most famous, of course, was gamma globulin, which you hear about now. We were the first ones to work with that in huge quantities. But we really weren't ready for that. In fact, we didn't even know what some of the fractions could be used for, so we stored them at 60 degrees below zero to wait for the day when we could work with them. But along the way we worked with other fractions that we knew we could utilize, including fibrinogen and thrombin and so forth, having to do with the clotting, which was important also.

There were a lot of things we accomplished that would never have been accomplished if the war hadn't taken place. It's a hell of a thing to say, but it's just like the NASA program today. One was the method of centrification. Originally we started by putting each individual bottle in a centrifuge. Centrifuging took 30-40 minutes. But then we developed a continuous method of doing this separation so what originally took about 20 hours now took two hours.

In this process, the red cells separated out. We had no use for the red cells, and they went down the drain, into the New Brunswick sewer system. If anybody wanted to check it, they'd think there was mass murder going on in the city.

Then we developed a product from fibrinogen that was like a white foam, like styrofoam. It could be packed into wounds and stopped bleeding that way. It wasn't utilized to any great extent, but it was the beginning of something.

One of the most interesting things about this work was the people that worked for us. We had all walks of life come in and work part time, from kids to people in their 70s. The most interesting group were the Rutgers professors. They wanted to help in the war effort. They were mostly fellows in their 50s. So I had the most marvelous group of guys you'd ever want to meet. They would work three or four hours, mostly in the evening.

We had ministers of various denominations who wanted to be part of the effort. I would match up a minister with a guy from the other side of town, and they became fast friends and helped each other. It was really a great sociological situation there.

Remember, we were doing all this in an environment of five degrees below. Eventually, I worked without my coat; I'd just gotten used to the temperature. The body can make adjustments. The big problem was when you went from the cold to the normal temperature, you'd get headaches. So we carried on and that was the work that I did during the war, the whole time.

"I said, 'Take the men back, Gardner. I'm dying.' I didn't want them to carry me out, then they'd all be killed by the sniper." —Franklyn Johnson

It was said that the D-Day fleet was the largest armada in the history of the world, and I think that's true. When we finally got to the top of the cliffs and could take a moment to look back, it was absolutely amazing-- ships everywhere. A storm was coming up, and they were bobbing, and they were getting ready to go back and load up again.

I was a first lieutenant, and I had an antitank platoon. We'd tried to bed our men down the night before, but I'm sure everybody was thinking about the next day and probably praying. We could have no lights, so nobody could read anything, divert himself that way. It was, as it always is in England, (laughter) it was wet. If not raining, it was maybe drizzling. The ship went across, and we were listed for H-Hour, but some troops were there already. I would guess it was probably engineers trying to de-mine the place.

There were railroad ties that were bound together and sunk in cement, in the sand, so that at any tide, even high tide, your boat would ground on it. Our vessel was grounded out too far. I know some of my men drowned, because in those days the straps and things to get rid of the equipment were not what they have today, and they couldn't get rid of their heavy equipment in time. We'd been told it was going to be shallow, and they were carrying all the ammunition they could.

They were just shooting at us, and all you could do was try to haul yourself and your men up. Pappy, my second-in-command, was killed immediately. A shell landed near him and he was gone. A number of others were wounded and we couldn't get them out of the water, so they drowned.

Then General Theodore Roosevelt and a man named Cota, Norman D. Cota, he was a colonel, later a brigadier general, they came along, and both of them exhorted the men, "You're going to die here. You've got to get up the cliff." Well, there was a little shallow place, just a tidal shallow that gave a little shelter at the time we were trying to land, so we had to get out of there.

We were getting fire from the right side, so we headed for a draw on Red Beach, that's a part of Omaha Beach, and if one is there now, the cemetery is immediately above it, and this was an old sort of farm road. There had been some beach houses that

271

had been turned into forts. We managed to work our way up that draw.

We'd probably lost about eight men by that time, and all the vehicles except one jeep were gone, and all the guns, so, in effect, we were infantrymen. We were on foot. We had no heavy weapons. We just had to use our rifles and went on up, those of us that made it, to the top, into a wooded lane.

I still have a memento of the occasion-- the second of my three Purple Hearts. I had apparently been hit on the hand by a spent metal fragment, and I put a handkerchief around my middle left finger, and it was all blood-soaked, and we went by a sort of temporary Medical Corps tent with a red cross in front of it. And the aide called out, "Lieutenant, you're wounded. You're all bloody." And he said, "Here, let me bandage you up." So he put on a decent bandage, and somewhere along the line, he took down my name.

I went and caught up with my men, who were slowly moving down the lane. The odd follow-up of that was that back in England, some time later, some general came along, and he was handing out medals, and a Silver Star was among them and another Purple Heart. I guess he gave me two, because the third one was when I was shot and captured, and I'd forgotten all about this darned thing, but he explained, "Well, you were wounded on D-Day," and I said, "Okay, now I remember."

We had moved inland some distance, and we were often under fire from snipers, and I was finally hit by one of them. The area is called Vidouville, inland maybe 15 miles. We'd fought our way in, and, by this time it was June 25. We had lost men, but we had moved in, and except for Pappy Henderson, none of my leadership was killed.

We heard tanks moving around, down ahead of us, and I went to the old man, the Colonel, and said, "There are tanks down there, and even though our antitank guns are not too potent, maybe we could get close enough to knock some off." I think, by this time, we'd been landing heavy stuff, and we felt reasonably secure about staying on the land, but it was still tricky, and we knew that Hitler and company were going to bring up their heavy stuff to try to knock us back.

The old man said, "All right, take a patrol and go out there. There's a new officer who joined us, Lieutenant Gardner; get some experience for him." So, we had, I think, about seven or eight men between us. I asked him to stay at the rear, I'd take the front, right behind two scouts. They, hopefully, would spot snipers and keep us moving toward where we could hear these tanks in the distance, sort of rumbling around.

It was all hedgerows, and we were sort of in a lane, but you had to keep looking both ways. All of a sudden, shots rang out. It was a sniper in a tree that we had overlooked. Both those scouts were killed, and I was hit at the same time. And all I had time to do was to say, "Gardner, take the men back," because we couldn't see anything.

Then, I made the near fatal mistake. I said, "Take the men back, Gardner. I'm dying." Well, this was because I knew it was pretty serious, and I was afraid he was going to try to get a couple of guys to carry me or something, and then they would all get killed by snipers.

That was a bad mistake, because when someone says that, and there are no witnesses to anything other than this guy lying on the ground with a lot of blood flowing out of him, you tend to believe it. There was kind of a rule that if you didn't have any information you carried the person for 30 days as missing. So as I found out later, my parents had an MIA report. With my being the only child, this was a pretty hard blow,

Then, after 30 days, with no new information, a Killed-In-Action report was sent back. In the meantime, I had been captured and carried, somewhat painfully, into a place called Rennes, which is sort of a rail center, and we went into a field hospital, I guess it was. I was in an ambulance, and I was in and out, mainly conscious, because when we'd hit a bump I knew damn well that there was something badly the matter with me.

I'd been hit under the left shoulder blade, in the lung, and that's why they later had to take out most of that lung. There were little windows in the side of the ambulance. I could see that we were moving through countryside, but I was in and out of consciousness, so my memory is rather ragged after that, but I do remember we were in a kind of temporary hospital. There were cots, and it was an old Catholic girls' school.

Anyway, they did take out the slugs. I don't know how many there were. I do have, in German, the report, the medical report. They took out most of the left lung, and the sad thing was, they did it without any anesthesia. They said, "Well," in what little German I could pick up, "all the sulfa and the other drugs, all the painkillers, have been destroyed by your planes over the roads in France, so it's your fault that we don't have it."

I think at the start they might have figured there was some information I could give them. I wasn't tortured or anything like that. I was slapped in the face a couple of times and asked what my unit was, and where was it going, and so on, and I said, "I don't know," because I didn't.

Meanwhile, I was unable to move. I was put in a bed, and fed, but this kept getting worse. I found out later it's what they call empyema, a growth of poisons and liquid waste in your lung cavity, and I figured that sooner or later, unless I'm rescued, this is it.

There must have been 600 or 700 American prisoners in that hospital. There were German guards, but the nuns took care of us. The food supply was running out, there was black bread and so on. Then, on August 8th, guns began to fire closer, and several of the guards left. It was pretty clear that we were going to be rescued. Well, of course, the question in my mind was, "Is it going to be in time?" because I knew this thing was getting worse all the time in my chest.

Sure enough, Patton's forces arrived, and they rushed us out of there on the hospital planes and got us back to the 15th Army Hospital Group, up in the lake country of England. The firing

274

and the battle just moved on-- the St. Lo breakthrough and later, the Hurtgen Forest, and the Remagen Bridge, which my boys were all involved in, but which I couldn't keep up with, except in the papers.

I went back to this hospital, and that's where the real operation took place, to clean out this mess that was in my chest, and a Dr. Merchant, who performed the operation, and I became friends, and he said, finally, "Lieutenant, we're going to have you ZI-ed. "That was the saying for, "Sent to the Zone of the Interior," back to the US, and I was idealistic enough or something, to say, "Well, come on, the guys are fighting into Germany now," and he said, "Look, you aren't worth anything to them anymore. You're going home." So, I was put on a plane and shipped back to the States, where I had several months of recovery in another hospital.

"I remember clear as hell the day the kamikaze hit us. He came skimming over the water, over the destroyers, coming right at us." --William Gutter

The *Belleau Wood* was a flattop, a small flattop but it was up there with the fast carriers. It was a cruiser hull that they converted, and it operated quite well. I'd been trained for bomb disposal, and that's how I got assigned to this new ship. Every regular Navy guy was busting his butt to get a duty like that.

Our captain was a terrific guy. He wasn't a trade school boy. He was a mustang; he came up from the ranks. Captain Alfred M. Pride. He was the man who was ordered by the Navy Department after World War II to prevent the Chinese from overrunning the islands of Quemoy and Matsu. Remember those islands? He ended up on the cover of *Time* magazine.

He was quiet and laid back, and I had only the greatest respect for him. When he got his promotion to Admiral, I was fortunate enough to be there. He was sleeping, and the radioman brought the orders up, and I said, "Do me a favor, let me take it

275

to him." So I go down and knock on the door. "Who is it?" I said, "It's Lieutenant Gutter, Admiral Pride." He opens the door, he says, "What did you say?" I said, "Congratulations, Admiral Pride." That was such a thrill for me, to be able to do that for that man.

I remember as clear as hell the day when the kamikaze hit us. You didn't have much time to think about it. Suddenly you look and you see this thing skipping over destroyers, skipping over cruisers, skimming the water, and it's coming right at you. That's the way they came in.

It hit us at the rear end of the ship, where we had planes stored. I don't know how many planes there were, and everything blew up in there. I used to stand watch back there until they switched me about 30 days before. And later I found a guy dead right where I used to stand back there.

Then the fires started to spread, and I fought fires from nine in the morning till 11 at night before we finally got them all out. There were 40 mms going off just from the heat, and things like that. You've got no place to go, no place to walk, and you're fighting for your life.

We had a young seaman second class named Tom, who had been assigned from boot camp right to the *Belleau Wood*, and we had been teaching him about bombs and things. Now when we were hit, the rear end of the ship was aflame. And below the deck, on both sides, was the ready rocket storage. That's where they stored the rockets that were ready to be loaded onto planes that were about to take off. Usually, it was a torpedo bomb.

The flames were pretty heavy back there, and a lot of guys were lost. And I thought, "Oh, my God, that rocket storage can go any minute. We've got to get somebody down there to make sure no flames get near those rockets." But nobody's around; they're all fighting fires. So I go down and look, and there's this young trainee, on his own, spraying down the torpedo bombs with water spray and cooling 'em down just as nicely as anyone could have done.

I said, "Tom, if you were a girl, I'd kiss you. Just stay with it, keep doing what you're doing." I put him in for a Navy Cross. They knocked it down to a Silver Star, but I'll tell you one thing. That was one proud day of mine when they presented it to him and I was still aboard ship.

We lost about 200 men that day, and most of them were buried at sea.

"At one end of town, the French were waiting for us with American flags. At the other end, they were kissing the Germans goodbye." *--Bert R. Manhoff*

The original 82nd Airborne was training near us, and when they were dressed, they wore a kerchief and they were very dapper. And we were in town one day, and some guy started to tease them about their cravats. That they were sissies. As sure as I'm sitting here, they walked over, they grabbed the guy, one guy on his arms, one guy on his shoulder, walked over to the telegraph pole and smashed him against the telegraph pole and let him lay there. They fixed their cravats and went right on.

Another story I was told about the 82nd. They had been pulled back into a rest area, and there was a WAC attachment there. They were running a dance and they didn't invite the 82nd Airborne. General Gavin wrote them a letter. He wanted to know why his men weren't invited to the dance. They wrote back, "We didn't want any of your high-priced killers." That was a mistake.

On the night of the dance, they sent in a commando squad. They cut down the posts so the roof of the porch fell down and nobody could get out. Then they barricaded the back door. What I was told is that later Gavin sent a check to the hotel from the division, paid all the repairs.

See, they were taught the same as we were, that you were a war machine and human life meant nothing to you under certain circumstances. We were trained the same way. I found no prob-

277

lem ordering death to Germans or anything like that. We were taught that way, and then I saw some horrible acts that the Germans committed. I saw a medic crawl out on a field with a big Red Cross all over him and they zeroed in on him with artillery. He was going out there to try to recover a wounded soldier and the soldier was dead already.

One time in France we were advancing, we were with Patton so you know we were far ahead. And being with the reconnaissance company, we were out ahead of the tank destroyer battalions. We came to a town and we could see down from the crest of a hill, and there were the French people lined up at this end of the town, where we were going to come in, and they were there with their American flags and their flowers. At the other end of the town, you could see them kissing the Germans goodbye. Kissing and embracing them. The sight was unbelievable.

I did not have a high regard for French or German people. I had a high regard for the English fighters, they were funny as hell. We were attached to the desert rats for a while-- the 2nd Armored, I think. Our job as recon was to go and find the German tank parks, come back and report them and they would knock them out.

So we found a tank park, we come back and I'm reporting now to this British sergeant, the typical one you see in the movies with the mustache and the rolled-up sleeves. Right out of Hollywood, you know. And he said, "Say, yank, what did you see?" I said I saw about four tanks down there. "Good," he said. "We'll flush them out, and you stand by and deliver a smashing blow."

We had a 37 mm gun. It would be hard to break that window with it. I said, "Wait, you got that wrong. We'll flush them out and you deliver the blow." He had a 90 mm gun on a Churchill tank that could knock this building over. Well, he looked at me and he smiled as if to say, Okay kid, we'll play it your way this time. He said, "You flush them."

It was tough enough for us to flush them out. We just went

down to show this bunch what we had and then ran like hell. So they ran the other way and they ran into the fire of those British tanks, and they were good.

Later we wound up with the Churchill tanks ourselves, with the 90 mm. And we went into one town and there was a sniper there and the captain of the gun company happened to be a Catholic and he was angry because the sniper was hiding behind a statue. The sniper fired from behind a religious statue. So he said, "We want him!"

I said, "I'm not going after him. You want him, you go get him." So they got him all right. And I was told that they tied the guy to a tree and shot a 90 mm shell at him. A 90 mm could remove this building. It must have been quite a sight. It's just as well I didn't see it.

I had two Brooklyn guys with me, and Kelly, an Irishman, and Kelly was funny. We were in Germany and we had taken over a house. Because I was Jewish, I was the interpreter. I knew "Where are the eggs?" and "How many rooms?" That was the extent of Yiddish that I could convert to German.

There was a young German boy in the house, bright as hell. Probably right out of the Hitler Youth. So Kelly and I decided, as long as we're going to be there, we're going to Americanize the people. We were there for quite awhile because we were so far ahead that we didn't know where the hell the rest of the Army was. Each night, we'd gather all the people in the town, and turn the radio on-- the broadcast in German about what America was doing. And the night that Roosevelt died, a lot of the Germans had been convinced his name was Rosenfeld.

So we educated this kid and he was bright, he knew every state capital of the United States. And we get ready to leave and he comes up to Kelly and he says, "Kelly, why are you fighting Hitler?" We thought we'd cleansed his mind, see. Kelly says, "I'm going to kill that kid." I said, "No, you're not." He said, "Does he deserve to live?" and he's all ready to kill him. I said, "I'll tell you what, Kelly, I got a better way to scare him."

279

They were so afraid of the blacks because they had been taught that the blacks were inhuman, so I said, "You go back and tell him 'Die Schwarz ihr kommen.' 'Black is coming.'" He goes back and tells this to the kid, and the kid turns white and goes running up to his mother. He was scared to death.

"I'd just heard 'Bombs away!' That's when I was hit. It came in the left side of the plane and went out the right side."   *--Alexander Nazemetz*

Early in the war, the losses were extremely heavy, to the point where I think they had debated whether or not this strategic bombing was really worth the terrible sacrifices in human life. Now my group had, I don't exactly remember the number, but I'll be very close. We had 3,500 flying personnel from the time they got over there in 1943 until the war was over in early '45. Of those, 1,700 to 1,800 were shot down. That's 50 percent, and, of those, about 800 were prisoners of war. We were only one of many groups, and I know they have debated this point.

My own feeling is that the Air Force did a lot of good, softening up the areas where the ground troops had to go. Certainly we must have destroyed the morale of the German people. I can't imagine anybody being happy about airplanes coming over for 10 or 12 hours at a time, in a single file, the way we flew, and then, have the RAF come over at night.

We went after oil refineries. That was in Merseburg. We went after marshaling yards. We went after tank factories in Kassel. I don't know what exactly our target was in Munich. But I remember we were flying for at least 20 minutes back towards England, and we could still see the smoke, and it was just as high as we were flying.

My last mission, my thirty-third, was the one when I got wounded. We went to Hanover, Germany, on the 14th of March. I remember that we had a chute in the aircraft through which we deposited what we called chaff. Radar was still a fairly new thing, so what this chaff was, it was lengths of aluminum foil, I think about a foot long, and very much like the tinsel on a Christmas tree, except that it was stiff. And some of the aircraft that we flew were equipped with this stuff, and we would come in with three or four boxes of it. And I, as the waist-gunner, was back there by the chute, so that would be my job.

I'd have just dropped the stuff out. When it's sprinkled down below the aircraft that way, the radar that the Germans were using would hit that first, and then bounce back, and therefore, they wouldn't get our altitude immediately. It would work for awhile, but they would soon see they weren't hitting anything, so they would check it.

Now, when I was doing that, I was on my haunches, just opposite the right waist position, and I heard the announcement, "Bombs away," from the bombardier. I looked out the window, and I saw the bombs coming down. At that moment, I was hit. It came right across from the left side, hit the throat mike I was wearing, and went out the other side of the aircraft. The reason I was wearing that throat mike was that the mike in my oxygen mask, after all these missions, wasn't working.

You sweat, even in that terrible cold. Ice forms on the exhalation outlets there, and I used to keep a handkerchief-- by mission 33 it was a pretty dirty handkerchief-- handy, and I would clean my oxygen mask with it and quickly put it back on my face, so, it wouldn't freeze.

I didn't know immediately that I was hit. My tail-gunner began to call me, and I tried to say, "I'm hit." But I didn't hear my own voice. I remember looking down, and I saw the throat mike on the floor, and I saw the brass springs, and I thought, "Now, isn't that funny?"

This is all happening in a split-second, mind you, and then I realized that I had taken my hand away, and my glove was all bloody. So I reconnected myself and tried to say, "I'm hit" again. The pilot told the radioman to go back and check on what happened to me. So he came back.

He was a big ruddy guy, a weight lifter. He took one look at me and turned pale. I couldn't see what happened to me. Now, I know about jugular veins. I knew where vocal cords are, and here I was, unable to talk. And he just went so pale, and I thought, "Jesus, what happened to me?"

And then he disconnected me. The bombardier came back, and he sprinkled sulfa on me, and he gave me half a syringe of morphine. I didn't hurt, so I didn't want it. I tried to tell him that through hand motions. I couldn't speak, so I was really scared. I thought something happened to the vocal cords, but I told him not to shoot red flares upon landing to indicate wounded on board. The crew chief would see that it was his airplane and he'd get scared, so I asked him not to do it, but would you believe, I saw the red flares go over.

The pilot asked permission to leave the formation so he could come in first, and so we landed. The doctor was there, and he said to me, "Did you spit up any blood?" and I said, "No," and then I think he said, "You were lucky." Outside, I heard a voice say, "Hey, Doc, you need the stretcher?" I spoke then, and I said, "No, I can walk," and I could walk. (laughter) I was in the hospital for three weeks.

"There were two crease marks across the back of my neck and four bullet holes in my field jacket-- two ingoing and two out." --Raymond Mortensen

There are five men in a Sherman tank, and we lived in the tank, which is why the tank had to be modified. When it was built, somebody put a basket around the bottom of the turret, so you couldn't get from compartment to compartment without rotating the turret to an opening in the basket. First thing when you went into a new tank, you cut out the basket. Now, you can get all over the tank.

In the turret there was the gunner, the assistant gunner, and the tank commander-- that was me. We had places to load the ammunition, and we also had to carry extra ammo on the floor of the turret. We carried food, water, and the gunner and the assistant gunner were down in the lower part of the tank.

Nobody got out of the tank to sleep, unless you got out to go in a house and sleep. We did a lot of that, like in Marburg. We had the town secured, and I slept in a nice, warm bed that night, (laughter) but otherwise I slept on top of the ammunition, and, usually at night we would get refueled and we would get resupplied with food, because, in an armored company, except if you're in rest area, you don't have a mess truck. They bring you up rations, like K rations or C rations, and you eat, the five of you, pretty much together, not with anybody else. We were a close-knit group. We were very close. You had to be close because you depended on each other.

One time, after the Battle of the Bulge, it had gotten warmer, and the snow had melted, and we were now in mud. I mean lots of mud. It was in the evening, and the Company Commander had gotten his orders for the next day from regiment, and he called each platoon leader to come to the command post and get instructions for tomorrow.

So I walked up there, and we had a meeting and decided what time we were gonna depart, who was gonna do what and when, and I started back to my tank, and all of a sudden artillery fire started coming in. Now, I'm standing as close to my tank as you are to me and all I have to do is get inside. I couldn't get up on the tank, because of the mud. I kept slipping down. I said to myself, "I'm gonna die out here because I can't get into the tank." So I crawled under, and I lived, but a week later, that was a funny thing. (laughter)

I've said my tank was the first one to reach the Rhine River, and this is how it happened. I had read that the Third Armored Division was the first unit to reach the Rhine in the First Army, and I was in the Third Armored. I didn't realize how close we were. We were a little bit north of Cologne, in a suburb, a little different town, and we're wandering through the streets of this little town, encountering no resistance, and all of a sudden, bingo, like that, I called the Company Commander, and I said, "Is what I'm seeing what I think it is, the Rhine River?" He said, "Yes. Can you see it?" I said, "Yeah." "That's it, you're there," and that's all it was. Now, the other people, the real heroes, were the people that captured the Remagen Bridge, which was south of us. All we did was get to the Rhine. We had to wait for the engineers to come and build us a bridge.

The place where I was wounded was a town called Worberg. It was late in the afternoon, and we were in column, one tank behind the other, and we'd come through the town and I was going through an underpass, and I came out and, "Boom," that panzerfaust-- antitank grenade-- hit us right in the seam, where the turret sits on the hull, and with that it comes in, and sparks are flying around.

I couldn't see. I put my hand up to my right eye, and it came away all warm with blood, and I thought, "My God, I've lost the side of my face." So I gave the command to bail out and we did. I went over the top, and the other guys went over the top, and we wound up in a ditch on the side of the road, which was full of rainwater, and crawled back to where it was safer.

The medics came and assured me that I hadn't lost my face, and I hadn't lost a lot of blood, and that was it Nobody else in the tank was hurt. They just pushed the tank to the side and kept right on going, and sent me back to the hospital.

They sewed me up, and I was supposed to go back to my outfit, but then they found that I had lost most of my hearing, so they sent me back to a general hospital in France, and I stayed there until that cleared up.

The only thing that was frightening was, right after the surgery, I was back in the ward, and I had gone to sleep, and I woke up, and I was feeling no pain. I went to sit up, and I couldn't get my head off the pillow. It was stuck. So a nurse came along, and she got some alcohol, and I had two crease marks right across the back of my neck, and, upon further examination, the back of my tanker's field jacket had four bullet holes, two that went in and two where they came out.

It probably happened when I went over the top of the tank, and he was firing and missed, but he came close. I didn't sleep for a couple of nights after that, knowing how close I'd come to being killed.

"We opened fire and hit the kamikaze as he was swerving back up, and he slid down the side of the ship we were unloading." --M. Leon Canick

We went through Solomon's Base, Maryland and down to New Orleans to Shell Beach where we did anti-aircraft training and through the Panama Canal to San Diego. Then we went to Hawaii, that's where we put our boat together. Our boat was in three sections on top of an LST. We put our own boat together.

After Hawaii, we were at Enewitok and Kwajalein in the Carolines. Then we saw Tinian, Guam, and Saipan in the Marianas. We staged in Saipan for Iwo Jima. We staged at Leyte in the Philippines for the invasion of Okinawa. Then we saw the island of Okinawa, and then Iwo Jima.

We had gotten lumber on one of our trips and it was getting hot as hell so the fellows built a platform across our after deck in the stern between the two sets of cabins. We had four different cabin spaces. And they put up a house and they had screens. It was really a very nice little room. Let me tell you, that was a blessing.

During the typhoon, I was standing on that platform for 16 hours. The roof was going to come off but we hung on to it, then we got ropes on it and we managed to save it. Ours was the only LCT that was still at anchor after the storm.

There were two typhoons. One was a very serious one, but it hit the land a little more than it hit us. Our conning tower was 30 feet high and waves were 65 or 70 feet high. They were really enormous. In the other typhoon, though, an LST, (now we weighed 150 tons, the LST weighed 2,000 tons) went out of control and was banging against us.

Ultimately, because I was letting my anchor cable go in and out to ride with the waves when she came alongside us, the water got sucked up in the anchor winch and that knocked that out. Thank God an ocean-going tug came along and pulled her off, otherwise they would have drowned us. Some LCTs had broken out of their anchors and cut the cable. Some of them were 75-100 yards from shore, and they never could pull them off.

We were in the landings on D-Day at both Iwo Jima and Okinawa. At Iwo Jima, I was on the LST, but right off shore, and we were at our guns. The most memorable thing was the raising of the flag on Mount Suribachi at Iwo Jima. The other most memorable thing was the fact that the Marines landed on Iwo Jima after 92 consecutive days of bombing and shelling. At five o'clock in the afternoon, they were almost wiped off the island because the Japanese had not been destroyed at all. What should have been a seven-day campaign took 30 days and huge numbers of casualties.

Some of the Marines slept on my boat on the way to Iwo Jima. One of them was a 25-year veteran and he was there at the raising of the flag, and then he was killed. That was the only thing I know about him.

At Iwo Jima there was hostile fire from the beach, but they really weren't aiming at us because we were obviously not worth wasting ammunition on. But on Okinawa, the kamikazes were there and they were striking. There was an LSM not far from us who, against regulations, opened fire in the smoke screens at one of the kamikaze planes that they could see. The kamikaze plane, in turn, followed the tracers right down to the ship and strafed them-- and damaged them heavily.

But we got shrapnel. We got pieces of metal that came on board. The constant noise of guns firing was awful! No one was particularly firing at us except that a kamikaze came at us when we were alongside a ship unloading her. You could see it coming directly down on us. And the fellows wanted to leave their guns. I made them stay with their guns, 50 caliber guns and the 20 mm antiaircraft guns. He came close to us but then he tried to swerve down and go up again so he could hit something worthwhile like a destroyer, but we shot him down. We got him half-way up through his crawling, and he slid down the side of the bigger ship.

"I wasn't armed, and I heard voices down there. I ran down the stairs yelling, 'Ich bin ein Jude.' That was my weapon." *--Nathan Shoehalter*

The first casualty I encountered as a medic was a kid whose foot was blown off. That was a shock to me because it wasn't bleeding. Just shot off, no shoe, nothing. I remember hitting him with morphine, telling him how lucky he was, he got that million dollar wound. Stuck the tags on him, the tag that said we had given him morphine, looked for other injuries. He said he didn't have any. He was awake, and we carried him off, put him on a jeep, and sent him back. God, there were a lot of them. I can't tell you how many, I don't remember.

My family saved all the letters I'd written home. Reading those letters again, I was overwhelmed by memories that I could never have shared with them. The horror and fear came rushing back. As I read my letters, I cried as I was never able to cry when I wrote them. I remembered what it was like to walk in a permanent stoop, a kind of running lope, so you could hit the ground at the first sound of 88s or rifle fire. The single thought was to find places that offered protection from enemy shells: a hole in the ground, a tree to hide behind, a fold in the earth.

I had naively assumed that fighting stopped at nightfall and resumed again at daybreak. I soon learned that warfare is incessant. The relentless din of artillery, rifle fire, and machine guns never stops.

I was a company aid man/litter bearer in an infantry division.

287

That meant that under the Geneva Convention I was not permitted to carry arms; all I had along with the three other members of the litter squad were morphine needles, lots of bandages, and sulfa powder, but no weapon.

The men we were relieving trooped wordlessly past, haggard, slumped, with glazed expressions. Their weapons were slung casually, their uniforms were filthy, they carried nothing more than their ammo belts and a raincoat. The only sounds were the whooshing sounds of walking and an occasional clink of rifle against helmet. Everything was done in darkness and silence because we were only a few yards away from the Germans.

I expected banter from the departing soldiers just like in the movies, a grin, a wisecrack, then on to the job of getting the war over with. Our silence was the silence of fear.

The morning after our entry into the line I helped load three bodies of our men who were killed the night before. It was the first time in my life I had ever seen a dead body. This was all new and horrifying.

Our first attack on a German pillbox was launched from a crossroads in the tiny French village of Gravelotte. I remember hearing the field telephone ring, and fearing that it might be from one of our platoons reporting an injury we'd have to go out and attend to. It was. And the four of us, in the blackest of nights, took off with our litter and only a vague description of where the injured man lay.

The assault started hours before dawn with an awesome artillery attack. As the hissing shells exploded with deafening roars, I remember thinking that if they hit a tree here in the woods, we'd be goners, dispatched by our own artillery fire.

Then, for some unfathomable reason, in the midst of this ferocious barrage, I had a vivid image of a phonograph album in the window of the Rivoli Music Shop on George Street in New Brunswick, New Jersey, where I went to college. The album jacket read "Komm, Susse Todt"--"Come, Sweet Death!"

As it got lighter and the firing from our artillery ended, I could see the bunker that was our objective. Rifle fire spewed from its ports, and we returned the fire. Then two of our men rushed up to the bunker's steel door and fastened "bangalore" plastic around it. When the device exploded, it blew the door from its hinges. A handful of enemy soldiers came out of the bunker and were led away with their hands up.

We lived in that pillbox for four days, without food or fresh water, and cut off from our division. We were reduced to drinking our own urine that we "purified" with halogen tablets. We had a wounded man who desperately needed plasma, and we had radioed for emergency supplies. They were finally dropped by an artillery spotter plane but we couldn't inject the plasma because we couldn't find a vein; he was so bloated. We tried everything, an arm, the ankle, his neck. I can still hear the burbling sounds as he drowned in his own fluid.

I was in the line for about 90 days. In the front, all the time, in harm's way all the time, 90 days, and it was really extraordinarily stressful. This one kid shot his toe off. Another one went into a catatonic state. I'll never forget that. I can see him sitting there in his uniform, just hunched up in that womb position.

You could never get to everyone who needed help. Once you got to somebody, there was always somebody nearby who was hit also. Remember, I was not a doctor. All I did was shove a bandage on a kid's gaping guts, tie it, throw in sulfanilamide. That's all, and get them out, just get them out. Treat as many as you could and get them out.

Now I'll tell you my special story. In a place called Munchen Gladbach, which we came on very rapidly-- it was a big city-- my job was to find a place where we could set up an aid station. I picked a place that had a plate glass window on it and grave stones, marble grave stones. I thought, "Oh, God, this is secure, because it's got power there."

So, remember, I'm not armed, and we're fighting, and there's all kinds of stuff going on in this little town. I rush into this store, and there's nobody there, and I hear voices, and I open up a door, and there's a cellar, and the voices are down there. I wanted this place as our aid station. It was beautifully secure, and everything was just right. I ran down the stairs yelling, "Ich bin ein Jude." That was my weapon.

Fortunately, it was just an old man, an old woman and a young girl. That was my gun: "Ich bin ein Jude," and. . .this is very painful.

(Interviewer's note: "After the interview, Mr. Shoehalter left the room weeping and walked down College Avenue.")

"There were two hospital ships, the Comfort and the Mercy. They dropped a bomb right down the stack of the Mercy." --William MacKenzie

On Okinawa, the bombardments were incredible. The people were literally shell-shocked. They had been bombarded, I guess, for weeks before we went ashore and we saw very little of them. War was such a private thing, you knew only what was happening around you. I don't know who, but somebody must have been in charge. Maybe it was the good Lord and he just pulled the strings. Somebody had to know what was happening.

We went up there on a Navy ship, but it was manned by a coast guard crew. In fact, this guy in the crew was from my home town, Little Falls, and I went up into the gun tub with him. It was the first time I'd ever seen 16-inch shells go through the air. God, they looked like Volkswagens going through the air.

I went ashore in the third or fourth wave. It didn't matter what wave it was. We were all in at once. We were with a Seabee battalion, and the first objective was the Kadena airport. About six o'clock in the morning we went ashore and we didn't hear a shot fired for about three hours, I guess. We just walked, and we were almost to the Kadena Airport before we heard the first shot fired. And then it got very muzzy.

I was working with the Marines to set up an arsenal, an ordnance place. There was no place to go on that island, unless you

290

were a cave dweller. You couldn't dig a hole. It was all coral.

This was one of the home islands, and that's why they were fighting the way they did. This business of whether we should or should not have dropped the bomb, I think we probably saved two or three million lives, give or take a million on each side, because they would have fought to the bitter end.

The fighting became furious, and it all runs together from about that point on, because day and night were the same. Every day they came in with the-- we called them saki divers-- the kamikazes. They were knocking off the ships, we could see them get blown up. I saw the *Birmingham* go, right out there in the water. And at night they were coming over and bombing and strafing. And we had no place to go.

One guy, Carleson his name was, I don't know how the hell we wound up together, and we got caught out in the open one night and we ran. There were a lot of caves in Okinawa. We ran into one, "Hey this is a good place." And we found a little shelf in the cave. So the next night we pulled in there and we rolled a bed roll out and I guess we spent about two nights there. And then it rained and the water came up and washed us out.

Out in the fields you had to try to dig, and you scraped dirt up around you to try to get underneath. I got hit out there one night. I got hit in the back of the neck with a piece of steel, and then I got hit in the leg. But there was no place to go so you just stayed. One night they dropped incendiaries and a guy about 30 yards away was hit, and he was burning and screaming.

We took off for the cave. We found out that some of those caves were tombs, and the Okinawans buried their dead in them, in urns. So our routine was that, if you found a place, you moved the urns out at night and then you moved them back in the daytime.

We went up to the northern end of the island and we cleaned that out pretty well. Then we came back. I guess the Army had turned to the south, the Marines went north. We thought we had secured the north, then we went down to the Yontan airstrip, which was just south of us.

Then things ground to a screeching halt. And it got very, very wild, because there was no place to hide and there was no place to go. And we're getting the bombing every night. And the saki divers in the daytime. And the Japanese were really dug in.

The Army was running into problems with the ordnance. They were just wearing the stuff out, 'cause it was just shoot, shoot, shoot. And I went down there with them and we were running out of stuff. We were dumping everything we had at them and they were dug in, they were really dug in. They had probably spent a couple of years digging those fortifications.

Again, I don't know who was in charge of the war at that point, but I remember going back and yelling to somebody that we were running out of ammunition. And somebody said, "Then go get some." And I was on a truck out to the beach. And there were a bunch of ships anchored off. And I went out and got on board an ammo ship.

I just got on board when General Quarters sounded. And they started making smoke, which they did to obscure themselves. I remember standing on the deck outside the radio shack. I wanted to get that ammo over the side and onto the beach because we needed it, but we couldn't move, because the Japanese divers were coming in. They were coming in at smokestack level. You could stand and watch them.

You'd wonder, Is he going to hit us? They go roaring overhead or veering off. And there was smoke everywhere from the guns firing. We had five inch guns and 3.5 guns and 50 millimeters and 20 millimeters all going at once and all this stuff happening. And then I'm thinking: what a hell of a way to run a war! And I thought "This has got to be it." I thought that several times.

I'm on an ammo ship, see? And if an ammo ship gets hit, that's it. There's no long lingering. (laughter) You're just a puff of smoke, just a puff of smoke. My main emotion during most of the war was fear interrupted occasionally by bouts of terror, and that was certainly one of them.

They hit a couple of ships near us, and then somehow or other I got ashore. We got the ammo down the beach there and we had to get it across a river, which was just north of the line. And I remember I was wading across carrying a part of a machine gun and I got hit by something and spun around. You know something's happening, but you don't want to know.

It was pitch black, but all of a sudden they were firing star shells, and it was like the middle of a stage with a spotlight on you, and you just have to go because you can't stay there. Somewhere along the line I ran into a corpsman, who bound up my arm where I'd been hit, and I kept going.

There were a lot of unlikely heroes. It wasn't a matter of bravery, or your juices or anything else. You did what you had to do. You might as well go forward as go back, 'cause you're not going to make it out of there anyway. And somewhere along the line I got hit again with some shrapnel in my legs. And somebody caught up with me along the way and said, "You're going back; you're getting out of here" or something like that.

And then the word got around that we were going out. There were two hospital ships. We could see them out there-- the *Comfort* and the *Mercy,* and they were lit up like the top of the Empire State Building. They were big white ships with huge red crosses on the side and there was a red cross on the stack. And floodlights all around.

We were supposed to go out to either the *Comfort* or the *Mercy* and just about dusk, I guess it was, the kamikazes came in and one of them dropped a bomb right down the stack of the *Mercy*, and I think the *Mercy* went down. The report later on was that the bomb wound up in an operating room and they were all killed in there. So they called us off.

They put us in a dugout. They'd used a bulldozer to dig a hole in the ground. I'd guess there were 25, 28 guys in there. And the intelligence was that we were probably going to go out the next morning. And sometime during the night we took a direct hit in that hole. A bomb. And I think five of us got out of it. That's what I recall.

They helped us out in the morning, and I remember it looked like a meat market. It was hard for me to believe that what I saw there was not a standing rib roast but what was left of a man. We got out to the *Comfort* and they took our clothes off and threw them over the side. But they couldn't separate me from my rifle and my helmet. (laughter) I wanted to keep those. And I guess I had them for a day or so.

As bad as I was feeling for myself and the other guys who were with me, there were others who were worse off. The picket ships, the destroyers out there, were our first line of defense, and they were being knocked off like pool balls. And those destroyer sailors, who'd been tossed into the water half burned, full of oil and everything else, were on this ship with us.

I have no idea how long it took to get from there to Guam. I was in the hospital there four or five days. Then we flew to Kwajalein, refueled, and wound up in Pearl Harbor.

"I went back toward the German line and found him. He'd stepped on a mine, blown off both legs. I had to find a way to get him back."   --Walter Denise

I was not anxious to go out on patrol with a large group because there's always noise, more noise than you expect. But they had cut the concertina wire, and we had gone through, and we were out there, four of us who were regular scouts from the battalion. And we were out with I Company. They put half the platoon up front, and the other half of the platoon behind us. So we were getting through and getting to the enemy side.

At that point, we could branch off. One part of the group would go to the left and the other part to the right. And two of us would go with each group. That was the intention.

So they cut the concertina wire, and we went through. I had no idea what was going on. We're back, you know, 15 to 20 people back. And we try not to be too close together because you're too vulnerable if you're right behind one another. So all of a sudden, one of the men saw a German and a machine gun or something, and shot him. And that's when all hell broke loose. And everybody started getting out.

At that, the four of us, who were regular patrolmen, stopped where we were and set up what we call a defensive position. We covered while the rest of the group evacuated out of there. And the concertina wire that they had cut was behind us now. And when the other people ran out, they ran into a different stretch of concertina wire outside of the break. They didn't know where the break was, and they set off some land mines. That's when we pulled out of there.

And then, when things got quiet, and we thought everybody was gone, then that's when we decided to go back. I found our lieutenant. He had been blown into the wire. I cut him loose. He said, "Look at my rear end." And I looked at it. And I said, "Well you've got a little cut there. But you'll make it back all right." But I said, "Take off and go now!" So he took off. And he fainted when he got back to our lines.

I then heard this kid crying, "Mama, mother!" I didn't like the sound of it, so I went back towards the German line, off on an angle, where he was. And he had stepped on a mine. Blown off both legs. And that's when I felt that I gotta get him back. I can't leave him here. It was imperative to my way of looking at it. In the meantime, the Germans were getting all set to do what they could to repulse us, or get rid of us, or kill us or something.

I asked him if he knew the Lord's Prayer and he said, "Yes." We repeated the Lord's Prayer for a long time. Fortunately, four tanks had been through there and left some ruts from their tracks. They weren't too deep, but they gave us some protection. And I got him back to the aid station.

This kid never passed out, and I thought it was remarkable from a medical point of view. The loss of blood, the loss of two legs, he should've gone out, if not died. And they were amazed that he was still alive. And he sat up and watched them cut the loose meat that was holding his one foot on. I thought then, "My, what the body can take. This is phenomenal."

He survived and went back. And he was very despondent. He said, "Well, why didn't you just leave me there." His mother wrote to Sgt. Benezet and me about how he had been so despondent; why we didn't just leave him there to die because he had, in essence, become a kind of a drag on society because he's a double amputee and lost an arm, too. I didn't know he'd lost his arm, too.

So we corresponded with the mother a couple of times, and later we learned that he moved back to Chicago and married and had a couple of children. And I think he was doing some kind of work at that time. And about four or five years ago, I heard he was coming to the reunion.

I still find it hard to talk about.

"I knew right away the sergeant was off his rocker. He kept beating on the ground and saying over and over, 'I can't take it anymore.' "   *--J. Domer Zerbe*

We were getting ready to attack the Gothic Line, and that was not going to be a simple situation up in these Italian mountains. My division, the 88th, had been in reserve, and then, about September 15-- this was 1944-- we moved through the 85th Division and went into the line.

The 85th had already taken some of the primary hills, but they had not taken the objective in others, so, bingo, in we come. And it just got tougher and tougher. After only a week or 10 days, the company commander ordered me to take the weapons platoon. Now our company strength at that point was two-thirds of what a company should be. And the Italian campaign was supposed to be a holding campaign!

So now I was in a tough situation. Where do you place the machine guns? Where do you put the mortars? I can't impress on you too much how easy it was for a few enemy troops, in the right positions, to hold us up. We would frequently have a whole company column-- that's one guy following another. You had no choice. You tried to ride the ridge lines and not have people down in the valley, because the Germans were excellent with their mortars. It was bad enough on the ridge lines, but at least you had more elevation.

Finally, on a very foggy day, we took Mt. Battaglia, an important terrain feature, and it was a surprise. The Germans didn't expect us in the numbers we got up there. I can see our regimental commander coming up the hill, saying, "Come on, keep moving, keep moving." Mount Battaglia was only eight miles from the Po Valley, and the Po Valley would give us respite from mountain, mountain, mountain.

At this point, I was company exec of E Company. G Company was in the lead, and they had taken the mountain top. There was the remnants of a 12th century castle on top. And E company, we were down to their right about 400 yards or so, spread out and dug in.

We were there for seven days, and in those seven days we lost two-thirds of our battalion. You just had to hold it through the mortar fire, through the artillery fire, and we did, but the poor devils in G Company, they had the toughest time. I lost a very good friend, Company Commander Bob Roeder, he was killed up there at the castle. He got the Medal of Honor.

That was a nasty, nasty week. The foxholes could never be deep enough. It was wet snow and rain, and they'd fill up with water. We had a lot of trenchfoot. They had trouble supplying us. We didn't get any food for 36 hours. Everything had to come up by mules; they selected guys out of each division, and they became mule-skinners. And to get up to us, they had to go through an open expanse of 250 yards, and the Germans would mortar that stretch 24 hours a day.

We lost so many men on that hill, and G Company lost even more because they were at the very top. We weren't getting many replacements. They were going to the Seventh Army in Southern France. So the unit strength got lower and lower and lower. And the morale was dipping. And then some of the units ran out of ammunition, and the burros couldn't get up to where we were. Hell, the Germans were even throwing big pieces of rock down, anything to keep us from getting up the hill.

We were finally relieved, and we got a few replacements, but we were never up to full company strength.

Then, about the third week in October, we went into the attack. G Company was on our left, F in reserve, and we were attacking. It was open, rock-strewn, but there weren't trees. It was like two small hills, but no trees for cover, just rock. We got our hill. We took some casualties, but we got our objective. G Company, you could watch over there, they were getting mortared to tears. They were maybe 600 yards away, but that's something in infantry; it is so hard to communicate, it is so hard to control. But we could tell they were taking a lot of casualties.

Late in the afternoon, a runner comes up and says, "Colonel Williamson wants you to take command of G Company." Well, I can only tell you, it wasn't a happy thought. I thought, "God knows what I'm going to see when I get over there." The runner's name was Byrd. He was from West Virginia. I remember him well, he was a good kid. He said, "And the Colonel wants me to lead you over there."

So, we got down off the crest, and we get about half way over there, and a damn machine gun starts popping right around our heads. When they're close, they pop right over your head. I foolishly was up just a little too high, and some German had spotted me. And I thought, "You damn fool. How dumb can I be?" And I get down off of the slope. I think some days that was the worst day of my life.

I knew the company commander, Ed Maher. He's dead, he's laying on the hill. The company exec was wounded. He was shot in the ankle, and he was going to be sent back. I found a platoon sergeant by the name of Barone, from North Jersey. He was leading the company.

Barone is in a slit trench, and I said, "What the hell's the situation? Where are the machine guns?" He points to where the machine guns are. Hell, the gunners were both dead on each machine gun. The mortar squad were in the back and they weren't firing, and there was still sporadic fire coming in.

So I'm laying in this same slit trench with Barone, trying to size up the situation, "Where are the automatic weapons, and how many able men do you think there are?" and so forth and so on. I was with him for half an hour, maybe, and all of a sudden, he starts to beat on the ground. I knew, right off, that he was off his rocker. He kept saying, "I can't take it anymore. I can't take it anymore. I can't take it anymore."

I sent the runner back with Barone. I said, "He's of no use to me at this point." So he went back, and I got riflemen on the machine guns. We got through the night all right. If the Germans had decided to counterattack, they'd have overrun us so easily, it would have been an easy game. But they didn't.

Eventually we were on the outskirts of Bologna. On a clear day we could see the Po Valley. We'd been in the mountains all winter, and it was a rough winter. From November on, I had diarrhea, and by Christmas Eve I had yellow jaundice and hepatitis, and I was shipped back to Naples, to the 300th General Hospital. Spent six or seven weeks in the hospital, then I was sent back up. And the spring push started about April 3, I think.

This time I took over the battalion I&R platoon. Our battalion had to go up a gradual slope-- Monterumici was the name of the mountain on one side, Mount Adone was the other one, and there was a saddle between these two. It was probably 1,000 yards from the line of departure up to the saddle, and that was a tough 1,000 yards. The Germans had had all winter to dig in, prepare. So we had a hard job getting up there.

The Germans used a Schu mine, and they looked like a small cigar box, and they were buried. When we left the line of departure, there was a lot of sandy area, and it was all planted with those mines. When the mine goes off, it knocks off your foot, or half of your foot. We had 11 guys in the first 20 minutes step on Schu mines and lose their feet. Fortunately, we were able to get some of them into a farmhouse on the slope.

We got up there, we made our objective, and from that point on, now the hills are getting smaller, down into Bologna, and the Germans are in total retreat. This is now the spring of '45. The war's only got to go until May 7th or 8th, and it's over.

"The ship was now sinking rapidly. The last thing I remember him saying was, 'Andy, I can't swim.' I never saw him again."   *--Andrew White*

Christmas Eve was approaching, and our cooks were preparing our turkey dinner. Turkeys were slowly roasting in our field kitchen stoves. We had turkeys and the trimmings for Christmas. They were big black stoves fired by kerosene and set out in the field.

I'm not sure the exact time, it might have been the 23rd, or early morning the 24th, they said there was a change in plans. We learned about the Battle of the Bulge and were going to replace the guys that were captured or killed in the Bulge, so we had to dump all that food out on the ground and pack up all our kitchen and military equipment and move out to Weymouth, near Southampton.

In the early morning of the 24th, we boarded a troop ship called the *Leopoldville*. It had been a cargo-passenger ship, considered a luxury liner of sorts, going to the Congo prior to the war, and I was in one of those holds where they had hammocks instead of bunks, since this was a British ship, but it was only a short trip across the Channel.

We weren't sure where we were going, but we knew we were going somewhere in France. It was a small convoy. I don't think there were more than one or two ships and about two or three destroyers.

We were approaching land and could see twinkling lights about six o'clock at night, when we heard this loud noise. I was down in the hold. We had heard depth charges before, but it sounded like more than that. We went on deck, the lights were still on, the motors had stopped, and we were told that either a torpedo or a floating mine hit the ship, but "don't worry."

We weren't too concerned, and thought we probably would be towed in to port or beached. No announcements or alarm of any sort was sounded. We saw the ships' officers scurrying about, and soon the crew, who were Congolese, were getting into the lifeboats, and they didn't know how to launch them. They were capsizing and dumped into the sea, kind of sad.

As time went by, the ship started to list toward the stern, and the destroyers were going around us in circles dropping depth charges. At one time, a British destroyer came alongside and tried to take men off, which was very difficult in the rough sea. Some men did jump across when the two ships bounced close together. Some missed and were lost at sea, but a lot of men were able to jump across.

I was in the forward part of the *Leopoldville*, standing on the rail, and I thought when the bows of the ships were near each other I could jump across, but it would have been suicide. I decided not do that. I figured it's better to stay with the ship until something happens.

After two hours or so, the ship was really sinking and some of the crew were trying to lower the rafts. I don't think any of the rafts were ever lowered properly. But none of the soldiers got into the rafts. There was never any kind of signal to abandon ship. About eight-thirty, or thereabouts, the ship was going down rather fast. We threw ropes over the side with knots in them, and this man, maybe a little older than I, decided to go down the side. The ship was now sinking rapidly.

He went down first and last thing I remember him saying was, "Andy, I can't swim." I never saw him again. But I kicked off the ship. Probably the water hit me first, before I got down

301

to it, but I kicked off and started swimming away. I did make some progress, and I looked back and saw the ship go down.

A lot of my friends were on that ship, and some of them stayed with the ship when it went down, but they were able to float to the surface. There was no suction that kept them submerged. We were all a bunch of young kids and every one of my platoon buddies that hit the water was saved.

Anyway, it was cold on that December 24th. The British were criticized that they did not immediately notify Cherbourg that we were sinking. Apparently, they notified England, but the message never got to Cherbourg. But that's history. The Americans in Cherbourg were also criticized because they were partying and couldn't believe a ship was sinking that close to shore, so there was a delay in sending any rescue vessels out. Eventually, they did come out.

I doubt if I was in the water more than 15 or 20 minutes, otherwise I would not have survived because of hypothermia. I saw a tugboat coming towards me, an American tugboat. I was yelling my head off and it went right by me. I doubt if anyone heard me.

After a little while, another tug came towards me. It was going fast. It almost passed me. I was yelling when all of a sudden someone on deck threw a rope with a life ring at the end of it. I grabbed it and hung onto it, but they wouldn't pull me in. They were dragging me like a surfer. But eventually I was dragged in.

Then I realized how cold I was. They told me to stay in the bow with a lot of other men who had been picked up. They gave me a blanket and I just huddled there. We weren't able to get into the cabin until later on. They gave us some coffee.

It was pitch dark when I was rescued. That's probably why they didn't see me, a little speck in the rough water. A lot of men panicked when they hit the water. There probably were hundreds of men in the water. I realized I could not help anybody, because if someone grabbed me, I would have drowned. So I decided to stay clear of all the crowds and just swim away.

You could float with a life jacket, but a lot of men panicked. I was a good swimmer.

We had no one in charge to tell us what to do. We did everything on our own. Some jumped into the water earlier, some jumped when the ship went down, and some stayed with the ship. But we never had any officer tell us what to do.

It was a tragedy that probably could have been avoided if they had acted sooner. There were 800 men lost out of 2,000. The sad part about it is there are families, even to this day, that don't know what happened to their loved ones, because the British were embarrassed and they asked Eisenhower not to publicize it back home. It never made the press.

It wasn't until about four or five years ago that a documentary was filmed for the History Channel and it went through this whole episode, and the British refused to show it. There was some recognition in Congress, but we always felt there should have been more recognition for the men lost on the ship. It was a tragedy.

Those who hit the water, and I was one of them, were awarded Purple Hearts for exposure. I still have mine and it helped in getting me home sooner because of the extra points. It helped me personally in a few other ways. We could have been up at the Battle of the Bulge, because the 106th Division, in which I had my basic training, was the division that was caught there, and my friends in the Recon troop were killed or taken prisoner. I could have been one of them. They were green troops. We were going to replace these men and we missed that.

"About 15 wounded guys were lying there. One of them was conscious, and he yelled, 'Watch it, there are trip wires all over here.' "   *--James Essig*

I had two functions as a combat medic. I started at the lowest level, which was litter-bearer, really. My job was to go out there where things were happening and give first aid right on the battlefield to these people, and then, remove them by litter, either by hand carrying or by mounting the stretcher over the hood of a jeep, which we did whenever we could.

We'd get them back to a forward aid station, and then from there they'd have an ambulance, or some other unit come, pick them up, and take them back for further treatment. The doctors were farther back. You didn't even have doctors at the forward aid station, usually. There were skilled medics that were working that part of it.

During our six months of combat, we lost a lot of men. We had about 120 medics in the regiment and probably 80 percent were casualties. At least 80. It might have been higher, either killed or wounded.

Later, I volunteered to become a surgical technician. I would get general directions from the medical detachment, but immediate decisions were through the company commander. As a litter-bearer, in that earlier part, I did a lot of that. I was under the control of the head people in the aid station, mainly the forward aid station. I never got to the rear aid stations or the hospital part. I never saw that. Officers, doctors, I really didn't have that much to do with them. They were back to the rear.

Talking about combat, I have experienced every sort of combat you can as a infantryman. I was under fire from small arms, a lot of mortar fire, a lot of casualties. A lot from artillery, they had 88s, the Germans. They were very deadly. Nebelwerfers, rockets, fired by the Germans at us in certain places. We were strafed, I was strafed a couple of times. I was bombed once.

I had plenty of experience with mines. I was going into an area where a lot of wounded guys were lying, there must have been about 15 of them, on the ground. Some had been hit by air bursts-- the shells hit trees and they explode in the trees-- and shrapnel. A lot of them had walked on mines. I was going to help one, and one of the fellows was conscious, and he yelled, "Watch it, watch it, there are trip-wires here, all over."

If I had just nudged this wire, it would have exploded in the

304

air. So you had that kind of mine, too, as well as the mine buried an inch or two in the soil. I ran into everything.

I can't even remember what came first. It was just one thing after another. It's unbelievable that I escaped, frankly. I remember some things distinctly, some injuries distinctly, that stand out in my mind. When somebody was hit in the stomach area and he was spilling his guts out, he was in pain. Another person we had on the litter and his brains were oozing out, and then, of course, we saw all kinds of persons with lost arms, and bleeding was the major thing we had to address. Some of these people you couldn't help.

You're under such fear at the time, but you're doing the job, and you have to be there. I said prayers, "Let's hope I get through this." I think the worst decisions were about whether or not to carry people out. There were a lot of serious injuries in a wooded area, hilly, and we were walking a great distance, and we had somebody on the litter who was obviously very far gone. That was the one, maybe, where I saw the brains and all. We just decided he had had it, there was no hope.

You could tell if a person was dead or alive by certain tests. You'd try for a pulse, or see if there was any breathing, and make a decision, and then, of course, you had to make a decision about who gets on your litter. You can only do so much. Some cases, they were conscious, and wounded in the arms and all, and you'd tell them to follow us, come with us, and they'd be able to walk back.

Who could we help the most? We gave whatever first aid we could, and then we had to move them back quickly, to get more advanced aid in the rear. This was hard. You had to make a decision pretty fast, and many times you are making it under fire.

On a hillside behind the village of Rimling, there were two quarries. One of the quarries had two American tanks in it. They were in position to fire back at the Nazis, who were attacking. This was at the same time as the Battle of the Bulge.

The fellow in the rear US tank yelled to us, my buddy and

me. He said, "We're moving out of here, we're under fire."
Meanwhile, right at the entrance to the other quarry were two
foxholes, each had a couple of wounded guys.

We got perhaps the worst case on the litter, and then we had
to time it, because the Germans were firing mortars at us. We
could hear the mortars being fired and counted so many seconds until the shells exploded around us. We pulled the litter
under the lead tank. The driver didn't know we were under his
tank, and we knew he was going to pull out of there in a minute,
but we were under the tank, and the shrapnel was hitting up
against the sides of the tank, so, we had some protection under
there, from mortars at least.

We allowed so many seconds, and we pulled our casualty out
and ran down the hill. Then Nazi artillery opened up with air
bursts as we're going down. We didn't get hit, but that's the
sort of thing. There were difficulties of getting to people. It's
tough. If there was a heavy blanketing fire, you just have to wait
'til it lets up a little bit.

There were many, many cases like that. One of the decora-
tions I got was for removing people over an area of a couple of
miles up and down hills in woods and under fire. Sometimes the
walking wasn't that good.

"The lieutenant got up and he was starting to tell us to get out when a shell burst and he got it right through the head." --Jerome Selinger

My company was the lead company. You'd have to understand the setup of an armored division. The tanks were supported by armored infantry, so it was tanks and half-tracks that
were in a column. And we were the lead half-track as we came
up to the Siegfried Line. There were three tanks in front of us,
but we were the first half-track.

We were told by the reconnaissance as we were going up, I'll
never forget this, that there was nothing up there but small arms

306

fire. And we went over the crest of the hill. And we started down the hill. And, I hear 'fshhhhhhh, boom' shell on one side and 'fshhhhhh, boom' shell on the other side. We were zeroed in by the German 88s that were behind the dragon's teeth, the concrete columns that were part of the Siegfried Line.

They hit the first tank with a direct hit. They hit the second tank with a direct hit. They hit the third tank with a direct hit. And then they hit our half-track with a direct hit on the front right fender of the half-track. Just before that, the lieutenant got up and started to tell us to get out. And as he got up, the shell burst, and he got it right through the head. A piece of shrapnel. So that killed him.

What happened then was a terrifying thing. Everybody tried to get out of the half-track. And some of the men jumped over the side. And the Germans were zeroing in with machine guns on the side. We must have lost 30 percent of the company right there.

For some reason, I don't know what gave me the sense to do it, I lay on the floor, and I just crawled out the back of the track. So I had the track in front of me. And I hit the ground and I rolled over, and you know how on the side of a dirt road there's always a depression? I just laid in that depression while the fire was going on above my head

I must have laid there about 10, 15 minutes, and the firing slowed down, and I started looking around and I didn't see any-body. So I got up and I ran. And the way we were taught under fire was to run a few paces and hit the ground. And get up, run, hit the ground. And I did that until I got back up over the crest of the hill. Then I looked down and I see the rest of my com-pany are all digging in. And they looked up at me, and they were surprised to see me because they thought I was gone. That was an experience I'll never forget.

I think there was one other survivor. While I was digging in, a medic was leading him back. He had shrapnel right through his abdomen area. And a couple of fingers were shot off. And at that time, one of the things that we really wanted, or felt that we needed, was cigarettes. And he came up to me with the medic there and he says, "Here, I won't be needing this anymore," and hands me his cigarettes. I'll never forget that.

"I was on my back, and the bullets were coming right across my nose. We were pinned down there for two days and two nights." *--Maurice Meyers*

My very first day of combat started at about four, five o'clock in the morning, and we crossed this little river, called the Meurthe River, and we got across, and I said to my buddy, "Boy, war isn't bad at all. There's nothing. I haven't even heard a shot." It was like a dream. I thought, "What am I doing here?"

Then we find ourselves in a wide open area, and a signal comes back, "Okay, everybody lie down," and so, I don't know what's going on, you know, I'm new at this, this is my first day. A few guys I see are digging holes, but I didn't dig any hole. There's no fighting, why should I be digging a hole?

All of a sudden, in comes a rain of mortar shells, and all hell breaks loose. These shells are moving up and down, right across, and there's one guy over to my right, and a shell comes in right on top of the two of us, and I call over and say, "Hey, are you all right?" And I saw he was dead.

I turned the other way, more shells are coming in. There's a guy over here who I knew, his name was Lowell, and I said, "Lowell, how you doing?" He says, "I'm hit." He starts laughing hysterically. He couldn't stop laughing. He was hit by a shell, and I don't know whatever happened, he lived, but I never saw him again.

Now I'm in between these guys, and the Germans are bracketing, and I am terrified. I'm digging with my nose into the earth and it was just the most horrifying experience. I can't even tell you how horrifying it was, and I didn't know what to do, how to do it, I was just terrified.

After a while, it let up a little, and I heard a sergeant, or a lieutenant, say, "Okay, men, let's go, let's go," and people are jumping up and moving forward, and I don't know what the hell I'm doing, so I'm going that way too. By that time, it had gotten light enough, and I saw that some of my buddies were already across this field, and they were at a bank that goes up to a road, and they were standing there, there were bodies all over the place, and they're hollering at me.

Finally, I understood what they're saying. They're hollering, "There's mines," and I was in the middle of a mine field. I just kept walking and people were getting blown up and killed all over the field. I walked right through this mine field. I came up to them and they said, "Boy, are you lucky."

I says, "Who's got a cigarette?" I don't even know if I smoked, and I took a cigarette, and, as I lit it, I hear a swoosh, and I looked down, and right between my feet is a mortar shell, and it didn't go off. This is like seven o'clock in the morning and I said, "What more can happen?" The day has just started. It was almost humorous, seven o'clock in the morning and I've almost been killed six times already. And that was my first day.

One of the biggest battles, and one of the most important ones in my life, was the crossing of the Rhine River. It was planned way in advance and we were told that we were going to have tremendous artillery coverage and everything.

Well, we got to some buildings not far from the river, and then, late at night, we moved down to the river, where boats were all ready, and Navy engineers, or someone, to drive these boats. Well, when we started going down this hill to the river itself, all hell broke loose. Our artillery was shelling them, but they really were plastering us.

A great many of our people panicked, and, instead of going down to the boats, they took off, went back up the hill, including our company commander. Well, I was with a few other guys, and I hear somebody call my name, and it was our executive officer, he was the second-in-command, and he was standing by a boat, and he waved me on. So I went, and I got in the boat with him, but, very few people did. They were all taking off. They were running away.

Then I saw our colonel, the regimental commander, standing there by one of the boats and holding a pistol in his hand on the engineer to drive that boat, because everybody was scared. I jumped in the boat with our executive officer, and we took off across the river, and some of the boats got sunk, some of them got hit, and our boat got rocked. The lieutenant got banged against the boat. He hurt his leg.

We landed on the other side, and there were very few of us, and we moved from the river, and we had about a mile to go into the town, and there were some buildings, and I captured 11 Germans and gave them to somebody else to take back.

We got into the town, and there were very few of us, and, throughout the night, more and more of our people came across as the engineers put in a bridge, and I directed artillery on some German tanks in the town that were holding up one of our platoons.

Well, anyhow, I received, later on, after the war, the Silver Star, "For gallantry in action," as they say, and I was very proud of the fact that I didn't chicken out.

A different type of battle that I was in was near the end of the war, we had to breach the Siegfried Line. Two of my friends and I were pinned down as we got in the middle of this line. It was pill boxes and all kinds of artillery, and we got pinned down, and we dug a hole in a matter of minutes, and saved ourselves, crawled into this one hole, three of us, and a German machine gun was in the back of us, shooting at us, and we got in the hole just in time.

As I lay there-- it was only a hole, maybe, 18 inches deep for the three of us-- this German was firing at us, and the bullets would come right across my nose and hit in the dirt. I couldn't get any lower, you see. I was on my back with my head against the earth and right across my eye would come bullets from the machine gun. He couldn't get any lower, you understand, because we were just below his range.

So we were there, we were pinned down for two days and two nights, and then, on the second night, we finally made a run for it in the dark. There were bodies all over.

It was interesting, as I think about it now, because the three of us in that hole were very close friends in combat, you might say, but such a varied group. You had myself, an Orthodox northeastern Jew; another was an Italian from a large, wealthy Italian family in southern New Jersey; and the third one was a redneck from Georgia.

The three of us thought we're all going to die together, and we had given up. There was no way we could get out. One of the most monumental statements I have ever heard in my entire life was said in that hole by this redneck, and he was my friend. He was a violent racist, there was no question, but we had done a lot of things together throughout the war, and we were close, and we're in the middle of the Siegfried Line, and he says, "I wonder what Jew built this fucking Siegfried Line," and I looked at him and laughed, and I said, "You're really something."

That was his interpretation of everything, that only a Jew could have built the Siegfried Line. He did not realize what was going on with Jews in Germany, but he was my friend, he was my buddy, and that is strange. Strange things happen in war.

"Those depth charges were so close they set off a torpedo in its tube, and it jumped the stops and the torpedo engine started."   *--Willim J. Godfrey*

On our very first patrol, off of Honshu, near the city of Sendai, right along the coast, the first day on patrol, May 1, 1943, we knocked off a freighter. And, we were pretty severely depth-charged, and I said, "Well, this is routine, you get depth-charged." And, from then on, depth charges became commonplace. And then we sunk a small patrol craft. And then another

311

small freighter.

Then we came back to Midway. And then, on the second patrol, we were in the Truk area, way out in Japanese-controlled water. We sunk a 7,500-ton aircraft ferry. We damaged a few more freighters. And then, on the third patrol, we sunk a 700-ton freighter. And in all these we were normally depth-charged, because these convoys were escorted by destroyers. But we managed to evade, go deep, cruise away silently. We always tried to be terribly silent. That was the main thing.

And then, the fourth patrol was really one of the best, and the fifth was outstanding. En route to the Palaus Islands, in heavy seas, before we got to our op area, we came across a big sub tender, in the daytime, and a large freighter-- I believe it was 6,000 tons-- and a destroyer escort.

Well, this was in about a force five sea. And this was the first time I'm the diving officer, controlling the depth at the Captain's orders. We had heavy seas and big swells. When you're just in trim, a little bit will let you go up, a little bit will let you go down. But, when you're in heavy sea, broaching is possible.

The periscope went under at 65 feet, and the Captain never wanted to expose too much of the periscope. So he would order "64 feet," "63 feet." And, I'm down there with the planesman and the blow manifold, and the fellow pumping, and blowing, and trying to maintain that depth so he could just have the periscope barely above the surface, because we didn't want to disclose our location.

It was quite hairy for me, the first time, although I had dived the boat on previous patrols. My main fear was broaching, but we held it, and he got two torpedoes into this 7,000-ton freighter. And we sunk it, and we put one torpedo into another freighter, I think it was 6,000 tons, but we didn't sink it. So we moved down a little ways and stayed in the area.

At night we surfaced. And we got the ship upstream in the moon, so the moon wouldn't silhouette us. And then, during surface action, I would go up on the bridge and con the ship, while the captain would alternate between the conning tower and the bridge. He'd go down and watch the solution of the torpedo data computer with the fire control party, and I would be up giving orders to the helm. He'd say, "Bill, come right 15 degrees of course this and that." And so we stayed on the surface.

The destroyer was circling this big freighter, which was dead in the water. So we waited 'til the freighter got over on the far side. We got into, I guess, less than about 1,500 yards, and we fired two torpedoes. It was almost dead on. And within 10 or 15 minutes, it sunk.

Then, while still on the surface, we turned tail and put four engines on the line, made about 20 knots, and we hauled out of there. We didn't get a chance to shoot at the destroyer, but our main mission was to get out to the patrol area. But right there, on our way out to the area, we sunk 15,000 tons of shipping, right there.

From there, we continued on to the Palaus area. And this was the real plum. We stayed right off the island of Palau, early in the morning, at periscope depth, within sight of the beach, and out comes this troop carrier, loaded with troops. We were at periscope depth. I'm holding the submarine at 61, 62, 63 feet. I don't think we were over 1,500 yards from the target. We fired two torpedoes; they both hit. The ship sunk within a minute, with, I don't know, a couple thousand troops aboard.

After that, we submerged and tried to get into deep water. We were depth-charged all day, but we laid close to the bottom and just cruised very slow, very quiet. That afternoon we started conducting a periscope patrol away from the beach. And a little Japanese patrol craft was sighted. And, somehow, I don't know whether he saw our periscope or not, but he came in, giving us big angles on the bow, back and forth.

I'm laying in my bunk, I'm off watch. And all of a sudden, two depth charges were let go, and we were only at 65 feet. I think he only had two onboard, or he might have sunk us, or he might have sunk himself. I mean, if he had any more depth charges, he'd have had us cold.

The control room was in a little bit of confusion. They hollered, "Mr. Godfrey to the control room." I dashed out, flooded the negative tank, and took us down deep, and got everything squared away. The Captain comes out of his bunk, and everybody got to work and we got everything under control. But we were pretty badly damaged. We had lights broken, we had some machinery deranged. But the worst thing of all, the depth charges were so close, and probably near the stern, they set off a torpedo in the torpedo tube, and it jumped the stops and allowed the engine in the torpedo to start.

Fortunately, it was in the after torpedo room, and, when a torpedo leaves a tube, it has to go so many yards and a little device in there, like a propeller, will arm it. It can't arm itself until maybe it's 400 yards from us, so we don't blow ourselves up. But the engine in the torpedo is run by alcohol and makes steam, to run a little steam turbine to drive the propeller.

We buttoned up the tubes. Our forward tubes and the outboard shutters on the tubes were damaged. That night, when it got dark, the Captain says, "Bill, when we get on the surface, I want four engines on the line." So we surfaced, and had the four engines on the line before we surfaced, and we headed back towards Midway.

Meanwhile, we sent a message to Commander of Submarines, Pacific Fleet, relaying what had happened, and explained the damage, and they recalled us.

In 28 days, we had sunk two big freighters and a big transport. We had a chief torpedoman who was the best in the Navy. Believe it or not, he was able to extract the torpedo into the torpedo room, and he routined it. He got it all ready so we could fire it again, charged it, filled it with alcohol and compressed air. And, for that, he received a commendation and a medal. That was 28 days of real intense activity.

And then, I guess, the best patrol was the fifth patrol. We were, once again, just a little bit south of Formosa. And on that patrol, our first contact was a six-ship convoy with two destroyer escorts. We were on the surface, and they were hull down, but with a high periscope and our small sub, they couldn't see us. We made an end around run on the convoy until it got dark.

Somewhere along the line, one of the destroyers dropped off, and at last, we tracked him. He was on the starboard quarter of the convoy, way back aft, away from us. So we surfaced, it was just a little haze. And we surfaced right on the track of the convoy. We were tracking them for six hours with our periscope and our radar. And then, here comes, out of this mist, instead of the freighter coming out, the first ship coming out is a destroyer, no more than 2,000 yards away. Two thousand yards at sea isn't too far.

So this captain of mine, I'm on the bridge conning the ship, he's climbing up and down the conning tower, and, when this destroyer comes out of the mist, we're all surprised. (laughter) And, he says, "Set torpedoes for six feet." We had them set for 10 feet, for the freighters.

The captain's up and down, and I'm on the target bearing transmitter, taking visual bearings on the main mast of the destroyer. So, he says, "Fire one, fire two." By God, they both hit. Lit up the sky. They blew the thing completely to pieces. In 15 seconds, it was gone. There was so much fire, it lit up the conning tower. And, down the hatch, the people in the conning tower said, "What happened up there?" (laughter)

So then we fired again. We had six torpedoes forward, we fired two more. We sunk another freighter and we damaged another one. And the *Pogy* is still on the surface. We're not going to dive. Now we turn and go away from the convoy. And one of the freighters was fairly fast and turned towards us. And, the Captain wanted to fire the after torpedoes, and he thought better of it when the freighter started firing on us. They must have had some small guns up forward. So then the Captain says, "Dive."

We have four engines on line going 20 knots. I dived down

into the control room and manned the diving station. And, boy, we go under water like a porpoise, (laughter) and went to 200 feet and evaded. We weren't depth-charged. Then we followed on up the coast, and we met two or three more convoys. On that one patrol, overall, we sunk something like 30,000 tons and damaged another 7,000 or 8,000, plus the destroyer.

A lot of us received an award or decoration. The Captain got his second Navy Cross. And then we went back to Pearl Harbor, and that's when I was transferred and ordered back to the same shipyard to go through the same procedure with a new submarine, the USS Kraken, SS-370.

"One of our doctors was operating on a wounded kamikaze pilot when the Jap grabs a scalpel and stabs the doctor. Killed him." --Raymond Finley Jr.

I went on the *Monssen*, and we were getting ready for the invasion of Lingayen Gulf. We went down to New Guinea first, a place called Lai, and ran the practice invasion, just with ships, not with their troops. They would take an area that looked like where you were going to invade and you would run a practice invasion there. You'd see the mountain over here, lowlands here, and all that sort of stuff.

The landing craft would go in, but they didn't have them full of troops. We were going to be laying on the outside as antiaircraft, because the kamikazes had started then. That was the beginning of the kamikazes, in the Philippines.

We went up, we had the troops for D-plus-two-day. We were the only destroyer in the group that we took, though we had some patrol craft, PCs. They were small. I don't know what they were going to do, other than keep the other ships in line, because they weren't set up for any real antiaircraft. They had a machine gun, but that's like throwing rocks at an airplane.

So we were the only destroyer. The LSTs were so slow that we'd have to zigzag to stay back with them. Then we would run

316

a zigzag on a zigzag, just to have more way, so if something happened we could get going quicker.

We had one Dutch captain as we were going up alongside the Philippines. We were already in sight of land, so they had to know we were coming. We could see them. They must have been able to see us. This one Dutch captain put his running lights on. He said, "Too close, too close. I need my running lights." We're yelling at him to turn them out. So finally we told him, "You turn them out or we'll shoot them out." He said, "No," so we took a 20 mm, and shot a couple of shots across his bow, and the lights went out quick.

The Japs were pulling another thing here that they hadn't done before. The freighters and supply ships were anchored off of Lingayen Gulf. The Japs were swimming out with dynamite strapped to their chests and carrying a big magnet. They'd come up to the ship, and the magnet would pull the Jap up next to the ship, and then they'd pull the cord and blow the ship up-- and themselves too, of course. They had no qualms about doing that.

When we got there on D-plus-two day, they had hit several of the ships, which I think survived, but they had big holes blown in them, and there was a lot of stuff damaged, and some men had been killed, but I don't think they sunk.

One ship I heard of caught five kamikazes and that just broke the ship up. There was no way she was going to do anything but sink. It just broke through bulkheads and ripped too much of it apart. Then your boilers explode and that takes care of another compartment.

An interesting thing with the kamikazes. They were trained, when they went against a destroyer, to try to hit her right in behind the bridge if they could. They would be getting into an engine room. They'd probably kill the captain and do the most damage. There was more of a possibility that way of sinking the ships, but many of the ships survived. A lot of the people didn't.

You didn't have to be out there long in the kamikaze thing.

317

We were losing destroyers during the Okinawa campaign. There were more Navy people lost than Marines and Army people put together, because of the kamikazes.

Another thing the Japs had done, which was recorded and sent to us on messages, the doctor is operating on a Jap, a flyer who has been shot down, to save his life. The Jap, being such a fanatic as he was, grabs the scalpel and stabs the doctor. In one case, he killed the doctor.

So we had shot this Jap down and we had him onboard. He'd been burned around the face, so we got him onboard, stripped him, and gave him a set of coveralls to put on. That's the other thing you did with a Jap. Even if he was okay, you put a ladder over the side and you stripped him over there, and stood back, because you don't know if he had a dynamite capsule under his clothing somewhere.

So we had this Jap, and the doctors were ready to work on him. The captain turned to me and he said, "You stay with the Doc, get the .45, and you have it right on that guy's head the entire time the doctor is working on him. If he makes any move at him, you shoot him."

So I'm sitting there, but I have to keep moving around as the doctor moves, because I have to be careful I don't shoot the doctor, or that the bullet would go through him and hit the doctor. It so happened the guy didn't do anything.

We had another incident on the *Norman Scott*. This fellow crashed. He got through the flack and he crashed, right in front of the *Norman Scott*. They swung over and picked him up. They went through the same routine of, "Take your clothes off," and so forth. He said, in perfect English, "All right. I'm not going to do anything. I'm not one of those." They took him to the bridge to see the captain.

In perfect English, he said, "I'm a graduate of the University of Michigan. I stayed in the United States for several years after graduation. I was going to stay there longer, but when I saw this happening, Japan is my homeland, so I came home to serve my

318

country. When they started this kamikaze nonsense, I thought that might be my only way out. I didn't know what they were going to do with me next. I didn't want to get into a situation where I was going to have to crash into a ship. I want to live. I didn't buy this thing."

He thought he might be lucky enough to get through the flack and ditch, which is what he did. He was saved. They kept him on board two or three days, then transferred him to one of the big ships.

"Then all of a sudden a voice said to me-- and this is how I know there's a God-- 'Chuck, I want you to lead a sin-free life.' "   *--Charles Mickett Jr.*

H Company was ahead of us, and we were relieving them. We're outside of La Spezia, in Italy, and they had a German fortress in the harbor of La Spezia. They were throwing these really heavy naval guns at us. Now, these were big guns. Artillery was what bothered us because, when they hit, they make a big hole and they throw shrapnel around.

After a while, I could tell just by the sound of the projectile where the shot was about to land. "Don't even worry about that one. That one is going to go over there." But these naval shells were aimed at us because we were coming up the hill and we were in their range.

So I hear this crack. Now, I don't know how long it takes before you hear the crack, because sound travels faster than the projectile, but, I could count to 42 before the explosion, and I said, "God, this one is mine." I started praying while I was counting. I didn't know I could do that, but I said the Lord's Prayer, I said Hail Marys, I said the Apostle's Creed, I said the Twenty-third Psalm. Today, if I were to try that, I wouldn't be able to finish one, but it was like something was pulling it out of my brain.

And then, all of a sudden, a voice said to me-- this is how I

319

know there is a God--"Chuck, I want you to lead a sin-free life." Out of the blue, "I want you to lead a sin-free life," while I'm counting. I say, "Lord, I can't promise you that."

Then I said to the Lord something like, "Lord, you know, I don't think my mom would like it if something would happen to me." I still didn't just have the guts to say, "Lord, I just don't want to die," and he said, again, "Chuck, I want you to lead a sin-free life." I'd never heard that terminology. I said, "God, I can't promise that." I said, "I just don't want to die," and I think saying that, and being honest, saved me.

See where your coat is over there? That's where it landed, a projectile the size of a 500-pound bomb. I'm covered with mud, I'm covered with sulfur smoke. First thing I do is I feel my legs, my arms, breathe a little to see if I'm alive, or if I'm in heaven, or wherever.

I said, "Thank you, God." You know, I made a deal with him. I didn't change too much in Italy, but when I came back to the USA I did. I can't steal, I will not lie. I feel that if I do anything wrong, I'm betraying the Lord, because really, I should be dead. I didn't even get a concussion, nothing.

I heard the voice one more time. Boy, the Lord and my guardian angel are keeping me out of harm's way. After the war, I'm working for Burroughs Corporation, putting computers in the First National Bank of Englewood. I worked the day before something like 20 hours, started that morning at six. Six o'clock the next morning, we finally got the computer up. I was in charge of computers for the district.

Don Reardon was the gentleman who was the technical support. We're leaving, we're driving in my 1963 Mercury station wagon. We're near Exit 11 on the Turnpike. I'm talking to Don, just like I'm talking to you, except I'm looking straight ahead, doing 65 miles an hour. Next thing I know, I hear a voice that says, "Chuck, Chuck, Chuck," and suddenly I wake up. I'm concerned about whether I hit somebody. I said to Don, "Thank you, Don." Guess what? He was sound asleep.

EPILOGUE

The stories told here represent a period of only 25 years or so. In the long reach of time, that brief but crowded era was less than a third of the life span of the storytellers. In 1994, when the interviewing began, most of the boys were in their 70s. The events they were describing occurred 50 or more years earlier. What had they done in those intervening years?

The national climate to which they returned was one of expansive expectation. After World War I, the world looked back with longing to its lost prewar Eden. After World War II, all eyes looked to the future. The bad times were gone, and the world of tomorrow was full of wonders.

The boys threw themselves into their new lives with energy, eager to make up for lost time.

They became engineers, businessmen, doctors, lawyers and communicators. More than anything else, though, they became corporate executives and educators.

It's not surprising that leadership abilities in the military led to leadership in the corporate world, and many followed that route. Lew Bloom became a vice president of a textile company; George Boggs, an engineering executive of Colgate Palmolive; Carleton Dilatush, the CEO of National Cork Company; Frank Kneller, a marketing executive with Colgate, Revlon and Noxel;

321

Bob King, a sales executive with Johnson and Johnson; Charles Getty, the comptroller of Revere Copper and Brass; Crandon Clark, the vice president of a van line; Domer Zerb, an executive with DuPont; Art Jiannine, Ralph Schmidt and Elliot Bartner, chemical or pharmaceutical executives.

About as many had careers in education, motivated perhaps by the hope that they could help prevent future wars. Nathan Shoehalter made his mark in radio as well as in the classroom. John Archibald and Lyman Avery were school principals; Frank Dauster, John Dowling and Tom LaCosta became Rutgers professors; George Reynolds remained a physicist and professor at Princeton; Lloyd Kalugin, Bert Manhoff and Vincent Gorman were educators at county or local level. Franklyn Johnson was founding president of Jacksonville University.

Vince Kramer, Wally Kaenzig and Ed Bautz stayed in the military; Kramer and Kaenzig later returned to Rutgers as Director of Alumni Relations and Dean of Students. Bautz remained in the military and rose to the rank of Major General.

Messrs. Ambos, Burke, Claflen, Finley, Gimpel, Godfrey, Sarraiocco and Van Aken had engineering careers; Messrs. Adams, Brandt, Forrest Clark, Denise, Goodman, Kindre, MacKenzie, Mercer, Nazemetz, Gross, Gutter, Hansen, Hill, Leuser, McCartney, Mickett, Mojo, Mortensen, Pape, Robinson, Rork, and Sobin held positions in business, government or communications. Dick Kleiner, a Hollywood reporter, wrote 17 books on movie personalities.

Five became lawyers-- Addison, De Masi, Kolodziej, Moss and Winter. Addison and Winter went on to be judges, and Kolodziej was a state assemblyman. Leon Canick and Maurice Meyers were MDs and Jerome Selinger, a dentist.

Bob Owen was a foreign service officer; Fred Wesche, an airline pilot; and Sam Blum, an IBM scientist who was elected to the National Inventors Hall of Fame.

Some are now deceased, but not really. They live on in the Rutgers Oral History Archives, where we all have equal rank.

THE RUTGERS ORAL HISTORY ARCHIVES

(Interviews online at http://fas-history.rutgers.edu/oralhistory/orlhom.htm)
RC- Rutgers College;NJC- New Jersey College for Women;CP- College of Pharmacy;GSA-Graduate School of Agriculture;GSE- Graduate School of Education;
RLS- Rutgers Law School;RLC-RutgersLawSchool/Camden;RSB-RutgersSchool of Business;R-Nwk- Rutgers/Newark;NJMD-NJ Med./Dent.;UC-University Col.

Thomas T. Adams, RC1942

Hon. Mark Addison ,RC1937

LtCol Howard K.Alberts, RC1943

John F. Ambos, RC1942

Frank Ambrosy

Mrs. Alice Jennings Archibald, GSE1938

John L. Archibald, RC1943

Robert Arnold, RC1950

Lyman Carewe Avery, RC1942

Thomas H. Bach, RC1950

Ogden C. Bacon, RC1950

Dr. Harold L. Baier, RC1943

Irvin Baker, RC1944

Mrs. Catherine Palmer Ballantine, NJC1945

Edward J. Barry Jr., RC1940

Henry E. Bartels, RC1945

Elliot Bartner, RC1943

M.G. William H.Bauer, RC1942

M.G. Edward Bautz, Jr., RC1941

Dr. John E. Baylor, RC1944

George H. Bebbington, UC1960

Richard L. Belford, RC1949

Alexander M. Bell, Jr., CP1942

Robert R. Bender, RC1941

Walter H. Berger, RC1938

Rev. John W. Berglund, RC1942

Col. Robert W. Billian, RC1949

Herbert I. Bilus, RC1942

Frederick Henry Bing

Charles F.Bishop, Jr., RC1949

Thomas J. Blanchet, RC1938

Lowell A. Blankfort, RC1946

Mrs. Adaline Glasser Bloom, NJC1941

Lewis M. Bloom, RC1942

Dr. Samuel E. Blum, RC1942

Prof.Theodore H. Blum, RC1951

Dr. Virginia Boardman, NJC1941

Prof.Raymond D.Bodnar, RC1951

William R. Boes, Jr., RC1939

Norman Towar Boggs II

George W. Boggs III, RC1942

Carl O. E. Bosenberg, RC1942

Warren J. Bowers, RC1949

Alfred V. Brady, RC1945

Floyd H. Bragg, RC1936

Norman Brandt, RC1942

Frank J. Brennan, Jr., RC1951

Leonard C. Briggs, RC1943

Herbert D. Brown, RC1936

Ms.Brigid Murphy BrownUC1989

Roscoe Brown

Harry A. Brown II, RC1949

Roy W. Brown, Jr., RC1943

Col.Walter R.Bruyere III, RC1939

Walter Scott Buist, Jr., RC1949

Herman E. Bulling, RC1944

Prof. W. Carl Burger, GSE

Victor J. Burger, RC1944

Dr. Jaroslav M. Burian, RC1949

Morton H. Burke, RC1945

Robert Bustamante

Dr. Robert L. Byram, RC1944

Robert L. Caleo, RC1952

Hon.Peter Daly Campbell, RC1950

VictorJ. Campi, RC1942

Dr. M. Leon Canick RC1942

Howard F. Canning, RC1949

Mrs. Alma Geist Cap, NJC1938

Stephen Capestro, RC1942

Hamilton C. Carson, RC1950

Dr. Kenneth Bard Charlesworth GSE1952

S. Robert Christensen, RC1942

Andrew J. Ciampa, RC,GSA1949

George L. Claflen, RC1942

Prof. Elizabeth Hughes Clark NJC1945

Crandon F. Clark, RC1944

Forrest S. Clark, RC1949

Russell W. Cloer, RC1943

Dr. Jay E. Comeforo, RC1944

Mrs. Jean C. Comeforo, NJC1945

John Conover, RC1949

John H. Cook, RC1938

Prof.David L. Cowen, RC1930

Peter D. Crane, RC1943

Hon.John F. Crane, RC1942

Lea M. Crawley

Dr. John A. Creager, RC1943

Edward F, Culwick, RC1949

Thomas R. Daggett, RC1942

Prof. Frank N. Dauster, RC1950

Mrs. Kathryn B. De Mott, RC Engrng 1945/46

Frederick Deibert, RC1942

Joseph DeMasi, RC1942

Sheldon Denburg, RC1949

Walter G. Denise, RC1948

Richard K. DeSante, RC1943

Casper W. Deschu, RC1944

LTC Carleton Dilatush RC1940

Prof. John J. DowlingJr, RC1942

Matthew Drag

Norman C. Dunbar, RC1943

Clifford L. Elling, RC1948

George Haddow Elwood, RC1949

William Epstein, RLS1939

Dr. Samuel J Errera, RC1949

Dr. James L. Essig, RC1948

Herbert S. Estell UC1945

Hon.Harry S. Evans, RC1947

John L. Fairbank, RC1940

Leonard J. Feinberg, RC1947

Edgar J. Feldman, RC1943

Ms. Frieda Finklestein Feller NJC1941

Robert M. Feller, RC1938

Lawrence J. Ferrero

Emmanuel L. Ferrito, RC1943

Nicholas W. Filippone, RC1945

Raymond A. Finley, Jr., RC1943

Robert J. Fischer, RC1949

Robert M. Fishkin, RC1949

Carl Fleming, RC1952

Richard K. Flitcraft, RC1942

LTC George H. Fralley, RC1944

Samuel R. Frankel, RC1949

Paul J. Frisco, R-Nwk

Dr. Harry A. Galinsky, RC1949

John A. Gausz, RC1946

Hon.Robert E. Gaynor, RC1940

Prof.Ludwig L. Geismar

Marvin I Gershenfeld R-Nwk1950

Charles R. Getty, RC1942

CAPT Richard C. Gies, RC1944

William S. Gillam, RC1940

Edward A. Gilliam, RC1943

Frank A. Gimpel, RC1949

Carlo J. Ginobile

Harry A. Glatt, UC1959

Ms. Nancy Petersen Godfrey NJC1944

CAPT William J.Godfrey, Jr. RC1940

Mrs.Lucille Miller Goff NJC1942

Dr. Sidney Goff, RC1942

Philip I. Goldberg, UC1968

Dr. Jerome Goldfisher, RC1951

Dr. Albert Goldstein, RC1951

Livy T. Goodman, RC1944

Alexander Gordeuk, RC1941

Dr. Irwin Gordon, RC1948

Vincent J. Gorman, RC1949

Robert A. Greacen, RC1941

Mrs.Annette S Greenblatt, NJC1945

Stephen Gregg
Ms. Marie Picker Griffin,UC1967
Prof.Paul Griminger
Herbert B. Gross, RC1942
Benjamin Gulko, UC1956
Samuel Gurstelle
Walter Gusciora GS-Rutgers 1972
Clark J. Gutman, RC1942
William Gutter, RC1942
Laurence F. Haemer
Reece E. Haines, RC1941
Richard M. Hale, RC1944
LtCol William G. Halliday,
    RC1949
Albert Handaly, UC1974
James G. Handford, RC1949
Leonard J. Hansen, RC1943
Dr. Harold J. Harris, RC1949
Mrs. Elizabeth Bacon Harris,
    NJC1945
Prof Thomas Hartmann
Mrs. Judith Harper Hassert,
    NJC1943
George T. Heinemann,UC1955
Col.William Carl Heyer,RC1925
C. Harrison Hill, Jr., RC1940
Donald M. Hillenmayer, RC1949
Curtis P. Hinckley
Richard W. Hitt, RC1948
Edward S. Hoe, Jr., RC1941
Robert L. Hoen, RC1949
Stokes H. Homan, RC1942
John F. Homan, RC1951
E. Robert Hoppe, RC1942
Fred R. Huettig, RC1950
John A. Hurlbert, RC1947
Benjamin P. Indick, RC1945
Leo C. Inglesby GS-NB1949
Robert Inglis, Jr., RC1943
Hon. Herbert W. Irwin, RC1943
Thomas C. Jackson, RC1943
Col. Jack H. Jacobs, RC1966
Alden F. Jacobs, RC1940

Dr. Arthur W. Jacoby, RC1949
Russell J. Janoff, RC1942
Ronald Jarvis, Jr., RC1942
Prof. W. Robert Jenkins
Dr. Paul B. Jennings, RC1945
Helge V. Jespersen, RC1948
Arthur D. Jiannine, RC1942
Kenneth E. Joel, RC1950
Robert E. Johnson, RC1941
Dr. Franklyn A.Johnson, RC1947
LtCol Wallace Kaenzig, RC1942
Kenneth M. Kaiser, RC1941
Dr. Lloyd Kalugin, GSE1975
Hon.Bernard A.Kannen, RC1950
Ms. Janice L. Karesh, NJC1945
Joseph W. Katz, RC1949
Charles F. Kellner, RC1935
Robert B. Kennedy, RC1942
William E. Kenny, RC1947
James T. Kenny, RC1942
Morton Kernis, RC1941
Fredrick Kerr RSB1950
William C. Kiessel, Jr., RC1947
Thomas A. Kindre, RC1942
Robert C. King, RC1942
David H. Kingston, RC1947
Clifford P. Kingston, Jr. RC1949
Harland B. Kinzley, RC1942
Richard Kleiner, RC1942
Barton H. Klion, RC1948
Joseph R. Knazik, RC1949
Franklin J. Kneller, RC1949
William Knox
Prof. Bernard W. Koft, RC1943
Melvin J. Kohn, RC1949
Edwin A. Kolodziej, RC1948
Jack J. Konner, RC1949
Rev. W. Wesley Konrad, RC1948
Dr. Charles W.Korbonits,RC1943
Dr. Lloyd B. Kornblatt, RC1944
Dr. Harold A. Kozinn, RC1949
Ms. Barbara Waters Kramer,
    NJC1942

Col. Vincent R. Kramer, RC1941
Dr. Harry Kranz, RC1945
Edmund Krawiczyk
Burton H. Krevsky, RC1945
GEN Frederick J. Kroesen,
    RC1944
Prof. Thomas LaCosta, RC1942
Charles R. Landback, Jr., RC1940
Dr. Michael J. Larkin, RC1942
Arnold I. Lasner RSB1949
Col. Robert G. Lauffer, RC1942
Henry H. Lawyer, RC1949
Prof.Solomon Leader, RC1949
Dr. Robert H. Leaming, RC1942
Dr. Milton B. Lederman, RC1942
LTC Ronald L. Ledwitz, RC1955
CAPT Joseph G. Lerner, RC194
Kurt G. Leuser, RC1942
Ms. S. Carol Levin, UC1978
Julian Levin, RC1947
Dr. Bernard G. Levine, RC1951
Mr. David Levy, RLS 1930
CDR John R.Lewis, RC 1942
Simon Liberman, RC1949
William C. Lilieholm, RC1948
William F. Llewellyn, RC1941
John Lofstrom
Raymond E. Logan, RC1950
Ralph E. Logan, RC1950
Peter J. Logerfo
Walter H. Lohmann, Sr., RC1949
Frank X. Long, RC1949
Robert L. Lowenstein, RC1944
Harvey S. Lowy, RC1948
Dr. Howard H. MacDougall,
    RC1942
Dr. Robert D. MacDougall,
    RC1942
William H. MacKenzie, RC1949
Robert B.MacPherson,Jr.,RC1942
Col. Christopher S. Maggio,
    RC1943
Bert R. Manhoff, RC1948

Richard Marlow, RC1942
Daniel Martin, RC1950
Dr.Dominic A.Mauriello,RC1942
Douglas L. McCabe, RC1944
Charles J. McCarthy, RC1949
Joseph B. McCartney, RC1942
Robert H. McCloughan, RC1942
Charles Walter McDougall,
    RC1942
Michael J. McIntosh, RC1944
Frank J. McIntosh, RC1944
Prof. Richard E. McKeeby,
    GSE1957
John A. Melrose, RC1942
Richard J. Mercer, RC1949
Albert Meserlin
Dr. Maurice Meyers, NJMD-Nwk
Gerald Michelson, RC1950
George Mickett, RC1949
Charles Mickett, Jr., RC1947
James R. Moetz, RC1949
D. Robert Mojo, Jr., RC1949
Dr.Donald A.Molony, RC1944
Mrs. Dorrit Weil Molony,
    GSE1948
Dr. Calvin Moon, RC1948
Mrs. June McCormack Moon
Raymond J. Mortensen, RC1944
Calvin H. Morton, RC1949
Simeon F. Moss, RC1941
Robert F. Moss, RC1942
Robert M. Moyerman, RC1949
Alexander Nazemetz, RC1949
Leslie C. Nelson, Jr., RC1949
Leonard Nemhauser, RC1948
Col.William C Neubauer,RC1941
Ms. Edna M. Newby, NJC1931
Herbert H. Newton, RC1941
Dr. Alfred Nisonoff, RC1942
Paul A Nolle, RC1950
Mr. Svenn A. Norstrom, RC1945
Robert F. Ochs, RC1949
Prof. John J. O'Connor

Dr. Robert C. Olsen, RC1942
Nicholas Oresko
Mrs. Mary Hance Owen,NJC1941
Robert I. Owen, RC1941
Elwood J. Palma, RC1940
Irving E. Pape, RC1943
James E. Parker, RC1948
Ms. Marjorie N. Pease UC1977
Philip A. Perlmutter, RC1949
Edward C. Piech, RC1949
Sam Piller, RC1943
Dr. John A. Pino, RC1944
Jules L. Plangere, Jr., RC1944
Eugene Polinsky, RC1941
Rev.Dr.Aaron S. Polinsky,
    RC1942
Dr. Irwin J. Polk, RC1949
Robert E. Pope, RC1949
Albert S. Porter, Jr., RC1948
ohn V. D. Poulson, RC1935
Dr. Allan B. Prince, RC1947
Col. William L. Prout, RC1943
Charles H. Prout, Jr., RC1941
Joseph H. Quade, RC1947
Fred H. Quantmeyer, Jr., RC1951
John C. Ragone, RC1942
Dr. Robert A. Ragotzkie, RC1946
Herbert L. Ramo, RC1950
Gerard J. Rau, RC1944
Walter B. Reichman, RC1942
Roy William Reisert UC1950
Dr. Norman Reitman, RC1932
Pat A. Restaino, RC1949
Dr. George T. Reynolds, RC1939
Mrs. Virginia Rendall Reynolds,
    NJC1943
John P. Reynolds, RC1949
Prof.Robert Rights R-Nwk
Walter E. Ringen, RC1945
Fred L. Ritter, RC1950
Ephraim Robinson, RC1941
Ms. Mary Robinson
David Robinson, RC1939

Theodore K. Robinson, RC1940
Daniel Rockoff, RC1940
Thomas R. Rogers, RC1948
CDR Paul W. Rork, RC1942
Dr.Morton M.Rosenberg,RC1938
Murray Rosenthal, RC1940
John G. Rosta, RC1936
Richard M. Roth
Benjamin B. Roth, RC1942
Nicholas G.Rutgers,IV, RC1950
Dr. Harold L. Saks, RC1950
Joseph B. Saldarini, RC1946
Mrs. Lita Saldarini
Robert Salvin, RC1949
Peter M. Sarraiocco, RC1949
Theodore W. Sattur, Jr., RC1942
Dr. Edward G. Scagliotta,RC1951
Seymour Schenkel, RC1942
John G. Scherholz, RC1949
Ralph Schmidt, RC1942
Earl F. Schneider R-Nwk1949
Col.Robert M.Schnitzer, RC1939
William C. Schnorr UC1953
Russell E. Schramm
John F. Schwanhausser, RC1949
Dr. Jerome Selinger, RC1945
Dr. Bernard Z. Senkowski
    R-Nwk1951
Walter H. Seward, RC1917
Nieson N. Shak, RC1946
Dr. Martin Sherman, RC1941
Prof. Nathan Shoehalter, RC1944
Jerry Shulman, RC1948
Ms.Helen Irwin Shuster,NJC1944
Dr. Carl N. Shuster, Jr., RC1942
Norman N. Siegal, RC1944
Dr. Seymour W. Silberberg,
    RC1942
Dr. Melvin Silverman, RC1949
Franklin S. Simon, RC1949
John E. Skinner, RC1949
Russell C. Smalley, Jr., RC1949
John Talbot Smith, RC1940

W. Kenneth Smith, RC1940
Col. Lawrence M. Smith
Richard M. Snethen, RC1943
Morton A. Sobin, RC1941
Ms. Alice Talbot Sofin,NJC1938
Abraham Soltz, RC1935
William R. Stalker, RC1945
Hon Laurence C. Stamelman,
    RC1949
Richard E. Stanley
Bernard E. Stark, RC1944
Dr. Joel R. Stern, RC1943
Dr. E. Theodore Stier, RC1949
Robert L. Strauss, RC1942
Werner Carl Sturm, RC1943
Franklyn Sullebarger, RC1950
William H. Suter, RC1943
Chester Szarawarski, RC1949
Dr.Armen Charles Tarjan,RC1944
Dr. Raymond P. Taub, RC1942
Roy Taylor
Lea E. Terry, RC1949
Dr. Charles B. Thayer, RC1944
George Wray Thomas, RC1942
Ms.Pearl P. Thompson, NJC1941
William Tomar, RLC1939
Col. Thomas S. Torresson, Jr.
Col. Charles S. Tracy
Saul Trager CP1949
Col.Eileen Witte Treash,NJC1949
Bert Tryon, RC1930
David Tudor, RC1940
Fred D. Van Aken, RC1950
Col. William G. Van Allen
    RC1936
Paul R. Van Duren, Sr., RC1949
John Van Kirk, Jr., RC1943
Harry C. Van Zandt, RC1944
Alfred Vardalis, Jr.
George T. Volk, RC1948
Richard G. Wagner, GSE1950
Ms. Helen M. Walkinshaw,
    NJC1952

Rev. Wilbur T. Washington,
    RC1949
LtCol Raymond A. Waters,
    RC1943
John T. Waters
Ripley Watson, Jr., RC1944
Ms. Margaret Harriet Waugh,
    NJC1944
Maurice M. Weill, RC1943
Dr. Joseph Weinstock, RC1949
Dr. Justin L. Weiss, RC1942
Dr. Leonard Weissburg, RC1943
Ms. Dorothy Salkin Welles,
    NJC1941
Hon. Melvin J. Welles, RC1940
William I. Wells, RC1943
CDR George R. Wells, RC1942
Mrs. Helen M. Wenger
LtCol Frederick Wesche, RC1939
Dr. P. Richard Wexler, RC1930
Charles V. White, RC1938
Donald K. White, RC1943
Andrew B. White, UC1955
Col. Charles Preston Whitlock,
    RC1941
John H. Wiles, RC1942
Jack M. Williams, RC1943
Dr. Abraham Wilson, RC1944
Hon.Roland A. Winter, RC1945
Charles T. Wittick, RC1949
Bert Wolf, RC1951
Prof. David C. Wood, RC1944
Carl R. Woodward, Jr., RC1940
Dr. Milton D. Yudis, RC1949
Robert H. Zeliff, RC1943
Paul Zell
J. Domer Zerbe, Jr., RC1943
William W. Zilka
MG Joseph Darrell Zink
    RLS1948
Stanley C. Zybort, RC1951

ISBN 141202592-3